Industrial Innovation and Firm Performance

NEW HORIZONS IN INTERNATIONAL BUSINESS

Series Editor: Peter J. Buckley
Centre for International Business,
University of Leeds (CIBUL), UK

The New Horizons in International Business series has established itself as the world's leading forum for the presentation of new ideas in international business research. It offers pre-eminent contributions in the areas of multinational enterprise – including foreign direct investment, business strategy and corporate alliances, global competitive strategies, and entrepreneurship. In short, this series constitutes essential reading for academics, business strategists and policy makers alike.

Titles in the series include:

Industrial Innovation and Firm Performance

The Impact of Scientific Knowledge on Multinational Corporations

Mario I. Kafouros

Lecturer in International Business and Innovation, Centre for International Business, University of Leeds, UK

NEW HORIZONS IN INTERNATIONAL BUSINESS

Edward Elgar
Cheltenham, UK • Northampton, MA, USA

Published by
Edward Elgar Publishing Limited
Glensanda House
Montpellier Parade
Cheltenham
Glos GL50 1UA
UK

Edward Elgar Publishing, Inc.
William Pratt House
9 Dewey Court
Northampton
Massachusetts 01060
USA

A catalogue record for this book
is available from the British Library

Library of Congress Control Number: 2008922098

ISBN 978 1 84720 220 8

Printed and bound in Great Britain by MPG Books Ltd, Bodmin, Cornwall

Contents

Abbreviations

2SLS	Two Stage Least Square
ABS	Antilock Braking System
BLUE	Best Linear Unbiased Estimator
CES	Constant Elasticity of Substitution
CRS	Constant Returns to Scale
DOI	Degree of Internationalization
DTI	Department of Trade and Industry
GDP	Gross Domestic Product
GNP	Gross National Product
IC	Integrated Circuits
ILS	Indirect Least Squares
ISC	Internet Systems Consortium
IT	Information Technology
LCD	Liquid Crystal Display
MNCs	Multinational Corporations
MNEs	Multinational Enterprises
MRS	Marginal Rate of Substitution
NIC	Network Information Centre
NSF	National Science Foundation
OECD	Organization for Economic Co-operation and Development
OLS	Ordinary Least Squares
ONS	Office for National Statistics
PPI	Producer Price Index
R&D	Research and Development
RF	Reduced Form
ROR	Rate of Return
SIC	Standard Industrial Classification
SSAP	Statement of Standard Accounting Practice
TFP	Total Factor Productivity
UK	United Kingdom
US	United States

Dedicated to my family

1. Introduction

1. THE RESEARCH TOPIC

It has long been recognized that technological innovation, either in the form of new products or in the form of new processes, may provide a firm a strong competitive advantage. Theoretically, it is accepted that the competitive edge that technological superiority gives may, in turn, allow a firm to improve its market share, output, productivity and in general its economic performance. In industrial practice, however, this theoretical prediction is often not confirmed. Investments in Research and Development (R&D) involve both technical uncertainty (will the new technology work?) and market uncertainty (will it be commercially successful?). Even when an innovation is both a technological and commercial success, the effects of intense competition, rivals' own innovations and other companies' imitations, mean that firms cannot always appropriate the advantages of their innovations. Additionally, the shorter life cycles of technologies and the rapid obsolescence of products force firms to improve their products continually, thereby increasing the associated costs significantly.

For these reasons, researchers distinguish between 'social' and 'private' returns to innovation and argue that although industrial research and development improves society's stock of scientific knowledge, its contribution to a firm's own economic performance may be limited (Griliches, 1979). Analysing firm-level data for a sample of UK multinational corporations (MNCs), this book offers a theoretical and empirical examination of the relationship between R&D capital (or stock of 'scientific knowledge') and firm productivity performance. To provide a better understanding of this relationship, the conditions under which multinational corporations benefit from innovation and their technological discoveries are investigated. These include issues such as the costs of industrial research, the time lag structure of R&D, the association between the Internet and R&D-efficiency, as well as the role of internationalization, product life cycle, firm size, type of industry and technological opportunities (all these research objectives are discussed in detail later in this introductory chapter). Additionally, the important role of competition in appropriating the benefits of innovation is theoretically and empirically examined. We argue that whilst innovation can be a strong competitive weapon for some organizations, it may only be a defense mechanism for others. We also discuss the extent to which the greater degree of internationalization of some corporations increases their ability to innovate and successfully exploit their technological developments.

Another issue that this book addresses is related to the importance of knowledge externalities (or spillovers). Researchers such as Jaffe (1986) and Scherer (1982) have argued that the technology and scientific knowledge of one firm may be beneficial to other organizations too. Similarly, Nelson (1982, p.467) argued that it is important to recognize that '... there is both a private and a public aspect to technological knowledge'. Accordingly, the scientific knowledge developed by R&D teams may affect not only the performance of those MNCs that undertake such activities, but also may impact on the performance of firms of the same industry or even of other industries. Previous empirical research has confirmed the existence of such spillover effects. However, although MNCs know that in order to unlock their full economic potential, they must search for and exploit external knowledge and technologies (Chesbrough, 2003; 2007), it is unclear what specific factors allow multinational corporations to build on and benefit from the discoveries of others. This book examines what the best MNCs do in order to profit from technologies developed by their rivals.

2. R&D, TECHNOLOGY AND PRODUCTIVITY PERFORMANCE

The importance of technology, innovative activity, and productivity has been emphasized many times. Many researchers have argued that it is unclear how different factors influence innovative capacity and, in turn economic growth. HM Treasury (2003, p.27-28) reports that the UK Government's economic ambition is that through a series of carefully directed and designed microeconomic reforms, firms will be encouraged to invest in technological progress and close the UK productivity gap. In brief, there is a need for better understanding of the process of technological innovation and the necessity to assess the impacts of the innovative activity upon a firm's economic performance. Productivity is regarded as one of the most important economic indices. At the firm-level, higher productivity means that an organization achieves a greater output from the same amount of input, thereby improving its performance. At the country-level, higher productivity can improve national welfare and the standards of living. However, past empirical findings are not encouraging, indicating that the world economy has experienced a continual deceleration of productivity growth (Crafts and

O'Mahony, 2001). As R&D is one factor that improves productivity, its evaluation has attracted wide interest.

One way to evaluate the role of R&D in explaining productivity performance is to conduct case studies. Even though such studies shed light on many qualitative issues, their findings cannot easily be generalized to other firms. In order to provide findings that can be generalized more reliably, the current study employs econometric methods to evaluate the economic returns to R&D. Many industry- and country-level studies have found the impact of R&D on productivity performance to be economically and statistically significant (Cameron, 2000; Griliches and Lichtenberg, 1984). Industry- and country-level studies are valuable because they provide evidence regarding the social returns to R&D (those returns to R&D that are forwarded to society). However, they cannot investigate the private returns to R&D (those that the firm itself gets for the money it invests in R&D), which is what ultimately matters from the point of view of a firm that makes vast investments in R&D.

The evaluation of the effects of R&D at firm-level is particularly important. Although one might expect the contribution of R&D to a firm's productivity performance to be positive, this may not always occur because the research efforts of a firm may be neutralized by those of its competitors (Chen and Miller, 1994; Porter, 1980). Indeed, whilst the majority of industry- and country-level studies found that R&D has significant consequences for productivity, many firm-level studies found that its contribution to productivity is often negligible (Griliches and Mairesse, 1983; Mairesse and Hall, 1996; Sassenou, 1988). The HM Treasury (2003, p.1) emphasizes the importance of using such data: 'At the firm level, there are wide variations in the productivity performance of different enterprises, which are masked by the national-level data. To understand fully the productivity gap it is necessary to examine the factors that contribute to productivity growth at the firm level'. Similarly, the investigation of knowledge spillovers using firm-level data is very important because it allows us to estimate the extent to which a firm (rather than an industry) benefits from the research efforts of other firms.

As it is unclear why some firms benefit from their research efforts (whilst others fail to do so), it is hoped that the contribution of this book to the development of the innovation research field will be significant. The increased understanding of the association between innovative activity and productivity should help managers and policy makers to appraise and direct science and technology policies (Cincera, 1998; Mohnen, 1999). The findings may also provide an insight to policy-makers, allowing them to identify the types of firms that should be aided and enabling the distribution of R&D-subsidies more efficiently.

3. RESEARCH OBJECTIVES

3.1 Main Research Objectives

The definition of R&D adopted here is that given by the OECD (2002, p.30): 'R&D comprises creative work undertaken on a systematic basis in order to increase the stock of knowledge, including knowledge of man, culture and society, and the use of this stock of knowledge to devise new applications'. Although in this book the words R&D and innovation are used interchangeably, as we will discuss in the next chapter the term 'innovation' implies the commercial success of a technology.

As discussed earlier, our main research objective is to estimate the impact of R&D on the productivity performance of UK multinational corporations. Although service firms undertake research in order to improve their processes, they rarely report their R&D expenditure in a systematic way. Hence, by necessity this book focuses on the manufacturing industry. We should also note that the measure of firm performance adopted here is that of labour productivity, measured by output per labour input.

In order to achieve its objectives and evaluate the returns to innovation, the current research adopts an approach that measures each firm's stock of 'scientific knowledge'. Although it is difficult to estimate knowledge in terms of units, scientific-knowledge as defined in this study is narrowed down to the knowledge produced from a firm's R&D department, making its estimation plausible (Schott, 1976). In the empirical analysis, we employ the method of Ordinary Least Squares method (OLS) and estimate a number of models that correlate output not only with the ordinary inputs of capital and labour but also with a measure of the stock of scientific. These models belong to the so-called endogenous group, and deal with the omission of factors which help to explain productivity growth. Two research samples are used. The first is composed of 107 UK multinational corporations, covering the eight year period from 1995 to 2002. The second comprises 84 firms covering the 14 years between 1989 and 2002.

We have already discussed that another important aspect of innovation that this book addresses relates to knowledge spillovers. By understanding whether the spillovers from certain industries and types of firms generate greater effects than spillovers from other industries and types of firms, policy makers might be able to eliminate the barriers that prevent the knowledge transmission between certain industries and types of firms (Cincera, 1998). This should assist in the circulation of knowledge by providing and disseminating information concerning the advances of technology and science through workshops and conferences (Mohnen, 1999).

An alternative approach is to estimate the impact of patents or actual innovations on productivity performance (as in the study of Griliches et al., 1987) rather than the impact of R&D. The reason why the book focuses on R&D is associated with the fact that both patents and innovations include an element of success. R&D projects however, are not always successful (and even when they are, their outcomes are not always patentable). When a firm invests in R&D, it cannot be sure that this investment will lead to patents and innovations. By trying to avoid focusing on successful firms, the book evaluates the impact of R&D investments and not the impact of patents or innovations.

It is also difficult to decide what measure of productivity – total factor productivity (TFP) or labour productivity – is most appropriate. Although it was initially believed that TFP was a better measure because it incorporated all the inputs of production, recent findings (Sargent and Rodriguez, 2000) suggest that both measures have their place, and that neither tells the whole story. The findings of Sargent and Rodriguez (2000) indicate that the choice of the measure of productivity should depend on factors such as the time period of interest and the comparability of capital stock data. Their analysis suggests that if we examine trends in the economy over a period of decade or so, then labour productivity is preferable. By contrast, if we examine long run trends of several decades, then TFP should be used. They also note that if the measures of capital stock are not comparable, then labour productivity should again be preferred. Given that the period of time analysed by this book does not include many decades and that the measures of capital stock are not very comparable (because they come from different industries), it was decided to focus on labour productivity.

However, there are two additional reasons why this book estimates the impact of R&D on labour productivity and not on total factor productivity. Firstly, as the majority of similar studies estimate the impact of R&D on labour productivity, the findings will be comparable to those of other studies, providing the opportunity to put them in context more easily. Secondly, the econometric framework used to investigate the impact of R&D on labour productivity allows comparison of the impact of R&D investments with that of other investments in ordinary capital (Griliches and Mairesse, 1984). Using the TFP framework would not allow that comparison.

3.2 Additional Research Objectives

The above research aims assume that the performance implications of innovation are similar for all multinational corporations. However, as many factors such as the production techniques, competitive pressure and product life cycles vary widely across industries, this assumption seems to be implausible. Therefore, the different impacts of R&D for four broadly defined industries (chemicals, mechanical engineering, electrical/electronics and transportation) are separately examined.

Additionally, after the work of Schumpeter (1950) who pointed out that innovative firms may operate more efficiently under imperfect (rather than perfect) competition, many researchers have suggested: (1) that the benefits of innovation are correlated with competitive pressure, and (2) that innovative capacity increases with firm size. This book empirically tests these theoretical predictions. This analysis is important both for scholarly knowledge and practice as it not only tests the validity of the Schumpeterian hypothesis, but also informs managers and policy makers about the role of firm size in innovative capacity.

Another issue that this book examines relates to the degree of internationalization of firms; that is, the extent to which firms operate beyond their national borders. It is often argued that companies that have a greater degree of internationalization have increased ability to both develop new technologies and to exploit the value of their innovations. We test empirically this theoretical prediction. We also examine whether the returns to innovation depend on the level of competition that a firm faces. Accepted theory indicates that a high level of competition may lead to lower returns to R&D. In contrast, lower competitive pressure may allow firms to appropriate the advantages of innovation better. In order to examine the validity of these propositions, we will initially construct a number of industry- and firm-level measures of competition. Then, by employing these measures, we will assess whether those firms that participate in markets where competition is low enjoy higher returns to R&D.

Additionally, in contrast to studies that assume that the costs of the inputs of R&D are similar across firms, our analysis takes into account the fact that some firms have to pay more for their industrial research. Because recent R&D price indices do not exist, many past studies employed the GDP price index in order to deflate R&D expenditures. Because the cost of R&D does not follow the general path of prices (Cameron, 1996), the use of the GDP price index does not allow researchers to measure the level of R&D activity accurately. To overcome this problem, the book investigates which firms needed to pay more for industrial research. The costs of R&D inputs are analysed and R&D price indices for 13 UK manufacturing industries are constructed.

The next issue addressed in this book relates to the role of technological opportunities. Technologically advanced firms have a better understanding of technologies (Kessler, 2003). Many researchers have also argued that they may be more capable of integrating the new research findings and technologies in the existing processes, and consequently may further increase their innovative capacity. Accordingly, it has been suggested that better technological opportunities and the integration of superior technology may allow an increase in the productivity of R&D (Iansiti and West, 1997). We examine empirically whether that is the case. Although this has been done before, the analysis offers new insights, contradicting earlier studies.

The book also investigates the time lag structure of R&D (for example: after how many years is the impact maximized? for what type of firms is it most immediate? and how rapidly do the returns to R&D decay?). The lag of R&D refers to the fact that time is needed to complete a project, introduce it to market (e.g. packaging, pricing and marketing), and gain a market share. Because of these reasons, the effects of R&D need time in order to be reflected and maximized. Because R&D lag can be defined in a number of ways (e.g. the lag between R&D and patents), it is important to note that this study investigates the time lag between R&D investments and their effects on productivity performance. Given that it may vary depending on the industry and the degree of internationalization of multinational corporations, the lag for different types of firms will be investigated.

Furthermore, there are findings that indicate that the impact of R&D on productivity declined between the 1960s and the 1980s (Hall, 1993). However, the 1990s witnessed major technological transformations that may have changed completely the contribution of R&D to productivity. Factors such as the Internet and the full computerization of organizations could have improved the processes of R&D. The last topic that the book addresses relates to the above arguments. It investigates the role of the Internet in explaining innovation performance. Specifically, the study develops and empirically tests a conceptual framework that explains how and why two features of the Internet (search and communication) improve three critical dimensions of R&D efficiency (cost, time and quality) and a firm's absorptive capacity (its ability to acquire and exploit external knowledge).

4. BOOK STRUCTURE

The book has 12 chapters. These are divided into three main parts: the value of innovation; conceptual and methodological issues; and empirical findings. The first part of the book discusses a number of theoretical perspectives and reviews past findings. The second part of the book deals with methodological and measurement issues. Researchers who wish to replicate the study using different data may find this useful. Finally, the last part of the book reports the empirical results of our analysis. The outline contents of each chapter are described below:

Chapter 2 discusses a number of issues essential to the understanding of the book, including the different types of industrial research, the stages of

R&D process, as well as the role of scientific knowledge and technological change. In addition, an overview of R&D investments and productivity is provided.

Chapter 3 sheds light on the theoretical relationship between innovation and corporate performance. It explains the ways in which investments in R&D may lead to increased market share and productivity. However, it also demonstrates that not all firms can benefit from innovation. Whilst some multinational corporations can turn innovation into a powerful competitive weapon, others find that the vast costs associated with innovation outweigh its potential advantages, indicating that for them, industrial research is merely a defense mechanism. We also show how highly internationalized companies frequently succeed in increasing both their innovative capacity and their ability to benefit economically from their scientific discoveries.

Chapter 4 provides a review of past findings and attempts to bring some of the previous results together. A number of methodological factors and sample characteristics that may influence the estimated impacts of innovation are also examined.

Chapter 5 is devoted to the examination of the costs of industrial research and development. Following earlier papers and the recommendations of the Frascati manual (OECD, 2002), it analyses the cost of R&D inputs and constructs R&D price indices for 13 industries over the period 1989-2002. By comparing the R&D price indices with the corresponding GDP and manufacturing indices, the analysis demonstrates that the use of inappropriate indices may (as one might expect) lead to imprecise results.

Chapter 6 This chapter presents the econometric framework and the models that the book employs in order to assess the contribution of R&D to firm performance. It also discusses how the inputs, the outputs and the innovative activities of firms should be measured.

Chapter 7 describes the research sample, provides descriptive statistics and explains how the main variables of the study were constructed. It also discusses the problems that emerged in the collection of the data and the measurement of the variables.

Chapter 8 presents the main empirical findings of the book regarding the impact of R&D on the productivity performance of multinational corporations. A wide range of factors that may influence the ability of an organization to benefit from innovation are examined. These include the role of competition, internationalization, firm size and technological opportunities.

Chapter 9 investigates the effects of innovation over time, as well as the lag structure of R&D. In other words, it examines how rapidly the returns to R&D decay, and after how many years they are maximized. Factors that may impact on this lag (such as the degree of a firm's internationalization and other industry-related idiosyncrasies) are also taken into account.

Chapter 10 is exclusively devoted to the exploration of knowledge spillovers. It investigates the extent to which the research efforts of other firms contribute to the productivity performance of multinational corporations.

Chapter 11 explores the theoretical association between the Internet and R&D-efficiency. Although data constraints make it difficult to provide econometric evidence, this chapter offers some preliminary findings that may be used as a basis for future research.

Chapter 12 summarizes the research findings of the book. Conclusions for both management and policy making are drawn, and opportunities for future research are proposed.

PART I

The Value of Innovation

2. The Process and Types of R&D and the Role of Scientific Knowledge

This chapter familiarizes the reader with a number of issues essential to the understanding of this book. Firstly, the different types of R&D are described. Secondly, in order to provide a better understanding as to how manufacturing firms put everything together in the development of new products, the different stages of R&D are presented. Then, we discuss the role of scientific knowledge and the concept of technological change. Finally, an overview of R&D investments and productivity in the UK and other industrialized countries is provided.

1. THE TYPES OF R&D

Industrial R&D embodies a plethora of activities. Both the US National Science Foundation (NSF) and the Organization for Economic Co-operation and Development (OECD) have divided R&D into three distinct types: (1) basic research, (2) applied research, and (3) experimental development. According to the Frascati R&D manual (OECD, 2002, p.30), basic research '… is experimental or theoretical work undertaken primarily to acquire new knowledge of the underlying foundation of phenomena and observable facts, without any particular application or use in view'. Mansfield (1968a) argues that the scientist who investigates what physical properties make an alloy of metals tougher, without aiming at a specific application, is carrying out basic research. As we will discuss in Chapter 4, even though basic-research projects require more time in order to be completed, they often generate significant economic returns.

Applied research, as defined by the Frascati manual (OECD, 2002, p.30) is '… original investigation undertaken in order to acquire new knowledge which will be directed towards a specific practical aim'. In other words, the aim of applied research is to generate knowledge that can be used for specific products and processes. Scientists, who investigate the conductivity of different materials in order to create a faster computer processor, are carrying out applied research. The last type of R&D is the so-called experimental development. According to the Frascati manual (OECD, 2002, p.30) experimental development '... is systematic work, drawing on existing knowledge gained from research and/or practical experience, which is directed to producing new materials, products or devices, to installing new processes, systems and services, or to improving substantially those already produced or installed'. A similar definition is given by Mansfield (1968a, p.45-46): 'Experimental Development aims at the reduction of research findings to practice, i.e. to develop new products and processes or improve the existing ones.' For example, scientists and engineers, who develop a computer screen that does not emit radiation, are carrying out experimental development. As Mansfield (1968a, p.45-46) points out, the development phase is usually more expensive than the research phase because it is difficult to turn an initial concept to a final product.

R&D can also be divided into product and process R&D. Product R&D aims to develop new products or to improve existing ones, as in the development of a new lower consumption car engine. In contrast, process R&D aims to develop new processes or to improve the existing ones. Because process R&D develops processes that bring the production costs down, it is considered as a cost-saving investment. There is also a distinction between business-funded R&D and public-funded R&D. Whilst business-funded R&D is usually directed towards applied research, public-funded R&D occurs when governments fund research usually in universities and in industries related to aerospace and defense (Cincera, 1998).

It is also worth discussing those characteristics of R&D that differentiate it from other investments in ordinary capital. First, the fixed set-up costs of R&D are very high. For that reason, they are usually seen as a fixed factor of production. This is known as the indivisible aspect of R&D (Arrow, 1962). Second, knowledge is often considered as a public good. Hence, it may be used by many firms or individuals (the non-rivalry nature of knowledge). Furthermore, the use of knowledge by one agent does not preclude its use by other agents (non-excludable property of knowledge; Arrow, 1962). Moreover, as Geroski (1995) argues, R&D not only involves substantial set-up costs and risk (as do all strategic investments), but also includes additional technological and market uncertainty. Technological uncertainty relates to the problem of converting a concept into something that works, whereas market uncertainty refers to the successful commercialization of the new product.

The outcome of R&D activities cannot be predicted easily. As the US Financial Accounting Standards Board (www.fasb.org) emphasizes, less than 2 percent of the new product ideas and fewer than 15 percent of product development projects are commercially successful. In addition, by looking at the history of inventions and innovations, both failures and success-stories can be identified. R&D for many large firms (such as Intel, IBM and GlaxoSmithKline) is considered to be one of their strongest competitive advantages. On the other hand, however, even when innovative activity is successful, it often takes so long to be completed that it engenders questions regarding its impact on a firm's economic performance. For instance, although nylon became a highly successful material, 12 years were spent in its development. Similarly, the laser diode became commercially successful approximately 17 years after its initial development.

2. THE PROCESS OF R&D

Having described the different types of research and development we now turn to the process of doing R&D. An understanding of the process makes it clear how different R&D activities are affected by factors such as external knowledge and the Internet. It will also explain how manufacturing firms put everything together in the development of new products and processes. Table 2.1 provides a description of the various activities that the R&D process embodies, starting from the initial concept-formulation of a product until its final introduction to market. Although Table 2.1 reflects the process of R&D as the researcher experienced it in the electronics industry, it is similar to the more general R&D process that other studies describe (Dahan and Srinivasan, 2000). Hence, it can to some extent be generalized to other industries. For instance, the technological components of the third stage could be electronic components for the electronics industry or chemical formulae for the chemical industry.

The first stage (conceptualization) includes activities related to the strategic orientation of the project. R&D individuals collect information regarding the products of competitors, current market trends and consumer needs. The information accumulated at this stage is of a factual nature, relating to the objectives, dimensions and characteristics that the product should have. For that reason, the R&D division needs to collaborate intensively with the marketing department and with senior managers in order to assess the market opportunities, decide how a technology can be used in order to meet a market need and generally turn the initial ideas into a product concept.

During the second stage (research) of the process, R&D teams collect the scientific information required for the project. They investigate as many external and internal knowledge sources as possible and collect information for the experiments and technological components required for the project. The collection of this information is critical. As Laursen and Salter (2006, p.131) emphasize:

A central part of the innovation process concerns the way firms go about organizing search for new ideas that have commercial potential. New models of innovation have suggested that many innovative firms have changed the way they search for new ideas, adopting open search strategies that involve the use of a wide range of external actors and sources to help them achieve and sustain innovation.

In the third stage (technology creation), the previously collected information is disseminated throughout the firm creating new knowledge which is finally transformed to new technological options and components. As Nonaka and Takeuchi (1995) describe, in order to empower this process, many Japanese firms organize R&D meetings and brainstorming camps in which employees can discuss and exchange information. During this stage, R&D teams carry out the necessary experiments and create the required technological options. They also communicate with suppliers to retrieve information for inputs, solve problems and order materials. This stage also includes evaluation and refining activities aimed at selecting the most appropriate technological options and components.

Table 2.1 The process of R&D

Stages	Description
1. Conceptualization	The initial concept of the project is formulated
2. Research	Collection of scientific information required for the project
3. Technology creation	New knowledge, technological options and components are created
4. Design	Design possible versions of the product
5. Prototyping	The first prototypes are created, debugged and tested
6. Development	The final product design is fine-tuned and implemented
7. Commercialization	The new product is introduced to market

In the fourth stage (Design), R&D teams collaborate, using the technological options and components created in the previous one. They also bring together the different parts of the research in order to design possible versions of the final product. They evaluate the designs of possible versions, choosing the most appropriate ones according to the objectives defined in the conceptualization stage. At the same time, they collaborate with other departments (such as marketing and the finance divisions) in order to decide which designs or versions of the products are closer to consumer needs and which are more profitable.

In the fifth stage (prototyping), the selected designs are put into practice and the first prototypes are created, debugged and tested. Implementers decide from a variety of possible versions the product that the firm will carry forward to the development stage. In the sixth stage (development), the R&D division collaborates with the production division and the final prototype is refined, fine-tuned and implemented. The last stage (commercialization) of the R&D process includes all those activities required to introduce the new product to market. These activities include the packaging, pricing, marketing as well as the feedback from customers which is essential in order to eliminate any faults that the debugging stage missed.

In their article, Nevens et al. (1990) provide an example from practice that reflects the stages described earlier. The authors discuss the case study of Hewlett Packard's desk-jet printer. They explain that this project started when the managers of Hewlett Packard read a market-research report that showed that consumers would welcome a device that printed at low speed but sold for half the price of other printers. Nevens et al. (1990) explain that Hewlett Packard formed a team of engineers, scientists and marketers to examine the technological feasibility and the economic potential of this project. This team evaluated the preferences of their customers as well as the benefits and disadvantages of the product.

Having collected the necessary information, Hewlett Packard's engineers and scientists worked on the development of various technologies such as the print head (which as Table 2.1 indicates is the third stage of R&D; that is, the creation of technological components). The next step was to design a prototype, which was used by the engineers of the firm in order to evaluate the performance of the device. Nevens et al. (1990) describe that when the research team confirmed the technical feasibility of the product, Hewlett Packard further expanded the project and tried to take into account customer's feedback, fine-tune the design, and improve the quality of the printer. At the same time, the marketing division of the firm worked on the necessary promotion, advertising and distribution activities in order to ensure the commercially successful introduction of the product to market (this refers to the last stage of the process of R&D in Table 2.1; that is the commercialization stage).

3. R&D AND THE STOCK OF SCIENTIFIC KNOWLEDGE

As noted in Chapter 1, it is very difficult to measure how much knowledge
exists in a firm. Following past research however (Griliches, 1979), this
study focuses on the knowledge produced from a firm's R&D department. In
other words, it is assumed that the level of a firm's stock of scientific
knowledge (or R&D capital) is a function of its past and current investments
in R&D (econometric details regarding the measurement of the stock of
knowledge are included in Chapter 6). The key role of knowledge in the
process of R&D has been emphasized by many scholars. Nonaka and
Takeuchi (1995) argued that as products become obsolete quickly, successful
firms are those that are able to consistently create new knowledge. Other
researchers adopted a 'search' perspective. Quoting Nelson (1982, p.452):

> In many verbal discussions, R&D capabilities are proposed to be related to the
> strength of knowledge. While this proposition can be interpreted in a variety of
> ways, a promising one is lent by models that treat R&D as a search that can be
> pursued to varying degrees and, perhaps, pointed in different directions, but with
> stochastic outcomes. In these models the expected R&D cost of a given (target)
> outcome is related to the expected number of elements that need to be drawn
> before that outcome is achieved. From this vantage point R&D capabilities can be
> recognized as connected with knowledge about how to search efficiently.

A number of interesting questions can be raised regarding the stock of
scientific knowledge. For instance, 'what is the true association between
scientific knowledge and R&D?' and 'can an aggregate measure of R&D
adequately represent scientific knowledge?' Although it seems reasonable to
assume that a firm can increase its scientific knowledge by investing in R&D,
it is by no means certain that a measure of R&D expenditures can adequately
represent the scientific knowledge of a firm. R&D expenditures can represent
the formal research effort. However, the scientific knowledge of a firm is
also determined by many other sources such as any informal research
(Griliches, 1979). Moreover, scientific knowledge can also be increased
through the learning by doing process. Quoting Baussola (1999, p.83):

> Many innovations are applied imperfectly when they are first introduced and are
> therefore improved gradually over time as a result of experience. This gradual
> improvement can be seen as an intrinsic part of the innovation process, running
> from research through development to production. Thus, scope for improvement
> may be discovered as a result of a learning process and not as a result of formal
> R&D activity.

Nevertheless, even though investments in R&D may generate scientific
knowledge, it should not be ignored that scientific knowledge is also an input

for future R&D. Accordingly, the efficiency of the process of R&D is closely related to a firm's capability to search, understand and exploit external knowledge. Indeed, many studies have shown that the productivity performance achieved by one firm depends not only on its own research but also on the level of the external pool of knowledge accessible to it (Griliches, 1992). Consistent with this view, the work of Nelson (1982, p.462) indicates that:

> Strong knowledge means ability to guide R&D effectively. Stronger knowledge enables a larger expected advance to be achieved from a given R&D outlay: alternatively, strong knowledge reduces the expected cost of any R&D achievement. Strong knowledge enhances efficiency both by enabling R&D to proceed on a generally better set of candidate projects, and by enabling the set worked upon to reflect more accurately particular demands and needs.

At this point, we should also explain that in addition to the knowledge generated by the R&D laboratories of private firms, another important stock of knowledge is generated by academic research. The interface between industry and the universities is important in promoting innovation. In line with this view, the work of Sorenson and Fleming (2004) demonstrated that academic publication is an important mechanism for accelerating the rate of innovation.

Particularly in applied sciences, the research priorities of academic researchers are closely related to the technological priorities and objectives of private firms (Nelson, 1982). The notion that various industries rely on academic research is also confirmed by the study of Mansfield (1991). Analysing data for the 1975-1985 period, he found that one tenth of new products could not have been developed in the absence of academic research. Nevertheless, the results of Laursen and Salter (2004) indicated that only a small number of organizations utilize directly knowledge from universities.

4. TECHNOLOGICAL CHANGE

To better understand this research, it is important to clarify and define the concepts of technology and technological change. Mansfield (1968a, p.10) argues that:

> Technology is society's pool of knowledge regarding the industrial arts. It consists of knowledge used by the industry regarding the principles of physical and social phenomena (such as the properties of fluids and the laws of motions), knowledge regarding the application of these principles to production (such as the application of genetic theory to the breeding of new plants), and knowledge regarding the day-to-day operations of production (such as the rules of thumb of craftsmen).

Based on this definition of technology, one can then argue that technological change refers to the advances of society's pool of knowledge. The process of technological change can be divided into three stages: invention, innovation and diffusion (Schumpeter, 1950). As Cincera (1998) emphasized the invention process corresponds to the generation of new ideas. But Freeman (1982) pointed out that although inventions (the creation of previously not-existent products, processes and systems) may be patented, they do not necessarily lead to innovations (which is the second stage of technological progress). An innovation, he argued, is accomplished only with the commercial application of the invention. Quoting Mansfield (1968a, p.99): 'An invention when applied for the first time is called innovation. In brief, invention has little economic significance until it is applied.' Finally, during the third stage (diffusion), the newly developed knowledge, products and processes are diffused across the market. New technologies however, can take many years in order to diffuse (Karshenas and Stoneman, 1995).

To accomplish its objectives, this study uses the so-called endogenous models of economic growth (these will be described in Chapter 6). In order to position the study better, however, it is worth reviewing other theoretical schools that have attempted to explain productivity and technological change. The first major attempt to study productivity began with the work of Cobb and Douglas (1928). The researchers introduced a production function that correlated output with capital and labour. Advances in the Cobb-Douglas production function took place when concepts such as total factor productivity were introduced in the literature by researchers such as Stigler (1947). Theorists of the traditional economic growth assumed that the growth of output was driven by increases in capital, labour and other materials.

In these models, however, only the growth of capital and labour was explained. The models assumed that technological change was determined exogenously, and tried to measure it by the so-called 'residual' that was left in the equation. In other words, advances in the state of technology were not explained. In his work, Robert Solow (1957) showed that technological change was the main reason for the economic growth of the US between 1909 and 1949. Even when researchers took into account changes in the quality of capital labour, technological change was still responsible for approximately the one third of the US economic growth (Jorgenson and Griliches, 1967).

Although exogenous models can measure the rate of technological change, they cannot investigate its determinants. For that reason, researchers such as Arrow (1962) tried to endogenize the role of technological change in new economic growth models. Four major perspectives of technological change have been considered by the literature (see Cameron, 1996): learning by doing, human capital, public infrastructure and R&D. The first one is based on the argument that a significant by-product of investments is knowledge about the production of goods. The rationale behind this concept is that firms add knowledge to the capital goods they produce. So when a firm invests in new machinery, it increases its state of knowledge and in consequence it becomes more productive ('learning by doing'; Romer, 1986).

The second camp of theorists argued that technological change can be explained by the fact that human capital incorporates knowledge that contributes to its continual improvement (Lucas, 1988). Because employees become more skilled, they can find better solutions to problems and can use machinery more efficiently, thereby resulting in higher productivity. A third explanation of technological change may also be provided by the investments made by governments (Barro, 1990). For example, public infrastructure such as transport networks could be seen as additional inputs in the production process which may further increase the output of firms. The fourth research camp includes studies similar to the current research, which attempt to explain technological change by considering R&D as a factor of production (Griliches 1979, Minasian, 1969, Terleckyj, 1974). A detailed discussion of the R&D econometric framework is included in Chapter 6.

5. R&D AND PRODUCTIVITY IN THE UK AND OTHER COUNTRIES

As discussed in Chapter 1, productivity is very important. It is the main determinant of national living standards (HM Treasury, 2003); it reflects how efficiently a firm can use available resources; and it improves the output (and consequently the economic performance) of firms. The rates of productivity growth are even more important for a country such as the UK because its level of productivity (whichever measure of productivity is used) has lagged behind in comparison with the levels of productivity of other industrialized economies.

For that reason, it is considered most important by the UK government to increase productivity more rapidly than its main competitors in order to close the productivity gap (HM Treasury, 2003). Figure 2.1 presents the average growth of labour productivity for a number of industrialized countries such as the UK, Germany, France, Japan and the USA. As this figure indicates, the productivity growth of these developed countries decreases during the last three decades, implying that it is particularly important to examine what conditions, policies and types of investments can accelerate the economic growth of these countries. The exception to the rule is the US. Its productivity growth increased during the last ten years. We should also note that the productivity growth rates of these countries were much higher before the oil crisis of 1973, after which they declined sharply. Although the productivity growth of the UK is not lower than that of other countries, its level of productivity is considerably lower. As the HM Treasury (2003) emphasizes, the UK needs to increase its output per head by over £6,000 to match the productivity performance of the US.

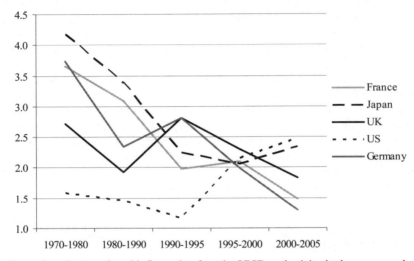

Source: In order to produce this figure, data from the OECD productivity database were used.

Figure 2.1 Labour productivity growth rates

Figure 2.2 depicts the R&D-intensity (gross R&D investments over GDP) for a number of industrialized countries. The R&D-intensity of the UK declined in the 1990s and early 2000s from about 2.1 to 1.8 percent. By contrast, the R&D-intensity of other countries such as the USA and Japan, either increased or remained relatively constant. In 2005 the R&D-intensity of the UK was lower than that of many other countries. The R&D-intensity of Japan in 2005, for example, is approximately 80 percent higher than that of the UK, being 3.3 compared to 1.8 percent. It should be noted however, that R&D-intensities are not always fully comparable because the composition of manufacturing and service sectors vary widely across countries. It is also interesting to examine the R&D-intensive industries. The UK R&D Scoreboard examined the top 1250 firms in terms of R&D. Table 2.2 reports some of the results, including the top 15 sectors and the percentage of total R&D investment by sector. Approximately 70 percent of the total R&D investments are undertaken by five industries (technology hardware, pharmaceuticals, automotive, electronics and electrical, and software) with the leading R&D industry being technology hardware at approximately 20 percent.

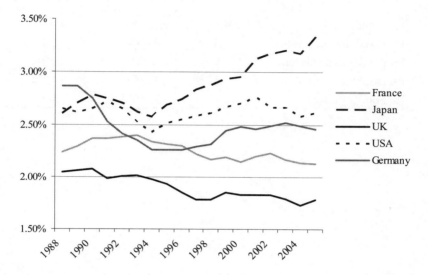

Source: In order to produce this figure, data from the OECD science, technology and patents database were used.

Figure 2.2 Gross R&D expenditure as a percentage of GDP

Table 2.2 The top 15 R&D-intensive sectors

Top 15 sectors	Sector R&D, £bn	1-year R&D growth	Sector R&D as % of global 1250
1. Technology Hardware	47.9	7.20%	19.20%
2. Pharmaceuticals	46.7	8.30%	18.70%
3. Automotive	43.9	5.10%	17.60%
4. Electronics & electrical	24.2	4.20%	7.40%
5. Software	16.5	8.90%	6.60%
6. Chemicals	11.6	-0.90%	4.60%
7. Leisure goods	10.7	1.70%	4.30%
8. Aerospace & defense	10.1	13.50%	4.10%
9. Gen. industrials	6.2	11.40%	2.50%
10. Industrial engineering	5.1	9.20%	2.40%

Table 2.2 continued

11. Health	4.5	12.50%	1.80%
12. Fixed line telecoms	4.4	6.00%	1.80%
13. Oil & gas producers	2.9	11.80%	1.10%
14. Household goods	2.5	7.50%	1.00%
15. Food producers	2.4	2.40%	1.00%

Source: R&D Scoreboard, UK DTI, 2006.

3. Innovation: A Competitive Weapon or a Defense Mechanism?

The development and application of innovations and new technologies is crucial to a firm's economic performance. However, 'increasing R&D investments alone does not ensure that companies will successfully exploit technology as a competitive weapon' (Frohman, 1982, p.97). In this chapter, we demonstrate initially how investments in R&D may improve a firm's performance. Nevertheless, we also argue that not all firms will benefit economically from innovation, as it is often only a defense mechanism, rather a competitive weapon. We also discuss a number of factors such as innovative capacity, internationalization, competition and appropriability of innovation that may influence the economic returns to R&D.

1. INNOVATION AS A COMPETITIVE WEAPON

Frohman (1982, p.97) argued that 'technology can be a powerful weapon on the battlefield of economic enterprise'. Indeed, both scholars and managers have recognized that R&D can provide a firm with a strong competitive advantage and, generally, that a firm's competitiveness depends on its ability to keep up in innovative products and processes (Pavitt, 1990). To explain more clearly how and why R&D improves competitiveness – and in consequence – firm performance, we start with the work of Cohen and Levinthal (1989) and Griffith et al. (2004) that showed that R&D has two faces: the conventional one of stimulating innovation and a second one of improving absorptive capacity. Adopting a slightly different view, we argue that R&D has both direct and indirect impacts on performance. These, in turn, give firms a strong competitive advantage (Figure 3.1). The direct impact can be most easily explained using economic theory, whereas the indirect one is better understood by demonstrating concepts such as dynamic capabilities from management.

The direct impact of R&D is easily identified. Investments in R&D lead to the creation of new technologies and generally to the development of a stock of 'scientific knowledge'. These technologies and knowledge can be used in many different ways in order to develop innovations and increase a firm's economic performance. A company can obtain a competitive advantage by introducing new products that better satisfy customers' needs and market demand. As a result of this, it can attract more customers and consequently increase its sales, market share and output. Higher output may also lead to a lower cost per unit as it often means that economies of scale will be achieved.

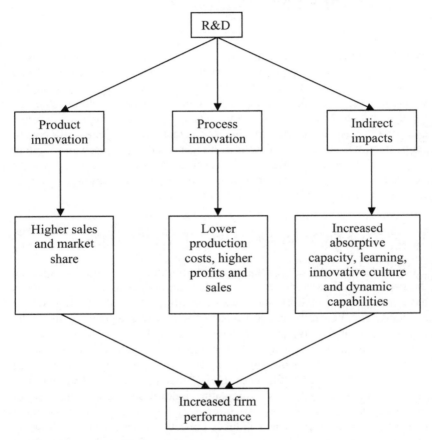

Figure 3.1 R&D and firm performance

The increased stock of scientific knowledge does not always result in technological breakthroughs. It may also be used simply to develop incremental (rather than radical) innovations and to improve a firm's existing products. Once again, a firm can either attract more customers or increase the prices for its products, which now have better quality, offering more value to its customers. For instance, Hewlett Packard, after the successful introduction of its Desk-Jet printer, succeeded in keeping its sales at a high level by improving its printing speed and by introducing more flexible versions of the original printer (Nevens et al., 1990). A firm can also increase revenues through the fees from patent licenses. A vivid example is demonstrated by IBM. In addition to the revenues that the company generates by selling its products and e-solutions, it also licenses technologies from six broad categories of patents (software, microelectronics, network and computing, server, display and storage).

We have discussed above the impacts of sales-generating innovation projects and explained to what extent a product innovation is reflected in a firm's sales. However, we have not discussed what happens when R&D results in a process innovation that reduces costs. Suppose that a firm invests in an R&D project that succeeds in reducing the manufacturing costs of an existing product by £20. The firm must then decide whether to retain the selling price of the product as it is, to reduce it by £20, or to reduce it by less than £20 (let us say, by £10). If the firm decides not to lower the selling price of its product, then the associated sales will remain constant. Output, and thus productivity, will remain the same and all the impact of R&D will be forwarded to profits.

By contrast, if the firm decides to reduce the selling price by £20, then the sales should be higher and a measure of productivity will fully reflect the impact of R&D. In the third case (that is when the firm decides to reduce the selling price by £10), R&D will not only contribute to sales but also to the profits of the firm. The case that allows us to adequately measure the impact of R&D on productivity performance is the second one. Nevertheless, as it is less likely that firms in the real world follow this practice, the impact of R&D on sales, output and in consequence on productivity is often underestimated because some of the advantages of R&D are reflected in profits.

We have demonstrated above how R&D impacts directly on firm economic performance. To adequately understand the total value of R&D however, we also need to appreciate the indirect impacts of innovation. The work of Cohen and Levinthal (1990) showed that R&D investments promote technological innovations and facilitate organizational learning. Specifically, Cohen and Levinthal (1990, p.128) argue that:

> The ability of a firm to recognize the value of new, external information, assimilate it, and apply it to commercial ends is critical to its innovative capabilities. [The authors] label this capability a firm's absorptive capacity and suggest that it is largely a function of the firm's level of prior related knowledge.

This argument is also confirmed by the study of Griffith et al. (2004).

Employing a dataset from twelve OECD countries, the researchers showed that R&D stimulates innovations and improves a firms' absorptive capacity. The notion of absorptive capacity has important implications for innovation management. Quoting Cohen and Levinthal (1990, p.148):

> The observation that R&D creates a capacity to assimilate and exploit new knowledge provides a ready explanation of why some firms may invest in basic research even when the preponderance of findings spill out into the public domain. Specifically, firms may contact basic research less for particular results than to be able to provide themselves with the general background of knowledge that would permit them to exploit rapidly useful scientific and technological knowledge through their own innovations or to be able to respond quickly – become a fast second – when competitors come up with a major advance (see also Rosenberg, 1990).

Similarly, Wakelin (2001) argued that innovative firms are qualitatively different from non-innovative firms. Indeed, there are significant differences between R&D-intensive organizations and other firms. For instance, the high number of scientist, engineers and technologists in R&D-intensive firms may promote an innovative organizational culture that assists the discovery of new knowledge and practices. This, in turn, may provide a strong competitive advantage.

In line with the above arguments, the literature on dynamic capabilities sheds light on a number of other indirect impacts of R&D. Using the resource-based view of the firm, Eisenhardt and Martin (2000) argue that the advantage of dynamic capabilities lies in the ability to turn resources into value-creating strategies. The researchers explain that main innovative processes, such as product development, increase a firm's dynamic capabilities. These capabilities promote innovation and a knowledge-creation environment (Eisenhardt and Martin, 2000; Teece et al., 1997). This argument also implies that those firms that develop their own technologies and innovations differ from the organizations that simply buy the technologies that other firms have developed (Brynjolfsson and Hitt, 2003).

2. INNOVATION AS A DEFENSE MECHANISM

The previous section discussed how and why investments in R&D give a firm a strong competitive advantage and accelerate its economic growth. However, 'How long and through what means can an organization expect to sustain its specific competitive advantage?' (Williams, 1992, p.29). Even though one might expect that the contribution of R&D to productivity performance would always be positive, this is not always the case. Not all firms enjoy high returns to their research efforts. But as Frohman (1982, p.97) asked 'Why is it one company may pursue a technological advance and later reap rewards in the marketplace while another may pump as many resources into a similar project and never make it to the marketplace?'. There are numerous factors that allow an organization to successfully benefit from its own innovations. In order to keep our discussion to a reasonable length, we group these factors into two categories: 'innovative capacity' and 'degree of appropriability'.

The first category includes those factors or variables that affect a firm's ability to develop and employ innovations and new technologies. This is closely linked to the efficiency of the R&D scientists and technologists and generally to the efficiency of a firm's R&D department to create technologically successful products. Firms must ensure that they can capture and create scientific knowledge more rapidly and effectively than their rivals. As we will discuss in Chapter 11, this efficiency also impacts on three critical dimensions of R&D (cost, time and quality). The second group of factors or variables influences the degree of appropriability. These factors affect the capacity of a multinational corporation to exploit, protect and appropriate its stock of scientific knowledge more successfully. Indeed, organizations that undertake R&D are rarely able to appropriate all the benefits of their research efforts (Geroski, 1995) and some of those do not return to the inventor but are forwarded to society.

There are many reasons that may explain why firms do not appropriate the fruits of their innovations (the main factors influencing the returns to R&D are also presented in Figure 3.2). The first relates to competition and to the fact that a firm's rivals undertake their own R&D. Hence, even if a product is technologically and commercially successful, its economic effect may be neutralized by the new or improved products of competitors. Many researchers have argued that when firms invest simultaneously in similar business practices which involve new knowledge, nearly all the benefits simply spillover to customers (Porter, 1980; Chen and Miller, 1994). Even though a manager might believe that higher productivity levels of competitors would not have a negative impact on the productivity of his firm, this often appears to be the case.

At this point, it is important to explain that this study (as well as past research) estimates a comparative – or relative – measure of productivity performance. This is because academic studies measure output (the numerator of any productivity measure) by employing either sales or value added. In other words, any measure of productivity depends upon sales. Consequently, when a firm's market share is taken away from competitors' advanced technologies, its measured (comparative) productivity may be lower (regardless that the capacity of the firm to produce remains the same).

These arguments are consistent with many previous studies. Aitken and Harrison (1999) emphasize that due to competition many firms are forced to reduce their production. The lower level of output shifts their costs curve higher, thereby leading to lower productivity. Similarly, McGahan and Silverman (2006) demonstrated that the technological innovations that a firm's rivals develop decreases firm performance either through 'direct market-stealing' or 'indirect appropriation through licensing'.

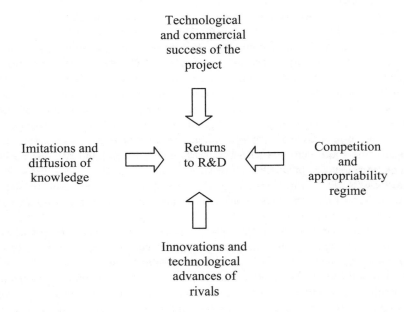

Figure 3.2 Factors that influence the returns to R&D

The appropriability issue and the neutralization of a firm's research findings also depend on the level of imitation and the effectiveness of intellectual property rights, as well as on the diffusion of innovations. Price (1996) emphasized that the efficient innovation management requires a good understanding not only of the technology itself but also of the evolution and diffusion of technologies. Theoretically, it can be argued that if an innovation is fully diffused then the returns to this innovation are either zero or negligible. Once again, although this innovation may still contribute to a firm's production capacity, it is unlikely that sales or market share will continue to reflect the associated benefits.

The rate of knowledge diffusion is important as it determines the extent to which, as well as how long, a firm can appropriate the benefits of its research activities. Williams (1992, p.30) argued that 'Many of the competitive pressures that an organization faces can be traced to the degree of sustainability of its products'. The researcher demonstrated the importance of blocking imitation by using resources such as geography, patents, company reputation and strong relationships with customers. By contrast, he showed that a firm's competitors can quickly duplicate idea-driven products such as cellular phones and walkman personal stereo. In such cases, a firm faces strong competitive pressures such as 'short product cycle times, rapid price reductions, stiff cost reduction targets, and eroding product profit margins' (Williams, 1992, p.32).

To understand the above arguments, let us give an example from industrial practice. Let us assume that Sony invests in a major R&D project and attempts to develop and manufacture a superior plasma television with excellent technical specifications. Let us also assume that the project is technologically successful. If there are no competitors in the global market (i.e. if Sony is a perfectly discriminating monopolist), its sales, market share and output will reflect the new product and thus capture not only the private but also the social returns to R&D. However, what will happen if there are competitors (say, Samsung and Philips)?

Although Sony may anticipate that its sales will increase by the introduction of the new plasma television, this will happen only to a lesser extent if Samsung and Philips also introduce a new and better television. In that case, given that some of the benefits of R&D will not return to Sony but will be forwarded to consumers, the proportionate change of sales, market share and output will be lower than the proportionate change of true output. As such, the true productivity advances will be underestimated. It also very interesting to analyse what happens to the scientific and technological knowledge created by Sony. If Sony has no competitor, the created knowledge will not be diffused. Hence, the firm can exploit the new knowledge for several years. However, what will happen in the real world in which firms such as Samsung and Philips are present?

After the introduction of the new television, competitors by using reverse engineering (or by examining the patents of Sony) will possibly study and analyse the techniques and methods that Sony used to design and manufacture it. In this case, a significant proportion of the knowledge that Sony created will be diffused and possibly used by its main competitors. Consequently, the new knowledge will depreciate and become obsolete faster. In markets which include many firms and have characteristics of perfect competition, it is sensible to expect that the knowledge of a firm will be diffused even faster and the increase of its sales will be negligible as intense competition will presumably force a firm to lower its prices (an empirical examination of the effects of competition is provided in Chapter 8).

Hence, as Williams (1992, p.29) argued 'Innovation can give a company a competitive advantage and profits, but nothing lasts forever. Success brings on imitators who respond with superior features, lower prices, or some new way to draw customers away. Time, the denominator of economic value, eventually renders nearly all the advantages obsolete'. Hence, we should appreciate that what is important is not a firm's level of R&D, but also the difference of this level from the average level of its rivals' R&D. In other words, these arguments indicate that whilst R&D for some firms may work as a competitive weapon or advantage, in technologically dynamic and competitive environments where firms are 'running to stand still', R&D may simply be a defense mechanism.

3. INTERNATIONALIZATION AND R&D

The previous sections offered a theoretical examination of the relationship between R&D, competitive advantage and firm performance. This relationship however becomes even more complex if we take into account that this research examines the performance of multinational corporations, which operate, sell and develop their products and processes in many different locations around the globe. The degree of internationalization of firms may influence both their ability to develop as well as to capture the value of technological innovations. In this study, the degree of internationalization (DOI) or multinationality is defined as the extent to which multinational enterprises (MNEs) operate beyond their national borders (Kotabe et al., 2002). However, it is difficult to find an appropriate proxy for measuring this because MNEs – depending on their strategic plan, firm size and industry – follow a different internationalization approach. For instance, MNEs that face intense price competition tend to internationalize their production more (in order to reduce production costs). By contrast, when product differentiation and innovation is more important, then firms may prefer to internationalize their R&D network.

The degree of a firm's internationalization plays a crucial role. Previous research indicates that multinational corporations have a number of firm-specific characteristics that allow them to better exploit and appropriate the benefits of innovation (some of these factors are also presented in Figure 3.3). Teece (1986) demonstrated that highly international firms obtain a wide range of complementary assets that allow them to convert a technological success into a commercial one, and consequently to outperform their competitors. Similarly, the theoretical framework of 'internalization' (Buckley and Casson, 1976) suggests that MNEs have distinct advantages that allow them to exploit their innovation-intensive products. These advantages refer to the ability of such firms to increase appropriation by using discriminatory pricing. It also refers to their ability to integrate the outputs of research and development with the marketing and production functions.

Consistent with the above arguments, the work of Santos et al. (2004) shows that multinational firms have the ability of combining technical know-how and market expertise. Another important factor that allows MNEs to enjoy good returns to their industrial R&D is the fact that they can offer their products to a large number of potential buyers. This argument is supported by Caves (1982) who argue that organizations that expanded to other countries received high economic payoff for their innovations. Consistent with this point, Lu and Beamish (2004) showed that when firms deploy their products in many countries can exploit their full value. MNEs can also enjoy higher returns to their research efforts by benefiting by economies of scale. Whilst domestic firms cannot cover the high costs of innovation (Hitt et al., 1994), highly international firms can lower such costs by performing many activities internally (Rugman, 1981), and by applying their process innovations to many production sites (Kotabe et al., 2002).

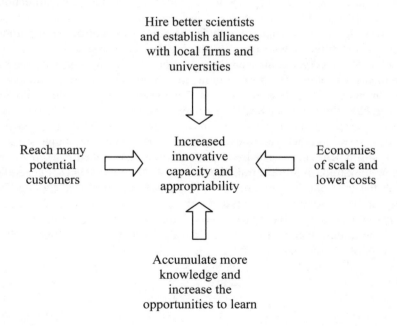

Figure 3.3 The factors that contribute to MNEs' increased innovative capacity and better ability to appropriate the value of innovation

In addition to the above arguments that suggest that multinational corporations can better appropriate and exploit the value of innovation, it has also been suggested that their internationalization and diversification allows them to improve their innovative capacity. They can do so by employing the specific resources and advantages of different countries (Hitt et al., 1994), and by establishing alliances with local firms and universities (Santos et al., 2004). Furthermore, the costs of developing new products and processes are usually lower for multinational corporations as they can buy R&D inputs from the cheapest available sources and locate their R&D departments in regions which are productive or in regions where the cost for resources such as land, materials and scientific talent is low (Granstrand et al., 1993; Kotabe et al., 2002).

MNEs can also increase their ability to innovate by (1) using know-how from different countries and scientists (Kafouros, 2006), (2) by accumulating more knowledge and by improving the opportunities to learn (Hitt et al., 1994) and (3) by hiring better employees and accessing skilled technical expertise (Cheng and Bolon, 1993). Indeed, as Kuemmerle (1997) argued, to ensure that they will innovate with the speed required to remain competitive, firms must exploit new findings from foreign universities, competitors and clusters of scientific excellence.

Nevertheless, even though a high degree of internationalization may give a firm competitive advantage, it should be emphasized that not all multinational corporations can benefit from R&D. MNEs face several problems and only a few firms can create a 'cohesive research community' (Kuemmerle, 1997). One problem is that the coordination and control of geographically dispersed R&D sites may increase the costs. The costs can also increase substantially because innovation managers and R&D employees need to travel to other R&D sites, suppliers, collaborators and universities. A second problem is associated with the unwitting dissemination of ideas and know-how from poorly-controlled departments (Fisch, 2003) and, generally, with the fact that the stock of scientific knowledge developed by one firm may spillover to rivals and other firms. Other studies have indicated that distance has a negative impact on the quality, frequency and speed of communication, thereby raising the risk of misunderstandings (Fisch, 2003; von Zedtwitz and Gassmann, 2002).

4. Evaluating the Economic Payoff of Industrial Research: A Review of Past Findings

As industrial Research and Development (R&D) is the engine that drives not only technological advances and innovation, but also economic growth and national welfare, the evaluation of its economic returns has attracted wide interest. This chapter reviews the relevant literature and attempts to bring some of the previous findings together. It also examines a number of methodological parameters and sample characteristics that influence the estimated returns to industrial research.

1. INTRODUCTION

This chapter has three main aims: (1) to survey the estimates of prior econometric research, (2) to structure other aspects of R&D described in the literature in a way which will help to put the findings of this research in context and (3) to investigate why the findings of previous studies vary so widely. As there are so many research fields related to innovation, it is impossible to bring all their findings together. In order to keep this chapter to a reasonable length, studies that use methodologies different from those used in this research book have not been surveyed. Similarly, the studies that explore the social (rather than the private) returns to R&D are also excluded. When necessary, smaller literature reviews are included in the next chapters. The next section examines the estimates of previous studies. As their comparability depends on the aggregation level of data (firm, industry or country level), this section focuses on micro-level studies. Besides the estimation of the effects of R&D, however, published studies also focus on aspects of R&D which are significant for corporate strategy and public policy. The third section reviews these aspects, exploring those factors that influence the contribution of R&D to corporate performance. The fourth section provides a summary of the factors that could bias the coefficient of

R&D. This may clarify why previous econometric estimates vary so widely. Finally, the fifth section provides the main conclusions.

2. THE RETURNS TO R&D: PREVIOUS FINDINGS

Two econometric specifications are usually used to assess the contribution of R&D to a firm's productivity performance: the R&D-elasticity specification and the Rate of Return (ROR) specification (Chapter 6 discusses these methodologies in detail). The first one is a Cobb-Douglas production function that correlates different measures of productivity not only with the conventional inputs of capital and labour, but also with a measure of R&D capital (or stock of scientific knowledge). The second econometric specification is a transformation of the Cobb-Douglas production function that includes the current R&D expenditure (rather than R&D capital). This specification allows the direct estimation of the rate of return to R&D (rather than the R&D elasticity). In other words, instead of assuming that R&D elasticity among firms is the same, this specification is based on the assumption that the rate of return to R&D is the same i.e. equal increases in output from increases in R&D. However, this makes its estimates not comparable to the estimates of the first econometric specification.

2.1 The R&D-Elasticity Estimates

Table 4.1 reports the results of previous studies that used the R&D-elasticity approach. This type of specification assumes that the disturbance term of the model is composed of two other types of disturbances: (i) a permanent disturbance specific to the firm, and (ii) a transitory disturbance (Cuneo and Mairesse, 1984).

Table 4.1 The findings of R&D-elasticity studies

Time Period	Study	Sample	R&D elasticity[1] (se)	R&D elasticity[2] (se)
1948-1957	Minasian (1969)	17 chemical firms (US)	0.26 (0.03)	0.08 (0.07)
1957-1965	Griliches (1980)	883 firms (US)	0.07 (0.01)	0.08 (0.01)

1963	Schankerman (1981)	110 chemical firms (US)	0.16	-
1966-1977	Griliches and Mairesse (1984)	133 firms (US)	0.07 (0.01)	0.08 (0.02)
1966-1977	Griliches (1986)	386 firms (US)	0.11 (0.02)	0.12 (0.02)
1973-1981	Sassenou (1988)	394 firms (Japan)	0.10 (0.01)	-0.01 (0.01)
1972-1977	Cuneo and Mairesse (1984)	98 high-tech firms (France)	0.14 (0.01)	0.08 (0.03)
1973-1978	Griliches and Mairesse (1983)	343 US, 185 French firms	-	0.02 (0.03)
1980-1987	Hall and Mairesse (1995)	197 firms (France)	0.25 (0.01)	0.08 (0.03)
		340 firms (France)	0.20 (0.06)	0.10 (0.02)
1974-1988	Adams and Jaffe (1996)	80 chemical firms (US)	0.08	-
1977-1989	Harhoff (1998)	443 Firms (Germany)	0.13 (0.01)	0.08 (0.02)
1981-1989	Mairesse and Hall (1996)	6282 obs. (France)	0.09 (0.006)	0.01 (0.01)
		6521 obs. (US)	0.24 (0.01)	0.17 (0.01)
1964-1990	Hall (1993)	16123 obs. (US)	0.03 (0.002)	0.02 (0.01)
1995	Dilling-Hansen et al. (2000)	110 firms (Denmark)	0.08 (0.02)	0.08 (0.03)
1994-2000	Wang and Tsai (2003)	136 firms (Taiwan)	0.19 (0.03)	-
1989-2002	Kafouros (2005)	78 firms (UK)	0.04 (0.01)	-

Notes:
[1] These estimates are based on the cross-sectional dimension of the data.
[2] These estimates are based on the time-series dimension of the data.

The decomposition of the disturbance term leads to two types of estimates. The first one is based on the cross-sectional dimension of the data, whereas the second one relies on their time-series dimension. The last two columns of Table 4.1 report both estimates. These findings indicate that usually (but not always) the impact of R&D on productivity performance is positive and statistically significant. R&D-elasticity varies from -0.01 to 0.26. In other words, when firms increase their stock of R&D by 1 percent, productivity performance is increased by up to 0.26 percent. The first researchers that used this method are Mansfield (1965) and Minasian (1969) (not shown in the table). Although the conceptual and empirical framework was not adequately developed in the 1960s, both studies confirmed the positive impact of R&D on productivity performance. After 1980, several studies by using the framework presented in Chapter 6 estimated R&D elasticity. For example, Griliches (1980) and Schankerman (1981) using US data estimated that R&D elasticity was 0.07 and 0.16 respectively. Cuneo and Mairesse (1984) and Hall and Mairesse (1995) using French data, found that R&D elasticity was 0.14 and 0.20 respectively.

There is also some scattered evidence for other countries, besides the US and France. Sassenou (1988), using a sample of 394 Japanese firms, calculated that R&D elasticity is 0.10. Harhoff's work (1998) indicates that for the German manufacturing firms, R&D elasticity is about 0.13. For a sample of 136 Taiwanese firms, Wang and Tsai (2003) found the R&D elasticity to be about 0.19, whereas Dilling-Hansen et al. (2000) using Danish data estimated that R&D elasticity is 0.08. Furthermore, the effects of R&D can vary widely depending not only on the country of study but also on the time period. As Hall (1993) found in relation to the US, the contribution of R&D declined from 0.10-0.15 during the 1960s and 1970s to about 0.02 in the 1980s. Similarly, the work of Mairesse and Hall (1996) verified that in both the US and France, R&D elasticity declined during the 1980s.

However, the estimated R&D elasticity does also depend on a number of methodological factors. One of those is double counting (R&D equipment and R&D employees are counted twice, one time in R&D capital and one more time in ordinary capital and labour). Cuneo and Mairesse (1984) showed that double-counting corrections increase the R&D-elasticity from 0.11 to 0.21. Hall and Mairesse (1995) found that when such corrections were made, the estimated rate of return was higher by 4 percent. Similarly, Schankerman (1981) found that double-counting biased downwards the estimates of R&D.

The definition of output is also important. Both Cuneo and Mairesse (1984) and Mairesse and Hall (1996) found that the use of sales instead of value added, attenuated the R&D elasticity from 0.21 to 0.14 and from 0.16 to 0.09 respectively. By contrast, the choice of the R&D depreciation rate does not appear to significantly affect the R&D elasticity. Many researchers, such as Griliches (1980), Harhoff (1998) and Kafouros (2005) have tried different depreciation rates (10, 15, 20 and 30 percent) and found that R&D elasticity remains stable. Indeed, even under the extreme assumption that depreciation rate is 100 percent, the R&D elasticity remains approximately the same (Hall and Mairesse, 1995). Another factor that may influence the estimated elasticity of R&D is the inclusion of industry dummies. Overall, taking into account the findings of previous studies (e.g. Griliches, 1986; Kafouros, 2005), it appears that the elasticity of R&D is lower when industry dummies are included in the analysis.

The last column of Table 4.1 reports the R&D elasticity which is based on the time-series dimension of the data. This elasticity is usually lower than the corresponding cross-sectional elasticity, and sometimes negligible. Cuneo and Mairesse (1984) found that R&D elasticity is reduced from 0.14 (cross-section) to 0.08 (time-series) whereas Harhoff (1998) found that it is reduced from 0.13 to 0.08. The principle reason for this phenomenon is the reduced variability that the time-series dimension of the data includes (Griliches, 1986). However, when the assumption of constant returns to scale is imposed, the difference between cross-sectional and time-series estimates is smaller.

2.2 The Rate-of-Return to R&D Estimates

Table 4.2 presents the findings obtained using the second econometric approach (rate of return). The rate of return to R&D usually varies from 0.00 to 0.56, thereby indicating that the contribution of R&D is usually, but not always, economically and statistically significant. Again, the major reasons for such wide variation are the differences between countries and over time. However, the wide variation is also the result of several methodological factors. As we will explain in Chapter 6, this specification is based on the R&D intensity of each firm. However, R&D intensity can be defined either as R&D over sales or as R&D over value added. Because value added is much lower than sales, the first ratio is considerably smaller than the latter amplifying the estimated rate of return. Nevertheless, in practice, the estimates of the sales and value added approaches are usually quite close.

The rate of return to R&D also depends on whether the assumption of constant returns to scale is imposed or not, whether industry dummies are included or not and whether productivity is measured as labour or total factor productivity (TFP). As with R&D elasticity studies, when the constant returns to scale assumption is imposed, the estimated rate of return to R&D is usually higher (Griliches and Mairesse, 1990; Sassenou, 1988). Conversely, the inclusion of industry dummies decreases the rate of return (Griliches and

The Value of Innovation

Mairesse, 1990; Odagiri and Iwata, 1986; Wakelin, 2001). When labour productivity is used instead of total factor productivity, the return to R&D tends to be slightly higher (Mairesse and Sassenou, 1991), but this is not always the case.

Table 4.2 The findings of rate of return studies

Time Period	Study	Sample	Rate of return to R&D (se)
1947-1957	Minasian (1962)	18 chemical firms (US)	0.25 (0.04)
1960-1976	Mansfield (1980)	16 oil and chemical firms (US)	0.27 (0.07)
1971-1976	Link (1981)	174 firms (US)	0.0
1973-1978	Griliches and Mairesse (1983)	343 firms (US)	0.19 (0.11)
		185 firms (France)	0.31 (0.07)
1975-1979	Link (1982)	97 firms (US)	0.31 (0.19)
1975-1979	Link (1983)	302 firms (US)	0.06 (0.04)
1971-1980	Clark and Griliches (1984)	924 business units (US)	0.18 (0.05)
1973-1980	Griliches and Mairesse (1990)	525 firms (US)	0.41 (0.1)
		406 firms (Japan)	0.56 (0.23)
1969-1981	Odagiri (1983)	370 firms (Japan)	0.26 (0.10)
1973-1981	Sassenou (1988)	394 firms (Japan)	0.22 (0.11)
1966-1973	Odagiri and Iwata (1986)	135 firms (Japan)	0.20 (0.11)

1974-1982		168 firms (Japan)	0.17 (0.06)
1976-1984	Goto and Suzuki (1989)	Drug and chemical firms (Japan)	0.32-0.56
1972-1985	Litchenberg and Siegel (1991)	2000 firms (US)	0.13 (0.02)
1980-1987	Hall and Mairesse (1995)	197 firms (France)	0.27 (0.06)
1977-1989	Harhoff (1998)	443 firms (Germany)	0.22 (0.07)
1988-1992	Wakelin (2001)	98 firms (UK)	0.28 (0.21)

It is also interesting to note that the estimated rate is actually the rate of return to gross R&D. In order to find the net rate of return, the depreciation of R&D must be subtracted from the gross rate of return. However, it is not clear which estimates (gross or net) are higher. A formal interpretation suggests that as the net rate of return is equal to gross minus depreciation, then the net rate of return should be lower than the gross return (Hall and Mairesse, 1995). Nevertheless, as the conceptual framework implies that the variable of interest should be a measure of the net R&D capital, by including the gross R&D capital (which is significantly higher), the estimated gross rate of return should be lower and not higher than the net (Hall and Mairesse, 1995). Unfortunately, the empirical findings are inconclusive too and do not clarify the contradictions of theory. Goto and Suzuki (1989) found that whilst many industries had a net rate of return higher than the gross, in some other cases it was lower. Hall and Mairesse (1995) found the net and gross rate of return to be very close. Harhoff (1998) on the other hand showed that the net rate of return is significantly higher than the corresponding gross return.

3. WHAT FACTORS AFFECT THE RETURNS TO R&D

Industrial research is not a homogeneous process. As firms implement R&D projects to serve their corporate strategy, these projects vary widely. So far in this chapter, the findings concerning the contribution of R&D on average has been discussed, without examining what particular factors affect the returns to R&D. This section investigates some of these factors. By relying on a concept-centred philosophy, it accumulates evidence from both firm- and industry-level studies. Table 4.3 categorizes these factors into six groups. Firstly, the effects of R&D depend on whether the industrial research that a firm undertakes is basic or applied R&D. As Iansiti and West (1997) point out, firms prefer to focus on applied R&D and to turn to universities and research institutes to help with the basic research. Unfortunately, the empirical findings are contradictory and do not shed light on whether the decision of firms to emphasize on applied R&D is optimal. The findings of Mansfield (1980) indicate that the rate of return to basic research in the US is 1.78 while the corresponding return to applied R&D is 0.10. The study of Lichtenberg and Siegel (1991) confirm this finding suggesting that the rate of return to basic R&D is 1.38 while the economic payoff for applied R&D is only 0.11. Similarly, Griliches (1986) found that although the average R&D elasticity is 0.12, the R&D elasticity of basic research is about 0.40 in the US.

Table 4.3 The factors affecting the returns to R&D

	1	2	3	4	5	6
Adams and Jaffe (1996)				•		
Clark and Griliches (1984)		•				
Cuneo and Mairesse (1984)					•	
Dilling-Hansen et al. (2000)			•			
Goto and Suzuki (1989)				•		
Griliches (1980)			•	•		•
Griliches (1986)	•		•			
Griliches and Lichtenberg (1984)			•			
Griliches and Mairesse (1983)				•		
Griliches and Mairesse (1984)					•	
Hall (1993)				•		•
Hall and Mairesse (1995)	•		•			
Harhoff (1998)					•	
Kafouros (2005)				•	•	•
Levy and Terleckyj (1983)			•			
Lichtenberg (1984)			•			
Lichtenberg and Siegel (1991)	•		•			•
Link (1981)	•					•
Mansfield (1980)	•					

Mansfield (1981)	•			•
Mansfield (1988)	•	•		•
Odagiri (1983)			•	•
Odagiri and Iwata (1986)			•	•
Singh and Trieu (1996)	•			
Wakelin (2001)			•	
Wang and Tsai (2003)			•	•

Notes:
[1] Basic versus applied R&D.
[2] Product versus process R&D.
[3] Company versus government financed R&D.
[4] Analysis for different industries.
[5] Technological opportunities.
[6] Firm size.

By contrast, Hall and Mairesse (1995), Mansfield (1988) and Singh and Trieu (1996), found either a negative or a statistically insignificant correlation between basic R&D and productivity. However, the evaluation of basic research is very complex. As Nelson (1959) argued, basic research may not solve practical problems but it may be used in the future as an additional R&D input. Thus basic research may be profitable only for diversified firms, such as MNEs, as their diversification may later accommodate the commercialization of whatever inventions may result. There is also an issue of the time lag of R&D effects as basic research typically needs more time in order to deliver benefits. Possibly, the impact of basic research may be low initially and magnified only after a number of years.

The returns to R&D also depend on whether the R&D undertaken is product or process R&D. The study of Clark and Griliches (1984) for the US showed that a higher proportion of product R&D leads to a lower rate of return. The findings of Mansfield (1988) are similar. He suggested that the efficiency of Japanese R&D could be explained by the high proportion of process R&D that they undertake (Japanese firms devote 2/3 of their R&D to process research whereas the US firms devote only 1/3). There are a number of reasons that explain the association of product R&D with lower returns. Firstly, as Clark and Griliches (1984) pointed out, intensive product R&D leads to an increased number of new products, which need a start-up and debugging phase. Hence, the established production processes are frequently disrupted, resulting in lower productivity. Secondly, as deflators do not fully account for product quality and variety, improvements of output resulting from enhanced product quality cannot be measured easily. Thirdly, the continual introduction of new products implies the adoption of flexible, less standardized processes, leading again to lower productivity (Clark and Griliches, 1984). It has also been argued that process R&D is not copied easily. Consequently, process R&D may be neutralized less easily by other firms' imitations (Kafouros, 2005).

A third factor that affects the R&D contribution is the source of funding. Levy and Terleckyj (1983) found that the elasticity of company-financed R&D in the US is 0.28 while the elasticity of government-financed R&D is 0.06. The studies of Griliches (1980 and 1986) and Griliches and Lichtenberg (1984) confirmed these results. Similarly, the findings of Lichtenberg and Siegel (1991) indicated that the rate of return to company-financed R&D in the US is 0.35 while the corresponding return to government-financed R&D is only 0.03. The results of Dilling-Hansen et al. (2000) for Denmark showed that the inclusion of a variable for company-financed R&D, increased the elasticity from 0.12 to 0.18. Moreover, Hall and Mairesse (1995) found a negative association between government-financed R&D and the productivity of French manufacturing firms. Griliches (1986) suggested that these results are sensible because firms invest in R&D only when the expected payoff is high and the risk is low.

However, care should be taken in interpreting the above findings. They do not suggest that governments should reduce R&D funding. As Link (1982) finds, government R&D is complementary to the firms' R&D spending suggesting that an increase in government R&D increases private R&D (in the US). Similarly, the results of Levy and Terleckyj (1983) showed that every dollar of government R&D stimulated an increase in private R&D spending by 0.27 of a dollar. In line with these findings, Mansfield's work (1984) indicated that each dollar increase in government funding of R&D leads to an additional average of six cents increase in a firm's spending for the subsequent two years; for each dollar cut, firms reduced their support by about 25 cents. Scott (1984) confirmed the above results. He rejected the hypothesis that company and government-financed R&D are substitutes and showed that government-financed R&D stimulates private investments. However, Lichtenberg (1984) provided contradictory findings for the US which indicated that increases in government R&D are usually associated with reductions in company-financed R&D. Maybe, as Mansfield (1984) suggested, we should not evaluate government-financed R&D separately but should view it as a factor that increases the profitability of company-financed R&D. This argument sounds plausible as governments do not distribute R&D funding randomly but principally to those firms that have already invested in R&D.

The fourth factor affecting the returns to R&D is the industry that a firm belongs to. The estimates of Griliches (1980) indicated that the R&D elasticity ranges from 0.03 in the US electrical equipment to 0.12 in the chemical industry. Kafouros (2005) found R&D elasticity to be 0.06 for UK mechanical machinery manufacturers but 0.15 for the electronics industry. The findings of Adams and Jaffe (1996) for the US chemical industry indicated that the R&D coefficient is about 0.13 for drug firms but only 0.04 for other chemicals such as plastics. Other studies such as those of Goto and Suzuki (1989) and Hall (1993) also explored this issue in Japan and in the US respectively. Overall it would appear that the coefficient of R&D tends to be higher for the pharmaceutical and electronics industries and lower for other industries such as metals.

There are also many studies that explored the role of technological opportunities by examining the differences between technologically advanced and low-tech firms. Griliches and Mairesse (1984) found that the R&D elasticity for US high-tech sectors is 0.22 whereas the corresponding elasticity for low-tech sectors is negative. In a similar vein, the findings of Harhoff (1998) indicated that high-tech German firms experience much higher R&D elasticity (0.16) than low-tech firms (0.09). Wang and Tsai (2003) reported results for Japan of 0.30 compared to 0.07. Similarly, the industry-level findings of Verspagen (1995) indicate that the coefficient of R&D is 0.11 for high-tech UK industries while it is insignificant for low-tech industries. Overall the empirical findings above appear to be consistent with the decisions of managers of high-tech firms to heavily invest in R&D as well as with the decisions of managers of low-tech firms to keep R&D investments at lower levels.

The final factor presented in Table 4.3 is firm size. A plethora of theoretical arguments are discussed in the next chapters that explain why the magnitude of R&D effects ought to be higher for larger firms. For instance, larger firms benefit from economies of scale, and have both technical know-how and managerial qualities that are important in determining a firm's speed of response to a new technique (Mansfield, 1968a). Although these theoretical arguments suggest that firm size is positively associated with R&D effects, the empirical findings of past studies are contradictory and have shed little light on the role of firm size. Link (1981) explored the above argument and found that the rate of return to R&D for US firms is positively associated with firm size. However, Lichtenberg and Siegel (1991) found that R&D coefficient is only marginally higher for larger US firms. Similarly, the findings of Cohen and Klepper (1996) support the notion that because larger firms have larger output, they can therefore apply the results of R&D to more products and processes and thus spread the cost. However, contradictory pieces of evidence are provided by Griliches (1980) and Wang and Tsai (2003) (for the US and Taiwan respectively). Both of these studies indicated no association between R&D and firm size. Hence, although the relationship between firm size and innovation has been examined for many decades, it is still a subject for debate.

4. WHY THE ESTIMATES VARY SO WIDELY

The previous sections indicated that the contribution of R&D to productivity
can vary widely. This significant variation is caused by two main factors. The
first one is the dissimilarity of samples, i.e. the different period, country and
industries that each study analyses. For instance, the R&D of one country
may indeed be more efficient than that of another country. The second factor
is the variation of the methodological specifications, such as the inclusion of
dummies, the assumption of constant returns to scale and double counting
corrections. Summary Table 4.4 presents both the sample and methodological
variations along with their impact on the coefficient of R&D. As it indicates,
the contribution of R&D appears to be higher for the R&D-intensive and
high-technology industries (especially chemical and electronics) as well as
for process and company-financed R&D. However, the findings appear to be
contradictory in relation to the effects of basic and applied R&D and the size
of firm.

Table 4.4 The effect of each methodological and sample variation

			R&D elasticity method	Rate of return method
Methodological variations				
1	Estimation method	Cross section dimension	↑	O
		Time series dimension	↓	O
2	Output definition	Value added	↑	↓
		Sales	↓	↑
3	Specification details	Lack of double counting corrections	↓	–
		Industry dummies inclusion	↓	↓
		Imposing constant returns to scale	↑	↑
		Depreciation	–	↕

4	Productivity measure	TFP vs. labour productivity	Not clear	Not clear
Other variations				
5	Type of R&D	Basic vs. applied R&D	↕	
		Product R&D	↓	
		Process R&D	↑	
6	Source of funding	Company-financed R&D	↑	
		Government-financed R&D	↓	
7	Industries	Chemical & electronics	↑	
		Metal & transportation	↓	
8	Firm characteristics	Hi-technology	↑	
		Low-technology	↓	
		Size of firm	↕	

Notes: The symbols denote: ↑ R&D contribution is higher, ↓ R&D contribution is lower, ↕ contradictory findings, – the R&D contribution is not affected, O cannot apply

The estimates also depend on the methodological specifications adopted by researchers. As Table 4.4 indicates, the R&D elasticity is higher when the cross-sectional dimension of the data is used. Using value added instead of sales results in higher R&D elasticity but a lower rate of return to R&D. By imposing the assumption of constant returns to scale the estimates appear higher, whereas the lack of double counting corrections biases the estimates downwards. Similarly, when the R&D coefficient is estimated with the inclusion of industry dummies, it tends to be lower. Although the depreciation rate does not affect the coefficient of the R&D-elasticity method, it does affect the ROR coefficient considerably. However, there are contradictions about whether this impact is positive or negative. And finally, although the measure of productivity (labour or TFP) may affect the estimates, it is not clear yet in which direction.

5. DISCUSSION AND CONCLUSION

This chapter surveyed the econometric literature regarding the relationship between R&D and productivity. First, it clarified why the estimates of the impact of R&D vary so widely and offered a summary table that presents the main possible biases and their effects on the estimates. Second and third, it answered two questions significant for management and policy making: (1) What is the exact contribution of R&D to productivity performance? and (2) What are the determinants of this contribution? The wide range of the estimated R&D coefficients give an ironic twist to the first question as it therefore cannot be answered adequately. Overall, prior research suggests that industrial R&D activities frequently contribute significantly to firms' productivity performance. This however does not suggest that all firms can benefit from innovation. Similarly, even when the R&D coefficient was zero, it did not necessarily mean that R&D was not important for firms' performance. As discussed later, it merely suggested that the effects of a firm's R&D activities may have been neutralized by the effects of its competitors' own research.

In contrast, the second objective of the chapter has been fulfilled more successfully. Although many of the factors affecting the returns to R&D have been known to researchers for quite some time, in a number of cases the empirical findings are still contradictory. What has been learnt by surveying the past literature, is that the contribution of R&D depends on a variety of different factors. The industry to which a firm belongs is important, as is the type of R&D undertaken, and the source of funding for the R&D. The data indicates that technologically advanced firms, especially in the pharmaceutical and electronic industries, are good R&D performers. This explains why their managers invested so heavily in R&D and emphasizes the importance of technological opportunities. The R&D contribution is also higher for process R&D and for company-financed R&D. However, the findings are contradictory concerning the role of basic and applied R&D. Similarly, the findings do not clearly support the theoretical predictions that the effects of R&D are positively associated with firm size.

Nevertheless, it is important to be particularly careful in interpreting the findings of the previous studies examined above. As discussed in the next chapters, the fact that R&D is correlated with higher productivity does not necessarily suggest that a firm can increase its productivity simply by investing in R&D. Firms that experience high returns to R&D may differ from those that do not, in ways which cannot be fully remedied simply by investing in R&D. For instance, the organizational culture and infrastructure of high-tech firms may be complementary factors that encourage such high returns to R&D (Teece et al., 1997).

The evaluation of the economic benefits and value of R&D is very complex. This chapter has surveyed the results concerning the impact of R&D on firm performance (as measured by productivity). However, the total value of R&D is not a single issue but may have many different facets. As well as the impact of R&D on productivity performance, it also affects business profitability, production costs and consumer value. Moreover, current methodology may give only a crude measure of R&D effects and may not capture further value hidden in R&D. As has been shown (Cohen and Levinthal, 1990; Kafouros, 2006), the mechanisms underlying industrial research do not just favor productivity performance, but can also facilitate business re-engineering and improve the capability of firms to collect, assimilate and exploit knowledge.

Knowing what has been covered by the past literature, allows the identification of a number of research gaps. To begin with, little past empirical work concerning the economic payoff to industrial research has taken into account the fact that many R&D projects are outsourced. So as well as a firm's internal R&D efforts, it would be interesting to evaluate the returns to R&D activities which are outsourced, either to other firms or to universities. This would allow the investigation as to whether the impact of in-house R&D is greater than the corresponding impact of the outsourced R&D.

Secondly, because there was little research done regarding firms' R&D in the 1990s and 2000s, it is likely that managers' decisions are currently based on the findings of the studies using data from the 1970s and 1980s, which indicated that R&D effects declined (Hall, 1993). For various reasons however, this picture might have changed in the 1990s and 2000s because of factors such as the Internet and the intensive firms' computerization. As Sterlacchini (1989) argues, energy-intensive processes have been replaced by information-intensive processes, changing the relationship between technological change and productivity. Another factor that most studies do not take into account is the time lag of the effects of R&D: because time is needed to complete a research project, to introduce its outcomes to the market, and to gain a market share, the impact of R&D may not be maximized immediately but may take several years. Although there has been some research regarding the time lag between patents and productivity (Hall et al., 1986), the time lag of R&D (the time between R&D investments and their effects on productivity) is largely unexplored (the following chapters examine this issue).

PART II

Conceptual and Methodological Issues

5. The Cost of Industrial Research and Development

To examine which firms had to pay more for industrial research, the costs of R&D inputs were analysed, and R&D price indices for 13 UK manufacturing industries were constructed. The results indicate that the GDP deflator, utilized in previous studies to convert R&D spending to constant prices, overestimated the inflation rate of R&D inputs. The findings also indicate that the inflation rate of R&D in industries such as textiles and minerals was higher than that in industries such as aerospace, office equipment and pharmaceuticals. As these results show that the costs of R&D inputs tend to rise more rapidly for low-technology firms, they also offer an alternative explanation of why previous studies found the returns to R&D to be lower for such firms. Given that numerous studies use R&D as a dependent or independent variable, the findings should be of benefit to a wide range of social scientists, government officials and managers.

1. INTRODUCTION

As industrial Research and Development (R&D) plays a critical role in the evolution of science and technology, the evaluation of its impacts on various measures of technological and economic performance has attracted wide interest. Indeed, there are numerous micro-level and macro-level studies that examine the relationship between R&D, patents, knowledge spillovers, innovation and productivity performance (Griliches, 1986; Sterlacchini, 1989; Geroski, 1991; Hall and Mairesse, 1995; Stoneman, 1995; Adams and Jaffe, 1996; Kafouros, 2005; 2006). However, as recent R&D price indices do not exist, previous studies utilized either the GDP deflator or a manufacturing deflator to convert R&D expenditures to constant prices.

Nevertheless, this approach does not allow us to measure accurately the level of R&D activity. As Cameron (1996, p.2) argues, 'It is not clear that the cost of R&D follows the path of prices in the economy as a whole'. Mansfield (1987, p.124-126) stresses the importance of R&D price indices by emphasizing that 'inaccurate price indices can result in substantial analytical and policy errors' and that 'little is known about the extent to which the results would change if price indices for R&D inputs were used instead of the GNP deflator'. Similarly, the Frascati Manual of OECD (OECD, 2002, p.218) emphasizes the importance of R&D deflators:

> R&D deflators are justified if it is believed that the cost of R&D has moved in a way that is significantly different from general costs and/or if trends in the cost of R&D have varied considerably among sectors or industries. In general, over the long term, it is reasonable to suppose that the implicit GDP (output) deflator would tend to increase less rapidly than a true R&D (input) deflator because of productivity increases.

These arguments, along with recent discussions concerning the capitalization of R&D in National Accounts of the UK and other OECD countries, engender a practical need for R&D price indices. This chapter aims to fill this void. Following earlier papers and the recommendations of the Frascati manual (OECD, 2002), it analyses the cost of R&D inputs and constructs R&D price indices for 13 UK industries over the period 1989-2002. It then compares them with the corresponding GDP and manufacturing deflators, and demonstrates how the use of inappropriate indices may lead to imprecise and biased estimates. The results are intriguing as they indicate that the cost that a firm has to pay in order to undertake R&D varies widely depending on the industry involved.

2. CONSTRUCTING R&D PRICE INDICES

Following the work of Schott (1976) and Bosworth (1979), this analysis uses a proxy price index for each R&D cost component. According to the Frascati manual (OECD, 2002), the three main R&D components are: (1) wages and salaries (w), (2) instruments and equipment (c) and (3) materials and other current inputs (m). A fourth R&D component relates to land and buildings. Because data on this component were not available, it was not included in the analysis. Nevertheless, as only 2 or 3 percent of the total R&D expenditure is spent on land and buildings (OECD, 2002), a significant bias is not expected from its absence. The price indices (p_w, p_c, p_m) for the three inputs of R&D were applied to their corresponding current expenditures (w, c, m):

$$wk = w \ (1 / p_w) \tag{5.1}$$
$$ck = c \ (1 / p_c) \tag{5.2}$$
$$mk = m \ (1 / p_m) \tag{5.3}$$

So the total R&D expenditure (T) expressed in constant prices is:

$$Tk = wk + ck + mk \tag{5.4}$$

In order to estimate the R&D price indices, the current R&D expenditures have been divided by the constant R&D expenditures, that is T/Tk. The price indices used for the three components of R&D (wages and salaries, instruments and equipment, materials and other current expenditures) are: (1) a labour compensation price index for the manufacturing sector, (2) a manufacturing capital price index, and (3) a price index that is appropriate for the materials used by manufacturing firms. All these indices were obtained from the UK Office for National Statistics (ONS). Following Bosworth (1979), we weight the price series by their corresponding current R&D expenditure. The implicit R&D price index (P) for an industry (j) and year (t) can be written as:

$$\frac{1}{P_{jt}} = \frac{w_{jt}}{T_{jt}}(\frac{1}{P_{wjt}}) + \frac{c_{jt}}{T_{jt}}(\frac{1}{P_{cjt}}) + \frac{m_{jt}}{T_{jt}}(\frac{1}{P_{mjt}}) \tag{5.5}$$

This index has attractive theoretical properties because in contrast to other formulations that through using fixed-weights overstate the rise in prices (Roberts, 2000), it takes into account that as cost and technological factors change over time, firms substitute some R&D inputs for others. Data concerning the expenditure devoted to the three different R&D inputs were available for 13 main UK industries. As Table 5.1 and Table 5.2 show, the spending devoted to each R&D component as a proportion of the total expenditure (denoted $w_\%$, $c_\%$ and $m_\%$) varied widely depending on the year and the industry involved.

Whilst the largest component for many industries was that of labour, the largest for others was the cost of materials. In a similar way, the spending devoted on each R&D component changed over time. In the case of textiles, for instance, the R&D component of capital increased from 4 percent in 1995 to 21 percent in 2002, showing that these firms started to focus on capital-intensive research and development. To estimate the indices more accurately, an attempt was made to retrieve industry-specific data on R&D spending per component for every year between 1989 and 2002. Unfortunately, only the total R&D spending per industry (T_j) was available between 1989 and 1994. For that reason, the annual expenditure per R&D component for these years was calculated by multiplying total R&D spending (T_j) for each industry by its corresponding mean values of $w_\%$, $c_\%$ and $m_\%$ for the years 1995 to 2002.

Conceptual and Methodological Issues

Table 5.1 Composition of R&D expenditure in 1995

Industry	Capital[a]	Labour[b]	Other Current[c]
Textiles	4%	33%	63%
Chemicals	12%	43%	45%
Pharmaceuticals	22%	32%	46%
Rubber & plastics	15%	43%	42%
Minerals	7%	48%	45%
Metal products	4%	46%	50%
Machinery	4%	44%	52%
Comp. & office equipment	13%	38%	49%
Electrical & electronics	6%	39%	55%
Communication	8%	45%	47%
Instrument engineering	6%	48%	46%
Motor vehicles	13%	37%	50%
Aerospace	6%	35%	59%
Average	**9%**	**41%**	**50%**

Notes:
[a] Capital includes plant, machinery, land and buildings.
[b] Labour includes salaries and wages.
[c] The 'Other Current' type of expenditure includes purchases of other inputs, materials and services.

Source: Office for National Statistics (ONS).

Table 5.2 Composition of R&D expenditure in 2002

Industry	Capital[a]	Labour[b]	Other Current[c]
Textiles	21%	53%	26%
Chemicals	10%	49%	41%
Pharmaceuticals	15%	37%	48%
Rubber & plastics	33%	31%	36%
Minerals	15%	50%	35%
Metal products	8%	43%	49%
Machinery	4%	53%	43%
Comp. & office equipment	5%	37%	58%
Electrical & electronics	4%	50%	46%
Communication	4%	49%	47%

Instrument engineering	8%	42%	50%
Motor vehicles	4%	48%	48%
Aerospace	6%	35%	59%
Average	**11%**	**44%**	**45%**

Notes:
[a] Capital includes plant, machinery, land and buildings.
[b] Labour includes salaries and wages.
[c] The 'Other Current' type of expenditure includes purchases of other inputs, materials and services.

Source: Office for National Statistics (ONS).

3. RESULTS

Table 5.3 and Table 5.4 show the estimated R&D price indices (base year = 2000) for the period between 1989 and 1995, and the period between 1996 and 2002 respectively. These indices are industry-specific for 13 different sectors of the economy. In line with the study of Jankowski (1993), the findings suggest considerable inter-industry variability in terms of the cost of R&D inputs. Over the 1989-2002 period, R&D inflation ranged between 14.9 percent for the aerospace industry and 37 percent for the textiles industry. The difference between the GDP deflator (see Table 5.5) and the industry-specific price indices is considerable in many sectors. For example, although the value of GDP deflator in 1989 was 69.6, the corresponding values of the R&D index for the aerospace, office equipment and pharmaceutical industries were 86, 84.2 and 84.4 respectively, confirming that the GDP deflator is a poor index for the deflation of R&D.

It is also noteworthy that the inflation rate of R&D in industries such as textiles and minerals has been higher than that in industries such as aerospace, office equipment and pharmaceuticals. As these findings show that the costs of R&D tend to rise more rapidly for the low-technology sectors of the economy, they imply that these firms have had to pay more for R&D inputs during the 1989-2002 period. This result has important implications for academic research as it offers an alternative explanation of why previous studies found the returns to R&D to be less positive for low-technology industries.

Furthermore, a weighted average of the constructed industry-specific R&D indices was estimated. This was compared with the UK manufacturing price index as well as with the GDP deflator that previous studies and the UK Office for National Statistics (ONS) usually utilize to convert R&D expenditures to constant prices. As Figure 5.1 and Table 5.5 indicate, the cost of R&D followed a trend significantly different from that of general costs. Although the GDP deflator was continually rising, the R&D index declined between 1995 and 1999. Further analyzing the costs of R&D, we found that the reason for this decline was the fact that the cost of materials used in industrial research decreased between 1995 and 1999.

Table 5.3 Industry-specific R&D price indices (1989-1995)

	1989	1990	1991	1992	1993	1994	1995
Textiles	74.8	77.6	79.9	80.7	84	87.7	105
Chemicals	79.5	81.6	83.4	83.6	87.1	90.9	99.6
Pharmaceuticals	84.4	86.2	87.3	86.5	89.8	93.5	101.6
Rubber & plastics	81.4	83.4	84.9	84.7	88.2	91.9	99
Minerals	79.3	81.5	83.4	83.6	87.1	90.9	100.9
Metal products	81.7	83.4	84.9	84.8	88.5	92.3	100.3
Machinery	81.4	83	84.6	84.6	88.3	92.2	101.1
Office equipment	84.2	85.6	86.9	86.3	90	93.8	101.2
Electrical	82.7	84.3	85.7	85.3	89	92.8	102.6
Communication	81.5	83.3	84.8	84.7	88.3	92.1	99.8
Instruments	79.8	81.7	83.5	83.7	87.4	91.3	98.9
Motor vehicles	81.6	83.4	85	84.8	88.4	92.1	101.9
Aerospace	86	86.9	87.9	87.1	91	94.9	104

Notes: The base year is 2000.

Table 5.4 Industry-specific R&D price indices (1996-2002)

	1996	1997	1998	1999	2000	2001	2002
Textiles	96.6	92.4	95.3	92.7	100	102.2	102.5
Chemicals	99.1	97.6	95.9	96	100	101.3	101.1
Pharmaceuticals	101.6	99.4	96.9	96.4	100	100.6	99.7
Rubber & plastics	99.8	98.4	96.4	95.8	100	101.1	100
Minerals	101.3	97.3	96.1	94.4	100	101.1	101.6
Metal products	100.2	98.4	96.8	96.2	100	101	100.1
Machinery	100.9	97.9	96.4	95.8	100	100.6	101.3
Office equipment	100	100.6	97.1	97	100	100.6	99

Electrical	101.7	98.5	96.2	96.3	100	100.7	100.9
Communication	100.3	97.8	96.5	96.1	100	100.6	100.7
Instruments	99.4	97.1	96.3	96	100	101.2	100
Motor vehicles	101.3	98.5	96.2	96.1	100	101.1	100.6
Aerospace	103.2	99.8	97.1	96.1	100	100.3	98.8

Notes: The base year is 2000.

Table 5.5 Manufacturing R&D price indices

	GDP	Manufacturing [a]	R&D Price Index [b]
1989	69.6	87.2	82
1990	75	91.4	83.8
1991	79.6	94.8	85.3
1992	82.2	95	85
1993	84.2	96.2	88.6
1994	85.3	98	92.4
1995	87.7	102.3	101.3
1996	90.5	103.7	100.7
1997	93.3	102.9	98.3
1998	95.9	101.5	96.4
1999	98.2	100.1	96
2000	100	100	100
2001	102.5	99.4	100.9
2002	105.5	99.3	100.4

Notes:
[a] This index excludes the following products: food, tobacco, and petrol.
[b] This index is a weighted average of the 13 manufacturing industries.

Source: The source for both the GDP and manufacturing index is the Office for National Statistics.

Figure 5.1 also indicates that the increase of the R&D index is higher than that of the manufacturing index. This result is consistent with the argument that as the manufacturing index is an output (rather than an input) index, it incorporates productivity increases. Thus, it tends to increase less rapidly than input prices (Mansfield, 1987; Hill, 1988). By contrast, the increase of the R&D index is lower than that of the GDP deflator. This shows that the cost of R&D rises less rapidly than the prices within the economy as a whole. This result is important as contradicts previous studies that examined earlier periods and found that the rise of the UK GDP deflator was less than that of the corresponding R&D index (Cameron, 1996; Schott, 1976).

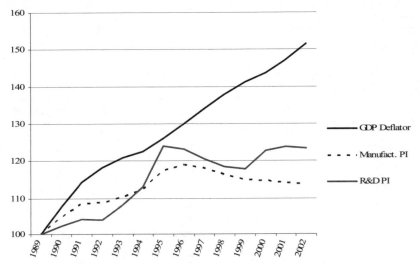

Figure 5.1 GDP, manufacturing and R&D price indices (1989=100)

The study also examined whether the constructed R&D price indices have a significant effect on real level of R&D activity. To do so, we initially applied the GDP and manufacturing deflators to data on UK R&D spending. The results showed that R&D growth over the 1989-2002 period was 17 percent and 55 percent respectively. However, applying the R&D price index to the data, we found that the real growth of R&D spending was actually 43 percent.

Nevertheless, the constructed price indices are subject to a number of limitations. Firstly, the trends in the wages of R&D employees may vary across industries. Because the salary price indices utilized are not industry-specific, some errors may creep in. Secondly, this study assumed that the price indices for basic, applied, process and product R&D are all identical. Data that are more detailed could allow future research to examine how the costs of these types of industrial research differ from each other. Thirdly, the trends in wages may vary across the categories of R&D personnel, such as researchers, technologists and supporting staff (OECD, 2002). However, as there are no official salary price indices for each category, the same index has been used for each of them, possibly resulting in some degree of inaccuracy.

4. CONCLUSION

Although inaccurate price indices may lead to substantial policy errors (Mansfield, 1987), previous studies utilized the GDP deflator to convert R&D expenditures to constant prices, and to estimate the real level of R&D activity. This chapter has contributed to research by analyzing the costs of R&D inputs, by examining which firms had to pay more for industrial research and by constructing R&D price indices for 13 UK industries. As the evaluation of the effects of R&D has attracted a lot of interest, a wide range of social scientists and policy makers could use the R&D price indices constructed in this study. Nevertheless, because the costs of the inputs of industrial research influence R&D budgeting, the findings are also important for managerial practice.

The study showed that when R&D expenditures are converted to constant prices using either the GDP or a manufacturing deflator, they are considerably distorted. This stresses the need for better R&D price indices. The findings also confirm those of Cameron (1996, p.219) who emphasized that 'the cost of R&D in individual industries can rise at very different rates from that in manufacturing as a whole'. Hence, to capture cost idiosyncrasies that vary across sectors, it is advisable to use the industry-specific R&D indices, rather than their weighted average.

The findings also indicate that the costs of R&D inputs tend to rise more rapidly for low-technology firms. This explains previous findings that suggest that the economic returns to R&D for low-technology firms are less positive than the corresponding returns for technologically advanced firms (Griliches and Mairesse, 1984; Harhoff, 1998; Kafouros, 2005). In other words, whilst it has been has suggested that technological opportunities increase the capability of a firm to benefit from R&D, the costs of R&D inputs may also play an important role in explaining why some firms enjoy high returns to R&D. This has clear implications for both scholars and practitioners. Firstly, researchers need to be cautious in attributing variations in the R&D-productivity relationship to technological opportunities. Secondly, the managers of low-technology firms should be warned that they have to pay more for R&D inputs. Finally, this result suggests that the government should intervene and reduce, possibly by means of tax credits and R&D subsidies, the private cost of R&D to such firms.

6. Modeling the Effects of Research and Development

This chapter presents the models that the study utilizes to assess the magnitude of the impact of R&D on performance. It also deals with a number of conceptual and methodological issues, and discusses how the inputs, the outputs and the innovative activities of firms should be measured. This chapter also includes a discussion concerning the ability of the econometric framework to measure the returns to R&D. This discussion involves two issues, the quality of price indices and the problem of appropriability.

1. INTRODUCTION

The previous chapters examined the theoretical relationship between R&D and productivity performance. As explained earlier, these predictions suggest that R&D investments lead to the creation of a stock of scientific knowledge (Griliches, 1979; Mansfield, 1984). A firm can use this knowledge in different ways to develop innovations and competencies, and improve its performance. By developing more efficient processes, for example, it can reduce the costs associated with the production of its goods. By introducing new products or by improving the quality of its existing products, it can increase its market share and sales (Mansfield, 1968a).

A firm can also increase its revenues through the royalty fees it receives from patent licenses. As well as these direct impacts of innovation on economic performance, scattered pieces of evidence indicate that it also has indirect impacts. Cohen and Levinthal (1990) suggested that innovation increases a firm's ability to capture, assimilate and apply external knowledge to ongoing projects. It has also been argued that innovative firms are qualitatively different from non-innovative firms (Wakelin, 2001), and that significant organizational adaptations that favor performance may be driven by R&D investments (Kafouros, 2005). Given that the research model that this study employs relies on the concept of production function, the next sections introduce three representative production functions (Cobb-Douglas, CES and Translog), and present the main econometric models.

2. THE RESEARCH MODEL

2.1 The Production Function Framework

The econometric framework that this study adopts has been used extensively during the last 30 years. As noted earlier, labour productivity may be defined as output (Q) over labour (L):

$$K = Q / L \qquad (6.1)$$

The rate of growth of labour productivity is defined as

$$\tau = \frac{(\Delta Q / \Delta t)}{Q} - \frac{(\Delta L / \Delta t)}{L} \qquad (6.2)$$

The main purpose of production functions is to determine the relationship between the inputs that a firm uses and its outputs. Hence, by using production functions we can assess what proportion of any increase in output can be attributed to increases in inputs (Thomas, 1993). This property makes production functions ideal for serving the objective of this research to assess the impacts of R&D. According to the neo-classical theory, the output (Q) of a firm is primarily a function of two inputs: capital (K) and labour (L).

$$Q = f(K, L) \qquad (6.3)$$

Where K expresses either a firm's capital stock or the flow of services of its capital stock; similarly, L expresses either labour input or the flow of services of labour. A main property is that the two inputs are substitutable and thus, a given output can be produced by many different combinations of capital and labour. The absolute rate at which one input can be substituted for another (without changing the output) is known as marginal rate of substitution (MRS):

$$MRS = -\frac{dK}{dL} = \frac{\partial Q / \partial L}{\partial Q / \partial K} \qquad (6.4)$$

However, as MRS is measured in terms of units of capital and labour, this raises estimation difficulties. An alternative measure is the so-called elasticity of substitution (σ) which is defined as the proportionate change in the capital/labour ratio divided by the proportionate change in MRS (see

Equation 6.5). If substitution between capital and labour is easy then the elasticity of substitution is high. By contrast, if the possibility of substitution is limited, then (σ) will be low (Thomas, 1993).

$$\sigma = \frac{d(K/L)}{K/L} / \frac{d(MRS)}{MRS} \qquad (6.5)$$

A problem that increases estimation difficulties is the fact that the relationship between input and output is not expected to be linear. In order to take into account this fact, researchers assume that the marginal products of capital and labour are positive but diminishing (the so-called law of diminishing marginal productivity). For example, if we keep the capital constant, the relationship between output and labour is similar to that of Figure 6.1. Another problem is the fact that capital and labour inputs are not predetermined. Given that a firm chooses its inputs, the variables of capital and labour are not always exogenously determined and many econometric problems arise (these are discussed later in the chapter).

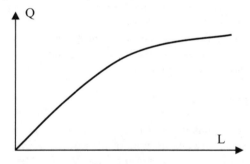

Figure 6.1 Marginal productivity of labour

The production function that has been used most widely (and which we will also use) is the Cobb-Douglas function (suggested by Cobb and Douglas, 1928).

$$Q = A\,K^{\alpha}\,L^{\beta}\,e^{\varepsilon} \qquad (6.6)$$

α and β are the elasticities of output with respect to capital and labour respectively, whereas ε is a disturbance term. The sum of α and β denotes the returns to scale. The term A is the so-called technical change that can be interpreted either as a residual which captures the disembodied technical change or as a measure of a firm's efficiency.

For instance, two firms can have the same α and β but the firm with the higher A can produce more. The technical progress of the Cobb Douglas production function is assumed to be neutral. That is, neither capital saving nor labour saving. However, we can examine whether technical progress is neutral by checking whether the growth in output affects the K/L ratio (Hebden, 1983). The elasticity of substitution (σ) of the Cobb Douglas production function is unity. Its main advantage is the fact that we can easily convert it to linear form by taking logarithms. In that case, it can be estimated using the Ordinary Least Squares (OLS) method:

$$logQ = logA + \alpha logK + \beta logL + \varepsilon \qquad (6.7)$$

If we assume constant returns to scale (CRS) (that is, $\alpha + \beta = 1$ or $\beta = 1 - \alpha$), and re-write the above equation in the form of labour productivity, then:

$$Log(Q/L) = logA + \alpha log(K/L) + \varepsilon \qquad (6.8)$$

A more complicated production function is the so-called Constant Elasticity of Substitution (CES). The main way in which this function differs from the Cobb-Douglas is that the elasticity of substitution (σ) is assumed to be constant but not unity. The form of the CES function is the following:

$$Q = \gamma \, [\delta K^{-\theta} + (1-\delta) \, L^{-\theta}]^{-1/\theta} \qquad (6.9)$$

the term γ can be interpreted as the A term in the Cobb-Douglas function, δ indicates the weighting of capital and labour, whilst θ is a substitution parameter related to the elasticity of substitution $[\theta = (1-\sigma)/\sigma]$. A third production function is the so-called Translog (or transcendental logarithmic) function, developed by Christensen et al. (1973). This function is a transformation of the Cobb-Douglas which assumes that σ is not constant over time (primarily because technical progress affects the ease (or difficulty) with which a firm may substitute capital for labour (and vice versa)). The general form of the Translog production function is shown below:

$$logQ = A + \beta_1 logK + \beta_2 logL + \beta_3 logK \, logL + \beta_4 (logK)^2 + \beta_5 (logL)^2 + \varepsilon \qquad (6.10)$$

If β_3, β_4, $\beta_5 = 0$ then Equation 6.10 becomes a Cobb-Douglas production function. If β_4, $\beta_5 = -\beta_3 / 2$ it becomes a CES function.

2.2 The Model

Until the late 1950s it was believed that advances in productivity could be achieved primarily through increases in capital and labour. However, a series of studies carried out by Robert Solow changed this perception. Solow's findings (1957) indicated that only 10 percent of the US productivity growth was attributable to capital and labour increases. The remaining growth could be attributed to the more efficient use of inputs and to technological advances. In the early 1960s, based on the studies of Robert Solow, efforts were made to assess econometrically the impact of R&D on productivity (e.g. Minasian, 1962). However, a detailed econometric framework was not satisfactorily developed until the late 1970s. The architect of this framework, Zvi Griliches (1979), presented a production function that correlated Output not only with the conventional inputs of Capital (Q) and Labour (L), but also with the level of scientific knowledge (R) or R&D capital (Equation 6.11). As discussed earlier, although one could argue that scientific knowledge is something which cannot be estimated in terms of units, scientific knowledge as defined in this book and in similar studies is narrowed down to the knowledge produced from a firm's R&D department and thus, its estimation is plausible (Schott, 1976).

$$Q = f(K, L, R, \varepsilon) \qquad (6.11)$$

A number of interesting questions can be raised regarding the properties of this model. One question relates to what should Q, K, L and R conceptually measure? Given that direct measures of these variables are lacking, researchers are usually forced to use proxies. For example, the majority of studies use the number of employees as a measure of labour. However, these proxies do not always represent accurately what they purport to measure engendering many problems (Griliches, 1984). These problems are discussed extensively in Chapter 7. Another set of questions relates to the stock of scientific knowledge (or R&D capital). What factors affect the level of scientific knowledge? How it can be measured? What is the association of scientific knowledge with R&D? Given that the scientific knowledge of a firm is unobservable, it is very difficult to construct a measure that can adequately represent it.

Another question relates to the functional form of Equation 6.11. The functional form that this study and the majority of other studies adopt is an extended Cobb-Douglas production function that includes in its inputs a measure of scientific knowledge (R). This production function after accounting for time (t) and firm (i) differences is:

$$Q_{it} = A \, e^{\lambda t} \, K_{it}^{\alpha} \, L_{it}^{\beta} \, R_{it}^{\gamma} \, e^{\varepsilon it} \qquad (6.12)$$

or by transforming it in logarithmic form:

$$q_{it} = a + \lambda t + ak_{it} + \beta l_{it} + \gamma r_{it} + \varepsilon_{it} \tag{6.13}$$

The lower case letters (q, k, l, r) denote the logs of the variables whereas α, β and γ are the elasticities of output with respect to capital, labour and scientific knowledge respectively. The term a is the residual of the Cobb-Douglas function (which should be lower given that one more factor of production is included); t is a time trend; λ represents the disembodied technical change, and ε_{it} stands for the disturbance term. However, in order to determine the differences between years, we follow Hall and Mairesse (1995), replacing the time trend λt by time dummies (D_{time}). Additional dummies are included in order to account for the industry effects ($D_{industry}$). Given that our objective is to estimate the impact of scientific knowledge on labour productivity performance, we reform Equation 6.13 in terms of labour productivity:

$$(q_{it} - l_{it}) = a + a(k_{it} - l_{it}) + \gamma(r_{it} - l_{it}) + (\mu - 1) l_{it} + D_{industry} + D_{time} + \varepsilon_{it} \tag{6.14}$$

Factor elasticities $\mu = \alpha + \beta + \gamma$ should equal unity, otherwise the assumption of Constant Returns to Scale (CRS) is rejected; that is, when $\mu\text{-}1$ is not 0. The advantage of imposing the assumption of CRS is that the problem of collinearity between K and L is circumvented (Thomas, 1993).

Although the Cobb-Douglas production function can be further reformed and expressed in terms of Total Factor Productivity (TFP), it is preferred to assess the impact of R&D on labour productivity. There are two main advantages of investigating the impact of R&D on labour productivity (rather than on total factor productivity). Firstly, it allows the comparison of the return to R&D with that of other investments in ordinary capital (Griliches and Mairesse, 1984). Secondly, given that the majority of studies use the labour productivity function, it allows us to put the findings in context more easily. An alternative functional form for the model could be the CES or the Translog production functions. However, there are several reasons that make the Cobb-Douglas production function more appropriate for this research:

(1) neither the CES nor the Translog production functions solve the problem of simultaneity which besets this and similar studies;

(2) as Griliches (1979) argues, complicated production functions are not attractive due to the poor quality of the data;

(3) complicated production functions, such as the CES, cannot be easily linearized by using a simple logarithmic transformation (as in the case of Cobb-Douglas function);

(4) the estimation of a CES, which includes many inputs, is very complicated;

(5) as noted earlier, other production functions, such as the CES and Translog, assume that the elasticity of substitution (σ) is not unity.

However, Thomas (1993) cites pieces of evidence from the studies of Fuchs (1963) and Griliches and Ringstad (1971) which indicate that σ is not significantly different from unity. The findings of Griliches (1964) are similar since they indicated that the CES should be rejected in favour of the CD function;

(6) because productions functions, such as the Translog, have more explanatory variables than Cobb-Douglas, the problem of multicollinearity is augmented;

(7) as Griliches and Mairesse (1984) emphasize, the use of more complicated functional forms will not really help as the main purpose is to estimate the coefficient of R&D.

Therefore, for all the above reasons but also for reasons of simplicity, it is preferred to use the extended Cobb-Douglas production function.

3. MEASURING THE STOCK OF SCIENTIFIC KNOWLEDGE (OR R&D CAPITAL)

3.1 The Main Measure

The main problem with the model is the measurement of scientific knowledge (R) (or R&D capital). As noted in Chapter 1, knowledge is something that cannot be realistically estimated in terms of units. However, there are two major proxies that can be used to measure the scientific knowledge produced by R&D departments: the number of patents and the R&D expenditure (Wakelin, 2001). The problem with the first proxy is the fact that research findings are not always patentable and even when they are, a firm may not submit patents for reasons of confidentiality. Hence, following many previous similar studies, the second proxy is adopted. This proxy is based on the assumption that the level of scientific knowledge is proportional to past and current R&D expenditures (RD) (Griliches, 1979). The scientific knowledge (R) at time t is defined as:

$$R_t = [W(B)RD_t]e^{\mu t+\upsilon} \qquad (6.15)$$

where $W(B)RD$ is a lag function of past and current R&D expenditures, μt is the trend of any other influences on the level of scientific knowledge, and υ stands for the random transitory component of scientific knowledge. As Griliches (1979, p.100) explains, if we substitute this equation to the production function we can absorb the trend μt into the general efficiency trend λt, and the component υ into the overall disturbance term ε. Thus, the remaining component $W(B)RD$ (the so-called R&D capital) is a function of past and current R&D expenditures.

In order to measure this intangible capital adequately, an additional issue should be addressed. If the R&D capital (R_{it}) of firm i at time t depends only on past and current R&D expenditures (RD), then:

$$R_{it} = RD_{it} + RD_{i(t-1)} + RD_{i(t-2)} + \ldots \qquad (6.16)$$

However, firms – in order to innovate continuously – have to abandon past knowledge and seek new knowledge. Over time, past research – like any other type of capital – depreciates and becomes less valuable primarily because past knowledge, findings and processes are replaced by new ones (Aghion and Howitt, 1992). Furthermore, part of a firm's research findings will be diffused, used and thus neutralized by other firms (Kafouros, 2005). Consequently, the net R&D capital is not equal to the gross R&D capital (which includes all the past and current R&D expenditures) (Griliches, 1979). In order to account for the declining usefulness of R&D, a depreciation factor δ which converts the gross research to net is usually introduced:

$$R_{it} = RD_{it} + \sum_{1}^{k} (1 - \delta)^k RD_{i(t-k)} \qquad (6.17)$$

The term κ represents the lagged year, and the weighting factor δ the geometrically declining depreciation. However, this approach has a number of drawbacks. First, this definition of R&D capital does not take into account the contribution of independent inventors who, as many researchers have emphasized, are very important if we want to measure advances in technology (Mansfield, 1968a; Schott, 1976). Second, this approach aggregates R&D expenditures linearly into R&D capital, ignoring the fact that the generation of new knowledge may depend non-linearly on previously accumulated outcomes (Wang and Tsai, 2003). Third, improvements made to products and processes by the employees of a firm are ignored if the costs of these are not included in a firm's reported R&D expenditure (Schott, 1976).

A fourth concern is related to the fact that R&D is in itself aggregated (in terms of composition). Reported R&D expenditures are the sum of different R&D activities, such as basic and applied R&D, product and process R&D, short-term and long-term projects, and small and large projects (Mansfield, 1984). Because the level of detail of the data does not allow the breakdown of R&D, it is important to make clear that the estimated R&D capital is the sum of all these different activities and, in consequence, this study investigates the average impact of different types of R&D on firm productivity performance.

At this point, there are two additional issues that should be introduced: the time-lag of R&D, and the role of external knowledge. We discuss the time lag of R&D in the next section. The second important issue that should be taken into account when measuring R&D capital is the impact of external knowledge on a firm's knowledge and in consequence on a firm's productivity (the so-called spillover effects). The spillover literature (Jaffe, 1986; Mohnen, 1999; Nadiri, 1993) relies on the argument that the general productivity of a firm and the productivity of its R&D department are both affected by the research efforts of other firms. As Griliches (1979) argues, the analysis of spillovers is complicated since we do not deal with one closed industry but with a number of industries which – depending on their technological distance – 'borrow' knowledge from one other. On the top of these issues, one should take into account that research is also undertaken by government institutions and universities. Later in this book, the spillover literature is surveyed, the spillover effects are modeled and their impact is investigated.

3.2 The Lagged Measure

The time-lag of R&D represents the average time between an R&D investment and the maximization of its impact. Research projects take time to be completed and cannot always have an immediate impact on productivity. As Griliches (1995) argues, the total time lag comprises three delaying factors: the time needed to complete a project (short or long-term project); the time needed to introduce it to market (e.g. packaging, pricing and marketing) and the time needed in order to gain a market share and to be reflected in revenues.

The length of this time lag is not yet clear. Pakes and Schankerman (1984) find that the mean lag is about two years. However, the time lag may not be the same for all firms, as it may depend on factors such as the industry and the type of R&D. For instance, the development time in the automotive industry was 60 months in the early 1990s but only 18 months in the early 2000s (Advanced Manufacturing, 2001). Similarly, it is sensible to argue that the time lag for basic research would be longer than that for applied research. A good approach is to estimate the lag from the data. In Chapter 9, the issue of time-lag is discussed again and the research data are used to estimate its structure.

In order to assess the time lag structure of R&D, one can simply incorporate in the model discussed earlier (see Equation 6.14) many measures of lagged R&D simultaneously. This approach however leads to multicollinearity and double-counting problems. Because of these problems, the effects of lagged R&D are estimated using an alternative avenue. The stock of R&D-capital has been a measure of current and past R&D investments (see Equation 6.17). This formulation assumed that the maximization of the impacts of R&D were in the year that the investment has been made. In other words, it was implicitly assumed that the impact of R&D on productivity performance was highest in the year that it was undertaken. This assumption, however, does not take into account that research projects need time in order to be completed and then to build up sales in the market (Ravenscraft and Scherer, 1982). A second assumption of this formulation was that the stock of scientific knowledge starts to depreciate immediately. Nevertheless, this assumption is not accurate as the new technologies that resulted from industrial research will be depreciated only after the completion of a project, rather than immediately.

Following Griliches and Mairesse (1984), we incorporate the time lag of R&D within the stock of scientific knowledge. Specifically, we construct a number of different lagged measures of R&D capital, in which the effects of R&D are similar to a bell-shape curve. In these measures, the effects of R&D are highest not in the current year (*t*), but in lagged years *t-1*, *t-2*, *t-3* ... and so on (that is, one year, two years, three years and so on, after the investment has been made). Instead of imposing a fixed peak for the maximization of the effects of R&D, we allow it to vary from one to six years. In order to construct these lagged measures of knowledge stock, we weighted investments in R&D differently, depending on whether the R&D was undertaken before or after the assumed 'peak' year.

The weighting of the industrial research undertaken before the assumed peak year followed the approach described in the previous section (a 20 percent depreciation rate). Theoretically, however, the weighting of the R&D undertaken after the assumed peak year should be different as this refers not to the depreciation of R&D investments, but to the fact that the impact of the stock of knowledge on firm performance is not maximized immediately but gradually. To weight this, a rate of 20 percent was employed. However, in order to examine the sensitivity of the results, a number of other lagged measures of R&D capital were constructed using the rates of 30 and 40 percent.

4. HOW MUCH ARE WE MISSING?

Motivated by the work of Griliches (1979), the discussion concerning the ability of the current framework to measure the returns to R&D is revived. This discussion involves two issues, the quality of price indices and the problem of appropriability. The first issue is associated with the fact that output (measured either by sales or by value added) cannot capture immeasurable improvements of output such as better product quality and variety. This problem is magnified in R&D-intensive industries since most of the price indices cannot fully account for the continual and rapid improvements of their products (Brynjolfsson and Hitt, 1996; Lichtenberg and Griliches, 1989). Although there are price indices (the so-called hedonic indices) that can to some extent solve this problem, they are rarely available.

This problem of inappropriate price indices occurs in several industries. In the case of the computer industry, for example, it is difficult for statistical agencies to take into account the improved resolution and lower emission of radiation that LCD (Liquid Crystal Display) screens offer. In the case of pharmaceutical industry, it is almost impossible to measure how much more effective a new drug is. Similarly, it is difficult to measure the value of the improved quality, safety and luxuries that a modern car offers, such as air-conditioning, satellite navigation and antilock braking system (ABS). A study that investigated how much we are missing by ignoring quality changes is that of Lichtenberg and Griliches (1989). Their findings indicated that the official US producer price indices (PPI) adjusted only the two-thirds of the true quality change. In other words, true productivity growth exceeds productivity growth based on the US producer price index (PPI) by an average of 34 percent.

As discussed in Chapter 3, another reason why the returns to R&D cannot be represented adequately is that of appropriability. Innovators cannot always appropriate the economic value of their discoveries (Geroski, 1995). Hence, some of the relevant benefits do not return to the inventor but are forwarded to society. As has been emphasized by Geroski (1995), knowledge has a non-rival nature. In contrast to a tangible good, knowledge can be used by many firms or individuals. Furthermore, knowledge is non-excludable (it is difficult for the producer of knowledge to stop other agents from using it). Thus, as Griliches (1979) argues, measured output goes up by the revenues received and productivity depends on the amount of returns that an innovator succeeds in appropriating for himself. There is an extensive literature that investigates the appropriability problem and suggests ways (e.g. patents and R&D-subsidies) to balance private and social rates of returns (Cockburn and Griliches, 1987; Levin, 1988; Stoneman, 1991). This issue, however, is outside the scope of the book.

Using examples from industrial practice, we demonstrated that the impact of R&D on sales (and consequently on the measure of productivity) is often underestimated as some of the benefits of innovation are reflected in firm profitability (rather than revenue). These examples also emphasized that depending on the market structure the estimated impact of R&D may vary. For instance, the impact of R&D on productivity performance is likely to be high for an industry in which the competition is low and a firm can easily appropriate its research findings. By contrast, we may – falsely – estimate that the contribution of R&D to productivity is negligible if the characteristics of the industry are similar to those of a perfect-competitive market. In summary, quoting Griliches (1979, p.99):

> Much of the reported R&D is expended in areas where its direct contribution cannot be measured. In an earlier paper (Griliches, 1973), I estimated these areas to account for about half of all reported R&D. An additional large component of R&D is aimed at final consumer product rather than process innovations and is reflected in productivity measures only to the extent that producers succeed in appropriating its fruits. Since much of the product of R&D is entirely unmeasured and much of the rest is mis-measured, it is not surprising that it has been rather difficult to find its traces in the data.

5. THE DEPRECIATION OF R&D

To calculate R&D capital, we need to know the pattern that its depreciation follows, as well as the rate of this depreciation. Pakes and Schankerman (1984, p.76) utilized patent data to investigate the pattern. They argued that if the density function of the distribution of revenues *f(r)* was lognormal, then the percentage of patents renewed in each year *P(t)* would be initially concave and then convex (see Figure 6.2).

On the other hand, if it followed the so-called Pareto-Levy distribution it would be similar to the curve of Figure 6.3. The authors cited evidence from the study of Scherer (1965) that indicated that the value of patents tended to follow a Pareto-Levy distribution. The findings of Scherer (1965) are also supported by the study of Federico (1958). The author uses data from five different countries and finds that the value of patents for four of them (including the UK) follows the Pareto-Levy distribution. Theoretically, one could expect that the value of patents should initially follow a Pareto-Levy distribution. After their expiration year (t_{exp}), however, this distribution should become steeper (see Figure 6.4) as a firm's intra-industry competitors and other firms from external industries will be able to imitate without significant barriers.

Although the last case might represent more accurately the pattern that the depreciation follows, it cannot be used as it requires data regarding the expiration of each patent. For that reason, we use Equation 6.18. This is consistent with the evidence of Federico (1958) and Scherer (1965) that the value of patents follows the distribution of Figure 6.3.

$$R_{it} = RD_{it} + \sum_{1}^{k} (1 - \delta)^k RD_{i(t-k)} \qquad (6.18)$$

However, the studies of Federico (1958) and Scherer (1965) investigate the pattern of the depreciation of patents (rather than R&D). Thus it is not known if this pattern is the same as that of R&D capital. Unfortunately, given that R&D capital is not directly observable, a proxy is needed in order to explore its pattern of depreciation and in our case the only available is patents.

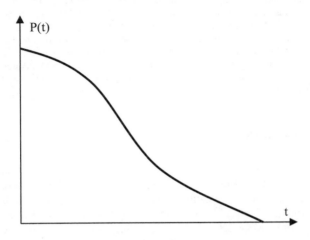

Figure 6.2 Depreciation curve 1

Regarding the second issue (the rate of depreciation), although it is clear that the R&D capital of a firm becomes less valuable over time, its rate of depreciation is not certain. Given that R&D capital is gradually replaced by new knowledge and is also diffused and thus used by other firms, it is sensible to expect that its rate of depreciation should be higher than the rate of depreciation of conventional capital (Griliches, 1979). Williams (1973, p.87-90) suggests that as private R&D investments are usually short-term, the impact of R&D should peak between three and five years and then decline rapidly. One can also argue here that the rate of depreciation should be higher after the year that the patents expire, since other firms can then imitate a firm's products without any significant barrier.

Although many studies set the depreciation rate δ at 15 percent per year, evidence suggests that the rate may be even higher than this. Moreover, past studies usually do not take into account the fact that the rate possibly varies not only from industry to industry but also over time, raising further problems. Attempts to estimate the depreciation rate of R&D capital were made by Goto and Suzuki (1989) and Pakes and Schankerman (1984). Pakes and Schankerman (1984) assume that firms renew their patents only if they are profitable and argue that a sensible rate is that at which the appropriable revenues for the innovating firm decline. They use two different sources of data to estimate δ: the first type of data are on the renewal of patents, taken from the study of Frederiko (1958), whereas the second set of data comes from the study of Wagner (1968) on the life span of R&D expenditures (covering five different countries including the UK and US).

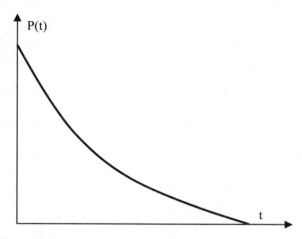

Figure 6.3 Depreciation curve 2

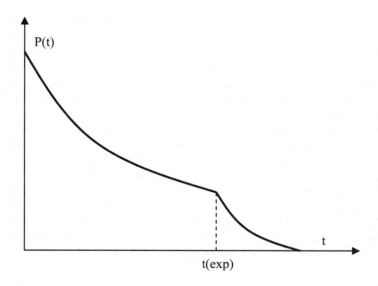

Figure 6.4 Depreciation curve 3

In each case it was found that the average value for δ was 25 percent, suggesting that the rate of 15 percent used by the majority of studies is low. Nevertheless, Goto and Suzuki (1989) emphasize that the cost of estimating whether a patent is profitable or not is very high because firms have to gather and analyse a lot of information. For that reason, they argue that large firms simply renew most of their patents. If true, the method that Pakes and Schankerman (1984) used may not be appropriate to calculate the rate of depreciation. However, it is difficult to agree with the argument that firms renew most of their patents. As previous research indicates (e.g. Nonaka and Takeuchi, 1995), a single product can embody as many as 300 different patents. In such cases, the renewal fees are not negligible and thus it is difficult to accept the assumption that firms do not evaluate their patents but simply renew all of them.

Goto and Suzuki (1989) suggest a different method to estimate δ. They use a survey by the Japanese Science and Technology Agency on the life span of technology. This survey includes the replies of firms regarding the time taken for their patents to generate revenues and the time taken for their products which embody patents to generate profits. Their estimates of δ are slightly lower than those of Pakes and Schankerman (1984), indicating that whilst the rate of depreciation is approximately 25 percent for high-technology industries, it is nearer 15 percent for other industries and can be as low as 8 percent for low-technology industries such as glass and metal manufacturers. However, the findings of both Pakes and Schankerman (1984) and Goto and Suzuki (1989) should be treated with care. As the former admit, given that the data came from patented innovations the estimated depreciation rate might not be representative for innovations that do not have a patentable nature. Another limitation is that these studies investigated only the depreciation rate of patents, i.e. the depreciation of successful R&D. Thus, they do not take into account the fact that only a small proportion of R&D investments lead to patents.

Hence, past research provides little clear evidence regarding the rate of depreciation that should be adopted for the current research. Taking into account the rate that the majority of studies use (15 percent) together with the findings of Pakes and Schankerman (1984) and Goto and Suzuki (1989) (from 15 to 25 percent), this study uses a rate of 20 percent. However, given that this choice is to some extent subjective, the next chapters also calculate R&D capital using the rates of 15 and 25 percent and investigate the impact of the depreciation rate on the estimates. As will be discussed later, the estimates are insensitive to the choice of depreciation rate.

6. THE METHOD OF ESTIMATION AND ECONOMETRIC PROBLEMS

There are several econometric methods for estimation. The method that this study (and almost all the similar studies) uses is that of Ordinary Least Squares (OLS). Although a number of instrumental variable methods such as the Two Stage Least Square (2SLS) and Indirect Least Squares (ILS) (also known as Reduced Form) can be used, they are not guaranteed to provide more accurate results. Griliches (1986) discusses this issue and argues that such techniques do not solve problems such as simultaneity, but shift the argument to the validity and exogeneity of these instruments. Additionally, the fact that the Reduced Form method is usually based on factor costs of the main inputs, engenders problems.

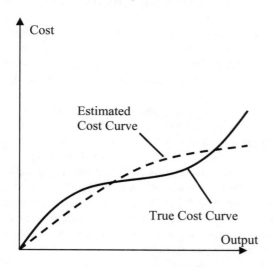

Source: Thomas (1993, p.316).

Figure 6.5 True and estimated cost curves

As Thomas (1993) argues, as there are increasing returns to scale for smaller firms and decreasing returns for larger ones, the pattern that the true total-cost curve has is similar to the heavy line of Figure 6.5. However, the cost curve that studies estimate is similar to the dashed line. This problem would be even greater in this research which analyses both larger and smaller firms whose returns to scale vary considerably. Moreover, as the decision regarding output and input is taken together, the estimates of simultaneous equation methods are biased because the simultaneous context of the model has been ignored (Hebden, 1983).

Taking into account the problems above, and given that the findings of studies that used methods such as the 2SLS and the Reduced Form (Cuneo and Mairesse, 1984; Griliches, 1964; Griliches, 1980; Sassenou, 1988) indicate that results were similar or only slightly better than those obtained from the ordinary method, there appears to be no good reason for rejecting the OLS method. Nevertheless, many econometric problems arise as many of the assumptions underlying OLS cannot be always fulfilled. We briefly review these problems below. The next chapters of the book discuss extensively the consequences of these problems and conduct a number of econometric tests to detect them:

(1) Multicollinearity. One of the assumptions of the classical linear regression model is that the explanatory variables must not be collinear (i.e. they must not move together), otherwise there are large standard errors and thus, it becomes difficult to calculate accurately the contribution of each input. In the case of multicollinearity, although the OLS estimator remains the Best Linear Unbiased Estimator (BLUE), there are high standard errors which make the estimates less precise.

(2) Simultaneity. Simultaneity is also very important as it can lead to inconsistent estimates. It is engendered by the fact that inputs (capital, labour and R&D capital) are not always exogenously determined as they must be, because there is a degree of feedback from output to input. This occurs when output is determined by inputs and, in turn, some inputs are determined by output (Gujarati, 1995). For instance, although output depends on past R&D, R&D also depends on past output. In such cases, referring to the so-called 'reversed causality' problem, we may end up estimating the impact of output on R&D expenditure rather than the opposite (Griliches, 1979).

(3) Heteroscedasticity. Another assumption of the classical linear regression model states that the variance of the disturbances must be equal (homoscedastic). However, this assumption is difficult to fulfil in a function such as the Cobb-Douglas because in addition to the three inputs of our model, other unobservable factors that affect a firm's productivity, such as managerial efficiency, are included in the disturbance term. Since these factors vary across firms, the variance of the disturbance term may be heteroscedastic. The consequence of heteroscedasticity is that although the OLS estimator remains unbiased, it no longer has minimum variance.

(4) Autocorrelation. This problem arises when the correlation between two disturbances is not zero, i.e. when the correlation of the

disturbances follows a (positive or negative) pattern. Similar to the case of heteroscedasticity, if there is autocorrelation, the OLS estimators are unbiased but not 'Best'.

(5) Specification bias. A specification bias occurs when a model is not correctly specified. This problem is primarily related to three questions: First, what is the functional form of the model? Second, what variables should the model include? Third, are the variables capable of measuring adequately what conceptually they should be measuring? The first and second questions have to some extent been answered as the extended form of the Cobb-Douglas production function has been tested over several decades. The third question is discussed in Chapter 7.

7. THE MAIN ECONOMETRIC SPECIFICATIONS

This section presents the two available types of econometric specification that can be used to estimate the impact of R&D on productivity: the 'R&D-elasticity' specification and the 'Rate of Return' (ROR) specification. Each method is beset by different biases and has its own advantages and faults. Therefore, it is difficult to claim that one method is superior compared to another or to claim that it yields less biased estimates. We prefer to use these methods primarily for three reasons. First, they yield estimates which are comparable with those of similar studies and thus allow us to put the research findings in context. Second, the two methods are complementary, so that possible biases of the first method may be investigated using the second one (and vice versa). Third, the findings of studies that used methods such as the Reduced Form (Cuneo and Mairesse, 1984; Griliches, 1964; Griliches, 1980; Sassenou, 1988) indicate that results were similar or only slightly different than those obtained from the ordinary method. Given that there is some research that focuses on the methodological variations (see Mairesse and Sassenou, 1991; Mairesse and Hall, 1996), we utilize these two approaches leaving space to concentrate on other important issues such as knowledge spillovers and the factors that affect the productivity of R&D.

7.1 The 'R&D-elasticity' Specification

This type of econometric specification employs Equation 6.14 to estimate the elasticity (γ) of output/labour with respect to R&D capital per labour (R&D-elasticity), i.e. to estimate the contribution of R&D capital to labour productivity.

Conceptual and Methodological Issues

$$(q_{it} - l_{it}) = a + a(k_{it} - l_{it}) + \gamma(r_{it} - l_{it}) + (\mu - 1) l_{it} + D_{industry} + D_{time} + \varepsilon_{it} \quad (6.14)$$

Where k, l and r are the logarithmic expressions of capital, labour and R&D capital respectively. This method assumes that the disturbance term ε_{it} is composed of two other types of disturbances. Firstly, a permanent disturbance (υ_i) specific to the firm and, secondly, a transitory disturbance (w_{it}) (Cuneo and Mairesse, 1984). The breakdown of the disturbance term leads to two types of estimates. The first is based on the levels of the data and uses their cross-sectional dimension. The second relies on the growth rates (or differences) of the data and utilizes their time-series dimension. The estimates that are based on the levels of the variables have the advantage of being unaffected by biases coming from the correlation between explanatory variables and the disturbance w_{it}. On the other hand, the estimates that are based on the growth rates of the variables are unaffected by υ_i disturbances (Cuneo and Mairesse, 1984). Another difference between the two types of estimates is their sources of variability. The first estimates rely on the level of the variables for a given year, so that most of the variability is provided by the differences 'between' firms for a specific year (Mairesse and Sassenou, 1991). By contrast, the variability of the second approach is provided by the differences of variables 'within' a firm over time.

The cross-sectional estimates can be computed using either the so-called 'total' method or the 'between' method. The first uses all the available firm-year observations (y_{it}) whereas the second relies on the firm-means (y_i) of the variables (Griliches and Mairesse, 1984). In practice, however, the 'total' and 'between' estimates are very close since most of the variability of data exists 'between' (rather than within) firms (Mairesse and Sassenou, 1991). That is, great differences in R&D expenditures can be observed between firms and not within firms and across years.

However, the cross-sectional estimates do not take into account the efficiency characteristics of the firm, such as managerial capability. A way to avoid this bias is to focus on growth rates (rather than on levels). This is equivalent to doing 'within firm' analysis (Odagiri and Iwata, 1986). As these estimates do not capture the variability outside a firm, this analysis is equivalent to adding firm dummies. Hence, we can take into account not only the characteristics of a specific industry but also the characteristics of each individual firm (Mairesse and Sassenou, 1991).

There are two types of time-series estimates, the so-called 'within' and the 'differences' (or growth rates). The 'within' estimates can be calculated using the deviations of the observations from their firm-means (i.e. $y_{it} - y_i$) whereas the second way uses the first or longer differences. The first-differences ($\Delta x_{it} = x_{it} - x_{it-1} = LogX_{it}/X_{it-1}$) are approximately the yearly growth rates (for small variations) whereas the long differences focus on the growth rate between the first and a longer year (Mairesse and Sassenou, 1991). Alternatively, some studies (e.g. Griliches, 1980) calculate a mean growth rate for the observed years.

Although the within and first-differenced estimates are close, it is not clear when the estimated R&D coefficient is higher. Sassenou (1988) finds that the within estimates are lower than the corresponding first-differenced ones whereas Hall and Mairesse (1995) and Mairesse and Hall (1996) find the opposite. The picture is clearer for the first and long-differenced estimates. The findings of Hall (1993), Hall and Mairesse (1995) and Harhoff (1998) indicate that longer differences tend to produce higher R&D coefficient. In general, longer differences are preferred by researchers since they tend to be more robust to measurement errors, heterogeneity biases and short-term fluctuations of the business cycle (Mairesse and Sassenou, 1991).

However, one important – but difficult to answer – question remains. Which analysis (between or within) will provide less biased estimates? The main advantages of analysing the time-series dimension of the data (within firm analysis) are that firm characteristics are not omitted, and that as we focus on the growth rates of the variables the problems of simultaneity and multicollinearity are to some extent circumvented. However, many researchers worry about the degree of bias and the robustness of this approach. Griliches and Mairesse (1984) argue that the collinearity between the conventional capital and R&D capital with time causes a lack of robustness. Similarly, Mairesse and Sassenou (1991) argue that some problems that might be less important in the cross-sectional approach (e.g., capacity utilization), may seriously bias the time-series estimates.

As variability (an essential requirement for the OLS estimation) is low in the time-series dimension of the data, the estimates that are based on the time-series dimension of the data are usually lower than those obtained by the cross-sectional dimension of the data. In consequence, given that variability is lower, the noise-to-signal ratio is magnified (see Griliches, 1979; Griliches and Mairesse, 1984). In summary, it seems that there is not a clear answer. It cannot be argued that the estimates of one approach are less biased that those of the other one. Each approach has its advantages but also its biases. For that reason, the coefficient of R&D will be estimated using both dimensions of the data.

7.2 The 'Rate of Return' Specification

The 'Rate of Return' (ROR) to R&D is an alternative type of econometric specification for the evaluation of R&D. Two main differences characterize it as compared to the previous one. Firstly, it uses the current R&D expenditure so there is no need to estimate R&D capital, and secondly, it calculates the rate of return to R&D instead of the R&D-elasticity. The last difference, however, make its estimates not comparable with the estimates of the previous method. The ROR method uses a transformation of Equation 6.13 that assumes equality of the marginal products dQ/dR across firms. Instead of assuming that R&D-elasticity among firms is the same, it is based on the assumption that the rate of return to R&D is the same i.e. equal increases in output arise from increases in R&D capital.

$$q_{it} = a + \lambda t + ak_{it} + \beta l_{it} + \gamma r_{it} + \varepsilon_{it} \qquad (6.13)$$

Since by definition the elasticity of R&D (γ) is equal to dQR / dRQ, the term γr can be rewritten as $dQRdR / dRQR$ or $dQdR / dRQ$. The fraction dQ/dR is the marginal product of R&D (ρ) that can be interpreted as the rate of return to R&D (however, as discussed below, this interpretation has its problems).

In order to avoid the measurement of R&D capital and simplify the model, most researchers (e.g. Clark and Griliches, 1984; Lichtenberg and Siegel, 1991; Odagiri, 1983) make the assumption that investments in R&D do not depreciate. Under this (rather extreme) assumption, the difference in R&D capital (dR) is equal to the current R&D investment (RD). As explained earlier, the term γr can be rewritten as $\rho(RD/Q)$. So the final form (expressed in terms of differences) is:

$$\Delta q_{it} = \lambda + a \Delta k_{it} + \beta \Delta l_{it} + \rho \frac{RD_{it}}{Q_{it}} + \Delta \varepsilon_{it} \qquad (6.19)$$

Where $\Delta x_{it} = x_{it} - x_{it-1} = log X_{it} / X_{it-1}$. In order to serve the objectives of the research, the above equation has been rewritten in terms of labour productivity:

$$\Delta (q_{it} - l_{it}) = \lambda + a \Delta (k_{it} - l_{it}) + \rho \frac{RD_{it}}{Q_{it}} + \Delta \varepsilon_{it} \qquad (6.20)$$

We should also note that some other studies (e.g., Mansfield, 1980) prefer to estimate separately the total factor productivity growth ($\Delta \Pi$) and then calculate the correlation between TFP growth and R&D using the following equation:

$$\Delta \Pi = \lambda + \rho \frac{RD_{it}}{Q_{it}} + \Delta \varepsilon_{it} \qquad (6.21)$$

The rate of return to R&D (ρ) that Equation 6.20 calculates, is actually the correlation of labour productivity growth with the ratio *RD/Q*, i.e. with R&D intensity. However, as noted earlier this interpretation is problematic. The term ρ is actually the rate of return to 'gross' R&D (because it was assumed that investments in R&D do not depreciate). In order to estimate the net rate of return to R&D, the depreciation rate of R&D should be subtracted from the 'gross' rate of return, i.e. $\rho_{net} = \rho_{gross} - \delta$ (Mairesse and Sassenou, 1991). But this is a main problem since the depreciation rate (δ) of R&D cannot be estimated accurately. Therefore, although by using this method we can avoid the estimation of R&D capital, the rate of depreciation remains a problem. Another ambiguity is the relationship between R&D-intensity and the observed productivity increase. The timing of this relationship possibly varies across industries and may not be always contemporaneous (Harhoff, 1998). Nevertheless, as Odagiri and Iwata (1986) explain, it still has the advantage of avoiding the possible bias due to simultaneous input-output decisions.

7.3 The Final Main Regressions

The previous sections described the two available types of specification that can be used to assess the impact of R&D on firm productivity. This subsection presents the main regressions that will be estimated in the next chapters. To estimate the impact of R&D on the level of productivity performance, the model below will be utilized. The coefficient of interest is the elasticity of R&D (i.e. γ).

$$(q_{it} - l_{it}) = a + a(k_{it} - l_{it}) + \gamma(r_{it} - l_{it}) + (\mu - 1) l_{it} + D_{industry} + D_{time} + \varepsilon_{it} \quad (6.14)$$

In order to calculate the R&D-elasticity that is based on growth rates, Equation 6.22 will be used. This is the same as the model above except that it is expressed in terms of differences.

$$\Delta(q_{it} - l_{it}) = a\Delta(k_{it} - l_{it}) + \gamma\Delta(r_{it} - l_{it}) + (\mu - 1)\Delta l_{it} + D_{industry} + D_{time} + \Delta\varepsilon_{it} \quad (6.22)$$

The final regression that will be utilized to calculate the rate of return to R&D (that is, its marginal impact) is Equation 6.23. As may be observed, it also includes dummies to represent the time and industry effects.

$$\Delta(q_{it} - l_{it}) = a\Delta(k_{it} - l_{it}) + (\mu - 1)\Delta l_{it} + \rho \frac{RD_{it}}{Q_{it}} + D_{industry} + D_{time} + \Delta\varepsilon_{it} \quad (6.23)$$

As noted earlier, to avoid the measurement of R&D capital and simplify the ROR model, researchers make the implausible assumption that investments in R&D do not depreciate and that the difference of R&D capital (*ΔR*) is equal to the current R&D investment (*RD*). However, as we will calculate R&D capital for the needs of the R&D-elasticity method, we will also estimate Equation 6.24 (in which the current R&D expenditure is replaced by the difference of R&D capital). We will then compare its results with those of Equation 6.23. This approach solves the interpretation problem regarding the rate of return to 'gross' and 'net' R&D. The findings of Goto and Suzuki (1989) who used a similar model show that estimates change radically when R&D capital (rather than R&D expenditure) is used.

$$\Delta(q_{it} - l_{it}) = a\Delta(k_{it} - l_{it}) + (\mu - 1)\Delta l_{it} + \rho \frac{\Delta R_{it}}{Q_{it}} + D_{industry} + D_{time} + \Delta\varepsilon_{it} \quad (6.24)$$

8. CHAPTER SUMMARY

This Chapter presents the econometric framework that is utilized to assess the impact of R&D on productivity performance. This framework is based on the concept of production function. The research model is an extended Cobb-Douglas function that besides the conventional inputs of capital and labour, includes a measure of R&D capital (or as many researchers prefer, a measure of scientific knowledge). This model can be linearized using natural logarithms and thus calculated using the OLS method. The measurement of R&D capital relies on the assumption that it is associated with past and current R&D expenditure. However, firms – in order to innovate continuously – abandon past knowledge and seek for new ones. Primarily for that reason, R&D capital – as any other type of capital – depreciates and becomes less valuable. But its rate of depreciation is still a topic of debate.

The most extensively used types of econometric specification for the research model are 'R&D-elasticity' and 'Rate of Return'. The first assumes that the elasticity of output with respect to R&D across firms is the same, whereas the second is based on the assumption that the rate of return to R&D is the same. As discussed earlier, it cannot be argued that the estimates of one approach are less biased than those of the other one. Each approach has its advantages but also its disadvantages. Although the estimates of the 'Rate of Return' type are not directly comparable to those of R&D-elasticity type, their advantage is that (to some extent), they avoid the possible bias due to simultaneous input-output decisions. Both types of specification will be estimated and compared in the following chapters.

7. The Data: Measuring Innovation and other Firm Inputs and Outputs

This chapter has two objectives. These are firstly, to familiarize the reader with the research data, and secondly to construct the research variables. To accomplish the first objective, the main characteristics of the data are examined (i.e. the level of aggregation, the richness, the reliability and the representativeness of the sample). The second objective is to examine what the output (Q), capital (K), labour (L) and R&D capital (R) should conceptually measure. This is actually a discussion of what proxies can be used in order to represent adequately these variables. In the first section of this chapter, the raw data and their sources are introduced, the two samples are described, and their representativeness is investigated. This section ends with a discussion of the problems of industrial classification and the accounting treatment of R&D expenditures. The second section describes how the research variables were constructed and discusses the problems of aggregation and double counting. The third section discusses the problem of deflation, whereas the last one provides descriptive statistics and identifies patterns of the data that cannot be easily seen without the use of these statistics.

1. DESCRIPTION OF THE DATA

Although the collection of firm-level data is time consuming, the estimation of the impacts of R&D at the firm-level offers numerous advantages. In contrast to industry- and country-level data, firm-level data allow us to measure the private (rather than social) returns to R&D. As they are less aggregated than the industry and country-level data, they are also better measures than those of the economy as a whole. Additionally, by going down to the firm-level we can collect a greater number of observations than could be obtained at industry-level. As Griliches (1979) has argued, firm-level data are also a good way to reduce the multicollinearity problem that besets macro-level studies. Another advantage relates to the measurement of output. Immeasurable improvements of output, such as product quality and product variety, are often overlooked in aggregate output statistics (Griliches, 1979).

Similarly, Brynjolfsson and Hitt (1996) showed that technological change is rarely found in aggregate output statistics. Furthermore, the variability that exists in firm-level data is greater than that in aggregate data (Griliches, 1979). This variability is essential for the accurate estimation of R&D effects. A disadvantage of industry and country-level data is that they do not allow us to separate those productivity improvements which are result of a firm's R&D investment from those which are general to a sector (Wakelin, 2001). In other words, it is not possible by using highly aggregated data to examine the differences across firms within an industry (Odagiri and Iwata, 1986). Indeed, the results of macro-level studies cannot be considered as representative of what is really happening at the firm-level. This is confirmed by many studies (e.g. Theil, 1954) which showed that there is no strong relationship between the firm-level and macro-level variables. Nevertheless, it should be acknowledged that firm-level data do have drawbacks. Firstly, they cannot be used to answer questions regarding the 'social' returns to R&D. Secondly, firm-level R&D data are often poor as they are collected from firms' financial reports rather than from government questionnaires (as occurs with industry and macro-level data; Odagiri and Iwata, 1986).

The estimation of the effects of R&D requires a panel dataset. For this purpose, we had to collect as much data as possible for MNEs that both belong to the UK manufacturing sector and that report their R&D expenditure. Three sources were used to collect the data: (1) DataStream: This is a database provided by Thomson. It includes financial reports and historical data for many UK firms. Most of the data were retrieved from Datastream. (2) The UK R&D Scoreboard Survey: The R&D Scoreboard is a survey of the UK department of trade and industry (DTI). It started in 1991, takes place every year and collects data for firms' output, profits, employees and R&D expenditure. (3) Firms' financial reports and websites: When there were missing data (i.e. observations which were not found in Datastream or the R&D scoreboard survey), the financial annual reports of firms were downloaded from their websites allowing us to close the remaining gaps. This was necessary for less than 1 percent of the data. The raw dataset consists of 192 firms in a 23-year panel from 1980 to 2002.

1.1 The Samples

Although 192 firms reported their R&D expenditure in 2002, only 16 firms reported it in 1980. Given that an ideal sample should include as many firms as possible (to reduce the selectivity bias) and have a long history (to explore the R&D time lag structure and impact of R&D over time), it was decided to construct two samples: a 'Large' sample (that includes many firms) and a 'Long' sample (that includes many years of observation). The 'Large' sample will be utilized to investigate most of the research questions whereas the 'Long' sample will only be employed to explore whether the impact of R&D on productivity has changed over time, as well as the time lag structure of R&D.

1.1.1 The 'Large' sample

This sample covers the eight year period between 1995 and 2002. There were 138 firms that reported their R&D expenditure in 1995. From these 138 firms, 31 were eliminated either because they were not multinationals or because they had many R&D-observations missing. Following the work of other studies (Griliches and Mairesse, 1983; Hall, 1990), all other missing R&D observations (no more than two per firm) were estimated by using the growth rate of R&D expenditure of the closest three years. As will be discussed later, many firms that invest in R&D may never report it. Therefore, believing that the sample might be distorted by including firms that reported zero R&D expenditure, it was decided that they should be eliminated.

Merged firms were not removed from the sample because after an investigation of firms' history (using Companies House and firms' websites), it was observed that during these eight years many of the large MNEs bought or sold smaller firms. As Griliches and Mairesse (1984) argue, however, by excluding these merged firms we may bias the estimates downwards. The final 'Large' sample is therefore composed of 107 firms over the 1995-2002 period (i.e. 107 firms X 8 years = 856 observations). The sectoral analysis of both the initial (unbalanced) and restricted (balanced) 'Large' sample is presented in Table 7.1.

1.1.2 The 'Long' sample

As noted earlier, two of the research objectives of this book are to investigate the time lag structure of R&D as well as whether the contribution of R&D to productivity changed over time. However, the eight year period that the 'Large' sample covers is not long enough for this purpose. Therefore, a 'Long' sample was constructed to provide information for a longer time period and to safeguard the estimates against any possible business-cycle bias (as it captures both recessions and revivals of the economy). This sample covers the 14 year period between 1989 and 2002.

The attempt to include more years of observation was not successful because although in 1989 there were 104 firms that reported their R&D expenditure, in 1988 only 31 firms did so. The reason why firms did not report their R&D expenditure prior to 1989 was the introduction of the revised Statement of Standard Accounting Practice in 1989 (SSAP-13, 1989). As Stoneman and Toivanen (2001) found, the revision of SSAP13 encouraged firms to disclose their R&D expenditure. However, as they argue, given that the accounting rules do not have the force of law, the reporting of R&D still remained voluntary.

Table 7.1 Sectoral analysis of the 'Large' sample (1995-2002)

Industry	Initial Sample		Restricted Sample	
	SIC 80 Code	No of Firms	SIC 80 Code	No of Firms
Metal products	22, 31	5	22 & 31	2
Minerals	23, 24	4	23 & 24	3
Chemicals	25	15	25	12
Pharmaceuticals	257	12	257	8
Machinery & mech. engineering	32	30	32	27
Computing & office equipment	33	3	33	2
Electrical & electronics	34	23	34	19
Telecommunication	344	10	344	9
Motor vehicle parts	35	8	35	6
Aerospace	364	6	364	6
Instrument engineering	37	10	37	7
Textiles	43	3	43	1
Paper & printing	47	2	47	2
Rubber and plastics	48	4	48	2
Other manufacturing	49	3	49	1
	Total	**138**	**Total**	**107**

Table 7.2 Sectoral analysis of the 'Long' sample (1989-2002)

Industry	Initial Sample		Restricted Sample	
	SIC 80 Code	No of Firms	SIC 80 Code	No of Firms
Metal products	22, 31	4	22 & 31	2
Minerals	23, 24	4	23 & 24	3
Chemicals	25	15	25	13
Pharmaceuticals	257	4	257	3

Machinery & mech. engineering	32	26	32	23
Computing & office equipment	33	2	33	1
Electrical & electronics	34	17	34	14
Telecommunication	344	6	344	4
Motor vehicle parts	35	8	35	6
Aerospace	364	6	364	5
Instrument engineering	37	5	37	4
Textiles	43	1	43	1
Paper & printing	47	2	47	2
Rubber and plastics	48	2	48	2
Other manufacturing	49	2	49	1
	Total	**104**	**Total**	**84**

From 104 firms, 20 companies were eliminated either because they were not multinationals or because they had many R&D observations missing. In line with the procedures followed for the first sample, merged firms were not removed and 39 missing R&D observations were estimated by using the growth rate of R&D expenditure of the closest three years. The final 'Long' sample comprised 84 firms over the 1989-2002 period (i.e. 84 firms X 14 years = 1176 observations). The sectoral analysis of both the initial and restricted 'Long' sample is presented in Table 7.2, whilst descriptive statistics for both samples are provided later in the Chapter.

1.2 Representativeness of the Sample

In 2002, the total private R&D investment of the whole UK manufacturing sector was £10.14 billion (ONS, 2002a). In that same year, the R&D expenditures of the 107 firms of the 'Large' sample accounted for £7.85 billions, approximately 77 percent of the total. Therefore, the possibility of having a serious sample selectivity bias is reduced. The fact that only 107 firms can represent the 77 percent of the total R&D expenditure may be regarded as surprising. However, it is consistent with the UK R&D-Scoreboard survey (R&D Scoreboard, 2003, p.24) which reports that in 2002 the top 37 UK MNEs accounted for over 82 percent of the R&D of the top 540 UK companies.

Nevertheless, the coverage of 77 percent of the total cannot guarantee that the sample is a random selection of the entire UK manufacturing sector. In order to be considered as representative it needs sufficient sampling variability. The sample biases that might occur are:

(1) Not all types of firms reported their R&D expenditure. This issue relates to the accounting treatment of R&D that is discussed later in the chapter.

(2) Given that sometimes only very large firms have the financial resources to invest in R&D (Mansfield, 1968a), it is possible to focus unintentionally on a sample exclusively composed of very large firms. However, such a sample is not consistent with the objective to investigate the role of firm size. Contrary to other studies (e.g. Griliches and Mairesse, 1984) which concentrate on larger firms, the research sample includes both larger and smaller firms. Approximately 55 percent of the sample are designated larger firms with more than 1000 employees, whilst the remaining 45 percent are designated smaller ones. Although a firm with less than 1000 employees might seem small in comparison to the largest MNEs that have many 1000s of employees, it still difficult to categorize a firm with 1000 employees as small (Mansfield, 1984).

(3) We also investigated whether the sample includes too many high-tech firms (from industries such as pharmaceutical, electronics and aerospace). It was found that 63 firms were technologically advanced, while the remaining 44 firms belonged in low-tech industries such as metals and textiles.

(4) Does the sample focus on specific industries whilst ignoring others? As Table 7.1 indicates, the sample is more focused on industries such as chemicals, electronics and engineering and less focused on industries such as metals, minerals and plastics. This bias engenders some interpretational problems as one cannot therefore claim that the return to R&D estimated in this research is the true average return to R&D of the UK manufacturing MNEs. On the other hand, it is clearly sensible to focus on industries such electronics and chemicals because the biggest part of industrial R&D is undertaken by them.

We should also note that because the research sample includes many R&D-intensive industries such as chemicals, electronics and engineering, it is reasonable to expect a higher average R&D-intensity than that found in the UK manufacturing sector as a whole. Indeed, whilst the average R&D-intensity of the UK manufacturing sector is around 3 percent, the corresponding intensity of the research sample is approximately 4.2 percent. The higher R&D-intensity indicates a sample bias to the side of R&D-intensive firms. Despite this, the sample does cover a wide range of R&D-intensities, between 0.2 percent (in the case of paper) to approximately 30 percent (in the case of some pharmaceutical companies). As for the 'Long' sample, its 84 companies invested £4.9 billion on R&D in 2002, and thus account for approximately 48 percent of the total. Although selectivity bias may be a problem, this is the cost paid for having a sample that includes many years. The sectoral analysis and the ratios of 'larger to smaller' firms and 'high- to low-tech' firms are similar to those of the first sample. By contrast, the R&D-intensity in this sample is lower (at 2.6 percent) and hence closer to the average R&D-intensity of the UK manufacturing sector overall.

1.3 The Problem of Industrial Classification

Although the classification of firms into sectors of the economy can be considered a straightforward procedure, it hides pitfalls that can seriously distort the estimates. Many firms are either diversified producing a wide variety of products, or change their main field of business over time. Given that the Standard Industrial Classification (SIC) does not fully account for these changes, one may end up aggregating dissimilar firms. Griliches (1984) suggested that although in the analysis of macro-level data some measurement errors may cancel each other out over the 1000s of observations, firm-level data is liable to be sensitive to the noise arising from the aggregation of dissimilar firms.

The decision regarding the main business field of each firm was taken using three different sources of information: (1) the two or three-digit SIC80 classification code (obtained from Datastream), (2) the R&D-Scoreboard survey and (3) Companies House. For about 70 percent of firms, the three sources reported the same business field, so classification was straightforward. Diversified firms were placed in the industry in which they had highest sales. However, the classification of the remaining 30 percent of the sample was more problematic. In many cases the difference between the reported business classifications was remarkable. For instance, Datastream classified one firm as part of the rubber and plastics industry, whereas both the Companies House and the R&D scoreboard survey placed it in the motor-vehicles sector. There were many similar examples that frequently provided no indication as to which industry the firm really belonged to.

This problem was investigated by examining the 'history', 'products' and 'about the company' Internet pages from each firm's website. Although this was a time-consuming procedure, it revealed important information. For example, the firm that belonged to both rubber-and-plastics and motor-vehicles industries, manufactured tires for motor vehicles. Similarly, another firm classified in both the metal-products and motor-vehicles sectors was a company that manufactured metallic bolts and nuts for motor vehicles. Unfortunately, these findings not only do not solve the initial problem but they engender additional ones, as they indicate that firm classification is to some extent subjective. It seems that in such cases the information on a firm's products provides limited help in the classification of a firm. So in order to resolve the problem, additional information for a firm's technological identity is needed.

The additional information that might complete this informational puzzle is the R&D-intensity of a firm. For example, in the UK the average R&D-intensity for the industry of rubber and plastics is approximately 0.4 percent, whereas the R&D-intensity for the motor-vehicle industry is 3 percent (ONS, 2002a). Given that the R&D-intensity of the firm of our example is more than 3 percent, it seemed more appropriate to include it in the motor-vehicles industry. The same practice was followed for all the firms whose history and products did not provide any insight for their true business field. It should be noted, however, that although this practice corrected several inaccuracies, some classification errors may still remain.

1.4 The Accounting Treatment of R&D Expenditures

As many of the research data were collected from firms' financial reports, the investigation of the accounting treatment of R&D expenditure is important in order to examine the selectivity bias and the quality of the data. Although the accounting treatment of R&D expenditure is a major problem for all innovation studies, it has not attracted much interest. In 1989 the revised Statement of Standard Accounting Practice (SSAP13 revised) was introduced in the UK. Stoneman and Toivanen (2001, p.124) explain in brief what it recommends:

> For accounting periods beginning on or after 1 January 1989, the new Statement of Standard Accounting Practice (SSAP13) recommended that UK firms separately declare their R&D spend in their annual accounts if the firm is a public company and meets two of the three following criteria: the balance sheet total exceeds £39m; turnover exceeds £80m; average number of employees exceeds 2500. Although there had been an earlier version of SSAP13 in place prior to 1989 that specified good practice for the accounting treatment of R&D in company accounts it was only with this revised Statement in 1989 that separate declaration was recommended.

As was noted earlier, although the Statement had a positive impact on the extent to which firms disclose their R&D expenditure, it did not have the power of law to force firms to disclose it. Hence, the reporting of R&D remains to some extent voluntary (Stoneman and Toivanen, 2001). The accounting problem of R&D is associated with two major questions: first, what factors influence a firm's decision to disclose or not its R&D expenditure? and second, what factors affect how much R&D a firm will report?

1.4.1 The issue of disclosure

The past literature (Dye, 1986; Stoneman and Toivanen, 2001) describes three major factors that affect the decision of disclosure. The first one is the impact of R&D expenditure on a firm's market value. For instance, a firm whose R&D spending did not lead to successful innovations may not report it in an effort to cover up the unsuccessful investment. A second factor relates to the costs involved in disclosing R&D expenditure. The higher these are the lower the likelihood of reporting it. The third one is the strategic impact that the disclosure of R&D may have. For example, disclosure of high R&D expenditure may alarm competitors and affect the first-mover advantage.

However, there are additional factors that may affect a firm's decision regarding disclosure. As there is a tax credit for R&D, a firm has a strong motive to report R&D expenditure. Government policy on R&D subsidies may persuade a firm to disclose its R&D, as it is unlikely to subsidize a firm that has not undertaken R&D before. It is also possible that a firm merely follows the practice of its competitors, reporting its expenditure if it belongs to an industry in which this is the normal procedure. Nevertheless, Stoneman and Toivanen (2001) who investigated this argument found no evidence to support it.

It is also reasonable to argue that larger firms are more likely to disclose their expenditure, as the SSAP Statement recommends that such firms should report their R&D expenditure separately. Because R&D effort in smaller firms is typically informal research, possibly mixed with other activities, it is rarely reported (for instance, engineers from the production department may develop a better production process which is never reported in R&D expenditure (Kleinknecht, 1987). As Kleinknecht (1987) found, although the Dutch official data indicated that the 91 percent of R&D is done by larger firms the real figure was 77 percent.

The issue of disclosure also relates to the sample selectivity biases of 'under-coverage' and 'item non-response'. The term under-coverage is usually used by statisticians to express the possibility that a certain sector of the relevant population is for some reason under-represented in the sample (Griliches, 1984). A major problem arises if the firms included in the sample are dissimilar to those not included. However, as we have already discussed earlier the sample can be considered as representative of the entire UK manufacturing sector as it covers 77 percent of the total private R&D and has sufficient sampling variability.

The problem of 'item non-response' arises when there are missing observations for a certain variable. However, the real problem is not the missing observations themselves but the fact that these observations may be missing for a particular reason (Griliches, 1984). Fortunately, the missing observations of the research dataset are very few and thus, this problem is minimal. In general, it could be seen that when a firm started to report its R&D expenditure, it continues to report it thereafter. This observation is consistent with the findings of Stoneman and Toivanen (2001) who observed a similar pattern.

1.4.2 What factors affect how much R&D a firm will report?

Another problem is the fact that even when a firm decides to disclose its R&D expenditure, there are numerous factors that affect the amount that the firm will report. This is another significant issue as it may affect the quality of the research data. Two factors that may lead a firm to over-report its R&D expenditure were discussed earlier (the tax credit for R&D and government policy on R&D subsidies). However, the most important source of distortion is likely to be the different methods of accounting treatment for R&D. There are also issues of comparability as the accounting rules vary from country to country. Nixon (1997) emphasizes that the Financial Accounting Standards Board (USA), the Accounting Standards Board (UK) and the International Accounting Standards Committee each recommend different accounting treatments for R&D expenditure. According to the SSAP Statement (ch.12), R&D expenditures can be reported using one of four different methods:

(1) Charge all costs to expense when incurred: In this case, R&D expenditures are regarded as expenses, they are written-off when incurred and thus reported at the end of each financial year. This is the treatment that the US accounting board recommends mainly because the future benefits are uncertain (the US Board cites evidence that less than 2 percent of the new product ideas and less than 15 percent of product development projects were commercially successful).

(2) Capitalize all costs: R&D expenditures are regarded as assets, they are capitalized and only a percentage of these expenditures is reported at the end of the year. This treatment is based on the argument that firms undertake R&D in the hope of future benefits. Hence a firm should capitalize R&D costs and match the total costs to the future benefits.

(3) Capitalize all costs when incurred providing specified conditions are fulfilled and charge all others to expense. In this case there are a number of conditions that must be fulfilled before R&D expenditure is capitalized. If these conditions are not met, R&D expenditure should be expensed.

(4) Accumulate all costs in a special category distinct from assets and expenses until the existence of future benefits can be determined. In this case, R&D expenditure initially remains in a special category but in future can be either transferred to assets (if some benefits arise) or written off (if no future benefits arise).

Although the accounting standards of the UK recommend that firms should write-off their R&D expenditures when incurred, they also suggest that the expenditures may be carried forward if future benefits are certain. However, firms should include a note in their financial reports to explain why future benefits can be considered as certain. Hence, the cost for a new R&D project can be reported by a firm either at the end of the financial year or over the next few years. Nevertheless, this treatment raises problems here, because firstly it distorts the quality of R&D data as it allows firms to manipulate the reported R&D expenditures and secondly, it is difficult to calculate the R&D capital of a firm that capitalizes its R&D expenditure because it does not report it immediately but over the next few years.

A study that sheds some light on the practice followed by firms in the UK, is that of Nixon (1997). This study found that 81 percent of UK companies write-off all R&D costs immediately (even when the certainty of future benefits is high). Nixon also cites evidence from the study of Gray (1985) that found that 83 per cent of respondents wrote-off R&D expenditure as it was incurred. Although these findings are reassuring, they cannot guarantee that all firms of our sample write off their R&D expenditures immediately.

Fortunately, Datastream has two separates codes for R&D, one for firms that immediately write off their R&D and a second one for those which capitalize it. The firms which capitalize R&D (very few) were excluded from the beginning and thus all firms in the research sample immediately write-off their R&D expenditure. This was confirmed by randomly selecting 15 firms of the sample and reading their financial reports. The SSAP Statement recommends that a firm's accounting policy on R&D expenditure should be stated and explained. It was found that the firms included a note in their financial statement explaining that R&D costs were written-off immediately.

It should also be emphasized that in many cases it is difficult for a firm to identify what types of activities constitute R&D. The SSAP Statement suggests that R&D activities are distinguished from non-research activities by the presence or absence of an element of innovation. However, this definition is not always sufficient to separate research from non-research activities. For instance, on the list of activities which are not considered as R&D is 'market research'. However, market research could equally easily be described as R&D because it is used not only by marketing divisions, but also by R&D divisions, in order to evaluate competitors' products and collect technical specifications. Therefore, even when two firms undertake the same R&D, they may report different R&D expenditures, depending on how they identify these activities.

2. CONSTRUCTING THE MAIN VARIABLES

Because direct measures of the main variables, such as output, capital and innovative activity do not exist, some sort of proxies had to be constructed from the raw data. However, proxies cannot always represent accurately what they purport to measure (Griliches, 1984). For instance, output can be defined either as sales or value-added. Similarly, there are many different types of labour (e.g. skilled/unskilled and educated/uneducated employees) and capital equipment (e.g. heavy machinery and portable computers). This section describes the construction of the research variables and discusses the associated problems.

2.1 The Output

The fact that the physical output of a firm comprises many different products makes its direct measurement impossible. Hence, monetary weights are usually used to aggregate the variety of output to a common measure. The majority of studies (e.g. Hall and Mairesse, 1995; Lichtenberg and Siegel, 1991) approximate output by using a measure either of sales or value-added (single or double deflated). The main drawback of the 'sales' variable is that it ignores the materials used in the production. A better measure is the 'single deflated value-added', which is the deflated measure of a firm's sales minus the raw materials and intermediate inputs used in the production. However, this measure has the disadvantage that although raw materials and intermediate inputs are considered as inputs of the production process, they are deflated using output price indices.

The third method (the so-called double deflated value-added) uses different deflators for sales from those for raw materials and intermediate inputs. Sales are deflated with output price indices, whereas raw materials and intermediate inputs are added to the inputs and thus deflated with input price indices. A study that sheds some light on the measurement of output is that of Stoneman and Francis (1994). The authors found that the methods of single and double deflated value-added can yield different estimates if input prices and output prices do not move together over time. Their findings indicate that double deflated value-added is a superior concept to employ for the measurement of productivity. Nevertheless, given that the research data do not include information for value-added, raw materials and intermediate inputs, the former measurement (sales) is by necessity employed here. Therefore, a record of output at constant prices was constructed by deflating the total sales of every individual firm (information on the deflation procedure is given later). A record of differenced output was also constructed in order to be used in the rate of return (ROR) specification:

$$\Delta q_{it} = q_{it} - q_{it-1} = logQ_{it} / Q_{it-1} \qquad (7.1)$$

The use of sales however, engenders some problems. By using sales instead of value-added, or alternatively by ignoring the raw and intermediate materials used in production, the estimated impact of R&D on productivity may be biased. The explanation for such bias is that at different levels of output, there may be economies in the use of raw materials. Hence, the relationship between sales and raw materials does not remain constant but varies depending on the output (Hebden, 1983). Cuneo and Mairesse (1984) and Mairesse and Hall (1996) find that the use of sales instead of value-added attenuates the elasticity of R&D. By contrast, the study of Sassenou (1988) indicates that the use of sales (instead of value-added) amplifies the rate of return to R&D. Additionally, it should be noted that the use of either sales or value-added engenders errors related to immeasurable improvements of output: even when output is higher, sales may falsely indicate that it has remained constant. As noted earlier, the estimated productivity depends firstly, on the extent to which sales can reflect the increased output and secondly, on the amount of returns that an innovator succeeds in appropriating for himself (Griliches, 1979).

2.2 The Capital Input

The measurement of Capital (K) input engenders similar problems. Many studies approximate it by using the Gross Fixed Capital stock, i.e. the cumulative stock of past investments in capital. However, capital theory suggests that (K) must be a measure of 'productive stock' implying that its efficiency declines as it gets older (Jorgenson, 1963). By ignoring the so-called 'wear and tear' effects, capital is overstated. A more accurate way to measure the capital input is the Net Fixed Capital stock, i.e. to take into account the depreciation of each asset, to split the capital goods into different age-groups and then weight them according to age (Hebden, 1983).

Although the majority of previous studies use either the Gross Fixed Capital stock or the Net Fixed Capital stock, these capital inputs are far from the conceptual one. The work of Jorgenson (1963) and the OECD Manual for Productivity (OECD, 2001b) suggest that capital input must be a measure not of capital stock but of the services flowing from it. According to this framework, the cumulative stock of capital produces a flow of productive services (the so-called 'capital services') which are the conceptual capital input for productivity analysis. These productive services are analogous to the discounted cumulative capital goods that a firm purchased or rented.

But how can we measure the capital services of each firm? The ideal method is to use the so-called 'rental price', i.e. the cost that a firm pays –

either to other firms or to itself – for having and using a number of assets (the so-called user costs). Following Griliches (1980) we approximate the rental price of capital services by the depreciation of Gross Fixed Capital stock, which is the actual cost that a firm pays for having and using its capital assets. The advantage of using the depreciation is that we can take into account the many different rental prices of each product. For example the depreciation of a product with a high rental price (e.g. a very innovative computer-cluster) will also be high. By contrast, the depreciation of a product with low rental price, such as a five year old lorry, will be low. The depreciation of Gross Fixed Capital stock would be a better proxy for rental price if it not confined to the change in value between two accounting periods, but instead, embodied the change of value due to a change in market value (OECD, 2001b). Unfortunately, the depreciation reported by firms does not incorporate such changes.

Another problem of this concept is the – implausible in the real world – assumption that capital services are proportional to capital stock. Even when two firms have exactly the same capital stock, the flow of capital services may be significantly different. For instance, one firm might use its machinery 16 hours per day (two shifts) while another one only eight hours. This phenomenon – known as capital utilization – can be caused by changes in demand conditions, seasonal variations or even by breakdown of machinery (OECD, 2001b). For that reason, a better proxy of capital input is the 'machine hours', i.e. the cumulative hours that the machinery of each firm was used. Nevertheless given that these data are rarely published, we confined ourselves to simpler proxies. Although the Gross and Net Fixed Capital stocks are an inferior measure of capital input (as compared to Capital Services), in order to provide a comparative perspective, the research model will be estimated using not only the Capital Services (that is our main variable of capital input) but also the Gross and Net Fixed Capital stock. It should be noted that these three definitions of capital input have been corrected for double counting. So the machinery devoted to the R&D division was deducted from the conventional capital.

2.3 The Labour Input

Similar problems arise when trying to construct a proxy variable that can adequately represent the labour input. The simplest and most usual measure of labour input is the number of employees. However, there are at least two major drawbacks that influence this proxy. First, it does not take into account potential changes in the number of the working hours caused by absence, overtime or part-time work. Second, it ignores the utilization of labour that may significantly vary over time and business cycles (OECD, 2001b). For that reason, a better measure of labour input is considered to be the total number of hours actually worked by all employees. This proxy however, has its own problems as it is based on the assumption that an hour worked by one employee contributes the same labour input as one worked by another one (OECD, 2001b). It therefore ignores the fact that the contribution of each employee depends on several parameters such as experience, effort, skills and education. This problem has also been emphasized by the US Bureau of Labour Statistics (1993) that pointed out that by measuring the total hours worked, we treat an hour worked by an experienced surgeon and an hour worked by a teenager at a fast food restaurant as equal amounts of labour.

For that reason, the heterogeneity of employees or hours worked is particularly important in order to construct a proxy that can adequately reflect the true labour input. A proxy that reflects this heterogeneity is the compensation paid to labour. For instance, a well educated and experienced scientist will not get paid the same as his assistant. Nevertheless, the compensation of labour is a sum of different types of payment that are often difficult to identify. It does not only include salaries and wages but it also includes non-wage types of compensation such as social security payments, training expenses and stock options (OECD, 2001b).

Following the productivity framework discussed above, two labour variables were constructed. The first one is the variable which is used by the majority of similar studies, i.e. the 'number of employees'. Because data regarding labour compensation were available, it was possible to construct a proxy-variable which might capture the heterogeneity of employees. Labour input is usually measured as total man-hours, weighted by their real wage-rate (Hebden, 1983). This is equal to the annual wages plus benefits that each employee receives. For that reason, we define the second labour variable as the total employment costs (deflated and corrected for double counting). The source of these data (Datastream) defines 'Total Employment Costs' as the sum of wages and salaries, profit sharing, social security costs and all other employment costs. Therefore, although it was known that social payments were included, it was not known whether or not other labour costs such as training expenses and stock options were included.

Although the use of employment costs may solve to some extent the problem of employees' heterogeneity, this variable is beset by biases that are no less important than the biases inherent to the 'number of employees' variable. These biases are associated with two assumptions that the 'employment costs' variable relies on: firstly, that the employees get paid fairly depending on their productivity and, secondly, that the average salary across industries and firms is similar. Both assumptions are highly unlikely, and may engender a serious bias. Managers do not always monitor adequately the contribution of each employee and thus do not always pay them fairly. Similarly, the assumption that the average salary paid is the same between industries or firms is unrealistic. In order to provide a comparative perspective, the model will be estimated using both the 'number of employees' and 'employment costs' variable.

2.4 The R&D Capital Stock

The estimation of R&D capital is based on the framework described in the previous chapters, i.e. it is based on Equation 7.2. There are two major problems associated with the calculation of R&D capital: the choice of the depreciation rate (δ), and the estimation of R&D capital for the initial year of the sample (1989 for the 'Long' sample, and 1995 for the 'Large' sample). The first problem has already been discussed earlier. Although the main measure of R&D capital employed is calculated using a depreciation rate of 20 percent, additional measures of R&D capital are also calculated using rates of 15 and 25 percent. Later on, the regression is re-estimated using these latter two rates, thereby investigating their impact on the coefficient of R&D.

$$R_{it} = RD_{it} + \sum_{1}^{k} (1 - \delta)^k RD_{i(t-k)} \qquad (7.2)$$

As for the second problem (the estimation of the R&D capital for the initial year of the sample), the practice that many studies adopt (Hall, 1990) is based on the assumption that the pre-sample growth rate (r) of the R&D expenditure is fixed at approximately 8 percent per year. If this assumption holds, the initial R&D capital is X times the spending of R&D in 1989 (or 1995, depending on the sample), where $X = 1 / (\delta + r)$. So if we assume that the depreciation rate (δ) is 20 percent and the yearly growth rate (r) is 8 percent then: $X = 1 / (0.20 + 0.08) = 3.57$. This suggests that R&D capital in 1989 was 3.57 times the R&D expenditure in 1989. This study however, does not follow that approach for a main reason. The assumption that (r) is fixed does not hold because this growth rate varies depending on the industry and the type of firm.

For 16 of the firms, R&D data go back to 1980, providing the opportunity to calculate their R&D capital more accurately. In order to correct the errors of the remaining firms, it is not assumed that the growth rate of the firms' R&D investments is 8 percent per year. Instead, the average growth rate of the earliest three years (1989-1991 for the 'Long' sample; 1995-1997 for the 'Large' sample) is calculated individually for each firm. This correction appears to be important as the growth rate of R&D investments was found to vary between 5 and 25 percent, depending on the firm. Finally, the R&D-

intensity of a firm (i) is defined as the ratio of R&D expenditure (RD) in year (t) over total sales (S) of that same year: $RI_{it} = RD_{it} / S_{it}$. However, as noted in the previous chapter, the rate of return to R&D will be calculated using not only the current R&D investment (RD) but also the difference of R&D capital (dR). In that case, the following equation will be used: $RI_{it} = dR_{it} / S_{it}$.

2.5 The Double-Counting Corrections

One practical problem arising in both R&D-Elasticity and rate of return (ROR) econometric specification, is that research employees and research equipment are counted twice, once in the conventional inputs of Capital (K) and Labour (L) and again in the input of R&D capital (Schankerman, 1981). Thus, R&D-equipment and R&D-employees should be subtracted from the conventional Capital and Labour inputs. The effect of 'double-counting' corrections on the estimated R&D-elasticity is important. The findings of Cuneo and Mairesse (1984) indicate that such corrections increase the R&D-elasticity from 0.11 to 0.21; Hall and Mairesse (1995) find that when the appropriate corrections are made, the estimated rate of return is raised by 4 percent. Similarly, Schankerman (1981) finds that double-counting biases downward the estimates of both R&D-elasticity and ROR specifications.

Although the double counting corrections are important for the accurate estimation of R&D-coefficients, the research data are not detailed enough to allow us to make such corrections. No information was available concerning either the number of research employees that each firm has (in order to deduct those from the ordinary employees), or each firm's capital which was devoted to the R&D division (in order to deduct it from the conventional capital). Even though actual data do not exist, it is possible to approximate the number of R&D employees and the amount of R&D equipment. Past findings have shown that R&D expenditure is primarily composed of three components: (1) equipment, e.g. instruments and computers, (2) employees, e.g. scientists, technologists and supportive staff, and (3) materials used for the every-day experiments (Mansfield, 1968a). Hence, we can break down R&D expenditures and thereby obtain an approximate measure for the stock of research equipment as well as the number of research employees.

As one might expect though, the composition of R&D is not always constant, but varies depending on country, industry and time. Data for the UK is available as a series of annual surveys on the breakdown of R&D, carried out by the ONS (ONS Business Monitor MA14). In line with the Frascati manual, the ONS surveys suggest that there are three main R&D components: Capital expenditure, Labour and other current expenditure. Capital expenditure includes the investments in plant, machinery, land and buildings; Labour spending includes the salaries and the wages devoted to

Conceptual and Methodological Issues

R&D personnel; and the other current expenditure includes purchases of materials and services. Table 7.3 and Table 7.4 presents the R&D breakdown for 13 major industries (for years 1995 and 2002 respectively). As expected the composition of R&D varies across industries and over time. For instance, approximately half of the money invested in R&D in 2002 by the chemical industry was devoted to research personnel. Yet the aerospace industry dedicated only one third of their total expenditure to this. Similar discrepancies can be observed relating to R&D equipment.

Table 7.3 Composition of R&D expenditure in 1995

Industry	Capital[a]	Labour[b]	Other Current[c]
Textiles	4%	33%	63%
Chemicals	12%	43%	45%
Pharmaceuticals	22%	32%	46%
Rubber & plastics	15%	43%	42%
Minerals	7%	48%	45%
Metal products	4%	46%	50%
Machinery	4%	44%	52%
Comp. & office equipment	13%	38%	49%
Electrical & electronics	6%	39%	55%
Communication	8%	45%	47%
Instrument engineering	6%	48%	46%
Motor vehicles	13%	37%	50%
Aerospace	6%	35%	59%
Average	**9%**	**41%**	**50%**

Notes:
[a] Capital includes plant, machinery, land and buildings.
[b] Labour includes salaries and wages.
[c] The 'Other Current' type of expenditure includes purchases of other inputs, materials and services.

Source: Office for National Statistics (ONS).

Although 33 percent of the R&D expenditure of the rubber industry is devoted to R&D equipment, the corresponding percentage for the electronic industry is only 4 percent. Similarly, the R&D composition varies across time. The spending for R&D equipment increased from 9 (in 1995) to 11 percent (in 2002), whilst the percentage devoted to R&D personnel increased from 41 to 44 percent. Unfortunately, there were no available data on the R&D breakdown for the years before 1995. For that reason, we had to calculate the average composition of each industry for the years 1995 to 2002 and use these average values for the missing years. In what follows, there is a description of the data on the composition of R&D that were used to make the necessary double-counting corrections.

2.5.1 Labour costs

The correction of 'labour costs' for double-counting ($L_{corrected}$) was straightforward. It was estimated by using the following equation: $L_{corrected} = L_{total} - L_{R\&D}$. Where L_{total} is the total labour costs that a firm reports and $L_{R\&D}$ represents the R&D labour costs. Although there were data on total labour costs, these were not available for the labour costs of the R&D division. For that reason, these costs were approximated by using the data on the composition of R&D.

Table 7.4 Composition of R&D expenditure in 2002

Industry	Capital[a]	Labour[b]	Other Current[c]
Textiles	21%	53%	26%
Chemicals	10%	49%	41%
Pharmaceuticals	15%	37%	48%
Rubber & plastics	33%	31%	36%
Minerals	15%	50%	35%
Metal Products	8%	43%	49%
Machinery	4%	53%	43%
Comp. & office equipment	5%	37%	58%
Electrical & electronics	4%	50%	46%
Communication	4%	49%	47%
Instrument engineering	8%	42%	50%
Motor vehicles	4%	48%	48%
Aerospace	6%	35%	59%
Average	**11%**	**44%**	**45%**

Notes:
[a] Capital includes plant, machinery, land and buildings.
[b] Labour includes salaries and wages.
[c] The 'Other Current' type of expenditure includes purchases of other inputs, materials and services.

Source: Office for National Statistics (ONS).

For example, if we want to make corrections for a pharmaceutical firm which during the year 2002 invested, say £1,000,000 in R&D, it is necessary to calculate how much of that £1,000,000 was devoted to R&D labour. As can be observed from Table 7.4, the average labour component for the pharmaceutical industry in 2002 was 37 percent. Hence, it would be estimated that this firm spent approximately £370,000 on research personnel (£1,000,000 * 37 percent = £370,000). Then, the corrected measure of labour may be estimated. This procedure was followed for all the firm-year observations. The effect of these corrections is significant as they decreased the initial labour input by an average of 7.5 percent.

2.5.2 Number of employees
The double-counting corrections for the 'number of employees' variable are similar to those made for the labour input. Employees who belonged to the R&D division ($N_{R\&D}$) were deducted from the total number of employees (N_{total}). Thus, the corrected number of employees ($N_{corrected}$) is: $N_{corrected} = N_{total} - N_{R\&D}$. Although there were data on the total number of employees, there were no data on how many employees each R&D division had. In order to approximate the missing data, we initially calculated the average cost per employee (L_{total} / N_{total}). Then, the number of research staff was estimated by dividing the R&D labour costs ($L_{R\&D}$) by the average cost per employee. So if the average cost per employee was £20,000 and the total R&D labour cost was £370,000, then the R&D division had approximately 19 employees (£370,000 / £20,000).

2.5.3 Net fixed capital input
The double-counting corrections for the capital input are much more complicated than those for labour input. In order to correct the 'net fixed capital' variable, the stock of net fixed R&D equipment ($NFC_{R\&D}$) had to be subtracted from the total stock of net fixed capital (NFC_{total}): $NFC_{corrected} = NFC_{total} - NFC_{R\&D}$. Although there were data on the ordinary net fixed capital, there were no data on the net fixed capital of the R&D division. For that reason, it had to be approximated. This was done using the perpetual inventory method, similar to that used in the estimation of the R&D capital variable. A source of inaccuracy is the fact that there is no way to know the annual depreciation rate of R&D equipment, particularly when considering the differences across industries. This depreciation is likely to be high as equipment such as computers and scientific instruments often become obsolete within six or seven years (Brynjolfsson and Hitt, 1996). They are likely, therefore, to depreciate at a rate of 15 to 20 percent per year. For that reason, the annual depreciation rate was set at 18 percent. Although there is no evidence to support this decision, it is to some extent reassuring that when

different depreciation rates (10, 15 and 20 percent) were utilized, the effect on the correction of the capital input was under 0.5 percent. After the estimation of the fixed capital stock used by each R&D division, this figure was deducted from the total net fixed capital of the firm, so that a corrected measure of it could be assessed. Once again, the effect of these corrections was significant (they decreased the initial capital input by an average of 6 percent).

2.5.4 Depreciation of capital input

Depreciation of capital input: In order to correct the 'depreciation of capital' variable, it was necessary to deduct the depreciation of R&D equipment ($Depr_{R\&D}$) from the total depreciation of conventional capital ($Depr_{total}$): $Depr_{corrected} = Depr_{total} - Depr_{R\&D}$. As the fixed capital of R&D division has already been estimated, the annual depreciation of this capital (as noted earlier, set at 18 percent) can be determined. Finally, the depreciation of R&D equipment was deducted from the total depreciation to yield a corrected measure of the variable.

2.6 The Problem of Aggregation

Another significant problem is the aggregation of different variables and types of data. The starting point of many aggregation errors is that it is impossible to construct a different variable for every single input and output of the production function. Hence, the study is based on the Lange-Hicks criterion that states that if two or more variables move together, they may be weighted and aggregated into a single variable. For example, because it is impossible to measure the numerous products that a firm produces, researchers focus on the firm's sales.

Aggregation errors are associated with the level of data acquired (firm, industry or macro-level). In general, as firm-level data are less aggregated, they are usually better measures than those of the economy as a whole. As noted earlier, technological improvements are rarely found in aggregate output statistics because product quality and variety are often overlooked (Brynjolfsson and Hitt, 1996). There is also much econometric research on the effects of aggregation. The study of Ando (1971) implies that the results obtained from macro variables are very poor compared to those obtained from micro variables. Zellner and Montmarquette (1971) showed that when the behaviors of economic entities are analysed using aggregated data, a distorted view is obtained because the aggregation involves a loss of information. Their findings suggest that estimators of non-aggregated data are more precise than those obtained from aggregated data. Other consequences of aggregation include a lower precision of estimation, a lower power for statistical tests, an inability to make short-run forecasts and a reduced likelihood of discovering new hypotheses about short-run behavior of the data (Zellner and Montmarquette, 1971, p.335). In addition, the results of other studies (e.g. Bryan, 1967) have shown that a high level of aggregation does not usually allow the exploration of time lag structures and, when it does allow it, they are significantly distorted. It has also been observed that the goodness of fit for aggregated data appears to have higher values than those for non-aggregated data. However, this finding is misleading because the improvement of goodness of fit in that case is strictly a mathematical effect (Zellner and Montmarquette, 1971).

Although this research book is based on firm-level data and consequently the above errors are avoided, a degree of aggregation still remains. The firms in the sample are multinationals, owning numerous smaller firms and operating in different countries across which economic and social parameters vary. The first problem is associated with R&D composition. As discussed earlier, R&D is in itself aggregated. Reported R&D expenditures is the sum of different R&D activities, such as basic and applied R&D, product and process R&D, short- and long-term projects, small and large projects (Mansfield, 1984). A good solution would be to break down R&D and estimate the impact of each type of R&D separately. Unfortunately, given that the research data are not detailed enough to allow this, only the average impact of different types of R&D on productivity performance can be estimated.

The second issue relates to the aggregation of heterogeneous firms that belong to different industries. In this case, firms have different production techniques and in consequence, it is unrealistic to try to fit the whole sample into the same production function. To avoid such error, the research sample is split into industries and the coefficients are recalculated for each industry separately. If we are dealing with a single industry, the methods of production are likely to be similar for each firm. In that case, as the coefficients should also be similar, it is more reasonable to use the R&D-elasticity method which assumes that elasticities across firms are the same. By contrast, when we work with the entire sample that is composed of firms in different industries, the coefficients are no longer necessarily similar and thus, it may be more sensible to use the rate of return (ROR) method that does not assume equality of the R&D coefficient across firms. In the following chapters, both methods will be used and their estimates will be discussed.

However, errors occur not only when we aggregate firms of different industries but also when we aggregate firms of the same industry. Firms experience different economies of scale and hence output and input expand at different rates (Thomas, 1993). In an effort to construct a sample of homogeneous firms, the sample will also be split into larger and smaller firms and the coefficients will be recalculated for each group separately. Similarly, the technological opportunities that a firm faces also play an important role (Harhoff, 1998). For that reason, the sample is divided into high-technology and low-technology firms and the impact of R&D is re-estimated for each group separately.

3. THE PROBLEM OF DEFLATION

The raw data presented earlier had to be corrected for price changes, i.e. they had to be deflated and converted to constant prices. Although the deflation process is straightforward (the value of interest divided by a price index), it can affect the research results. As has been emphasized before (Griliches, 1979; Griliches, 1984), output price indices are a major source of distortion as they are often erroneous. This problem – which is associated with the earlier discussion on output – arises when the official price indices do not fully account for immeasurable improvements of products whose quality and variety often change very rapidly over time. For example, the price of a personal computer may remain constant, even though its technical specifications have been improved (e.g. it may have a faster processor). In that case, the real price of the computer is lower because although consumers pay the same price, they buy a better product (the so-called quality-adjusted price decline, see Brynjolfsson and Hitt, 1996). In these or similar circumstances, technological complexity does not allow the accurate measurement of the true underlying price change. Hence, output is badly measured (measured output tends to be lower than true output). A solution to this problem is the use of the Hedonic price indices. These take into account not only the changes of prices but also the changes of quality. Griliches (1984, p.15) describes this approach:

> The common notion of quality change relates to the fact that many commodities are changing over time and that often it is impossible to construct appropriate pricing comparisons because the same varieties are not available at different times and in different places. Conceptually one might be able to get around this problem by assuming that the many different varieties of commodity differ only along a smaller number of relevant dimensions (characteristics, specifications), estimate the price-characteristics relationship econometrically and use the resulting estimates to impute a price to the missing model or variety in the relevant comparison period. This approach, pioneered by Waugh (1928) and Court (1939) and revived by Griliches (1961) has become known as the 'Hedonic' approach to price measurement.

It has been observed that Hedonic price indices increase the estimated productivity growth. When, for example, the ONS applied the US Hedonic deflator for computers to parts of the Index of Production, the index increased by 2-6 percent over 1995-1999. This is equivalent to an annual growth rate difference in the whole economy of up to 0.3 percent (Vase, 2001).

However, given that there are no Hedonic price indices for the UK, a downward bias of the estimated impact of R&D on productivity might occur. Similar problems arise when firms are diversified and their output is a mix of completely different types of products. The fraction of those firms' output which does not belong to their main business field has to be deflated using a different price index. However, data on firms' output which allow such detailed deflation rarely exist in the real world. As noted earlier, additional errors arise from the deflation of R&D expenditure. As official price indices for R&D expenditure do not exist, we were forced to estimate our own R&D indices (see Chapter 5). The paragraphs below describe the deflation procedure for each variable.

Table 7.5 Output price indices

Industry	SIC80 Code	ONS code
Metals	22	POKQ
Minerals	23, 24	POKP
Chemicals	25	POKN
Basic pharmaceutical products	257	PPOJ
Fabricated metal products	31	POLK
Machinery	32	POKR
Computers and office equipment	33	POLM
Electrical	34	POLN
Telecommunication	344	POLO
Motor vehicles	35	POLQ
Aerospace	364	PQKF
Instruments	37	PQHL
Textiles	43	POKZ
Printing material	47	POLE
Plastic and rubber	48	POKO
Other manufacturing products		PLLV

The deflation of sales was straightforward. The annual sales of each firm were divided by an output price index to yield a measure of output at constant prices, i.e. a measure of deflated output. Most of the price indices which were used are 2- or 3-digit industry specific and they were provided by the ONS (Table 7.5). However, as discussed earlier, it is difficult to know to what extent these indices are properly associated with the output of the relevant industry. Given that there are many different price indices for the deflation of output, their effect on the estimates is further investigated later on.

The procedure followed to deflate the different capital inputs (i.e. gross fixed capital, net fixed capital and depreciation of capital stock) was similar to that of sales. The capital input of each firm was divided by a fixed-capital price index to yield a measure of capital at constant prices. Given that the ONS has two different price indices for fixed-capital (see Table 7.6), two different measures were constructed. Once again, the impact of each price index on the research estimates will be investigated later.

As was discussed earlier, two different variables of labour input were constructed. The first variable (number of employees) does not need deflation. In order to deflate the second one (labour costs) we followed a similar procedure to that employed for the deflation of sales and capital. The price indices of labour were collected from ONS. Three appropriate price indices were found (see Table 7.6): (1) compensation of employees, (2) average earnings for the whole economy and (3) average earnings for the manufacturing sector. Three measures of the 'labour costs' variable were constructed (one for each of the three price indices).

The absence of any official R&D deflator besets all studies that assess the impact of R&D on productivity performance. Although most studies use the GDP price index to deflate R&D expenditures, as discussed earlier this practice engenders many problems. In contrast to previous research, this study utilizes the R&D price indices constructed in Chapter 5.

Table 7.6 Capital and labour price indices

Price index	ONS code
Fixed capital (A)	YBFG
Fixed capital (B)	YBFU
Compensation of employees index	YBGD
Average earnings (whole economy)	LNMQ
Average earnings (manufacturing sector)	LNMR

4. DESCRIPTIVE STATISTICS

4.1 Splitting the Sample into Sub-Samples

In order to be able to answer the questions 'On which sectors of the economy has R&D greater impact?', 'To what extent is the impact of R&D greater for high-technology firms?' and 'Is the impact of R&D greater on the productivity performance of larger firms?', the 'Large' sample was divided into a number of sub-samples.

4.1.1 Different sectors of the economy
To investigate to what extent the impact of R&D on labour productivity performance varies between different sectors of the economy, the 15 two-digit (and in some cases three-digit) industries of the 'Large' sample were merged into five broader groups (Table 7.7).

Table 7.7 The five main sectors of the 'Large' sample

Sector	SIC 80 code	No of firms
Chemicals	25, 257	20
Machinery and mech. engin.	32	27
Electrical and electronics	33, 34, 344, 37	37
Transportation	35, 364	12
Remaining	22, 23, 24, 31, 43, 47, 48, 49	11
	Total	**107**

These broader groups are: (the numbers in the parentheses are the Standard Industrial Classification codes SIC80): (1) Chemicals: This group is exclusively composed of chemical (25) and pharmaceutical (257) firms. (2) Machinery and Mechanical Engineering: This group includes firms that manufacture machinery and mechanical equipment (32). (3) Electrical and Electronics: This one is composed of firms from the industries of computing and office equipment (33), electrical and electronics (34), telecommunication (344) and instrument engineering (37). Although one could argue that the industry of instrument engineering does not belong to this group, a more detailed examination of these firms revealed that they are very close to those of electronics industry. (4) Transportation: This sector includes firms from the industries of motor vehicle parts (35) and aerospace (364). (5) Remaining: The last group includes all the remaining industries, i.e.

manufacturers of metal products (22 & 31), minerals (23 & 24), textiles (43), paper & printing (47), rubber and plastics (48) and other manufacturing firms (49).

4.1.2 Low- and high-technology firms

In order to examine the role of technological opportunities, the sample was also divided into low- and high-tech samples. Following similar studies (e.g. Griliches and Mairesse, 1984; Harhoff, 1998), the low-tech sample includes industries such as metal manufacturing, minerals and mechanical machinery whereas the high-tech sample includes industries such as chemical, electronics and aerospace (Table 7.8). The low-technology sample includes 44 firms whereas the remaining 63 firms belong to high-technology industries.

Table 7.8 High and low technology samples (1995-2002)

Industry	SIC 80 code	No of firms
Low-Technology Industries		
Metal products	22, 31	2
Minerals	23, 24	3
Machinery & mechanical engineering	32	27
Motor vehicle parts	35	6
Textiles	43	-
Paper & printing	47	2
Rubber and plastics	48	3
Other manufacturing	49	1
	Total	44
High-Technology Industries		
Chemicals	25	12
Pharmaceuticals	257	8
Computing & office equipment	33	2
Electrical & electronics	34	19
Telecommunication	344	9
Aerospace	364	6
Instrument Engineering	37	7
	Total	63

4.1.3 Smaller and larger firms

In order to examine the role of firm size, the sample was divided into smaller- and larger-firms sub-samples. Following Griliches (1980), the sub-sample of smaller firms includes all firms which have fewer than 1000 employees (in 1995) whereas the second sub-sample comprises firms with over 1000 employees. Smaller firms account for 45 percent of the whole sample; the remaining 55 percent are larger firms. As noted earlier, however, although firms which have less than 1000 employees are only a small fraction of other firms which may have a six digit number of employees, they still cannot be considered as small firms.

4.2 Additional Cleaning of the Data

To provide a dataset that can be fitted to a regression, some additional cleaning procedures had to be followed. Following previous studies (Griliches and Mairesse, 1984; Hall and Mairesse, 1995), both samples were cleaned according to the criteria given below: (1) For the needs of cross-sectional specification, the extreme values of the levels of the main variables were removed, i.e. output per labour, capital per labour, labour and R&D capital per labour. Only the extreme observations were removed, not the entire eight years from 1995 to 2002. This criterion removed approximately 3 percent of the total observations. (2) For the needs of time-series specification, the extreme values of the growth rates of the main variables were removed. Again, only the extreme observations rather than entire eight years from 1995 to 2002 were removed. This criterion removed approximately 2 percent of the total observations. (3) Any observations for which the growth rates of sales, capital, labour or R&D capital were less than minus 80 percent or greater than plus 300 percent were eliminated. Only 0.1 percent of the total observations were removed by this criterion. (4) Any observations for which R&D-intensity was more than 60 percent were removed. Only 0.1 percent of the total observations were eliminated by this criterion. (5) Any observations for which the growth rate of R&D-intensity was less than minus 80 percent or greater than plus 300 percent were removed. This criterion eliminated 0.3 percent of the total observations.

As shown by Chang and Tiao (1983), extreme values can bias the estimates and distort the statistical significance. Indeed, when the impact of extreme values on our estimates was investigated, we found that their inclusion biased upward our estimated R&D coefficients by two percentage points or more. On the other hand, however, by excluding these extreme values we reduce variability which is essential for the ordinary least squares (OLS) method. For that reason, the elimination of extreme values (i.e. using criteria one and two) has been done for each sub-sample separately, e.g. we eliminated the extreme values of the 'large-firms' sub-sample, of the 'small-firms' sub-sample, and so on.

4.3 Main Descriptive Statistics

This section highlights patterns in the data that cannot readily be identified without the help of descriptive statistics. Table 7.9 presents a set of basic descriptive statistics for both 'Large' and 'Long' samples. As previously mentioned, the R&D-intensity of the 'Large' and 'Long' samples is 4.2 and 2.6 percent respectively. This difference is reflected in the 'R&D capital per employee' which is £16,000 for the 'Large' sample but only £10,000 for the 'Long' sample. The mean number of employees is 7950 for the 'Large' sample and 9300 for the 'Long' sample whereas the mean values of 'sales per employee' and 'capital services per employees' are similar for both samples.

Table 7.9 Main descriptive statistics (mean values)

	Sales/ Employee	Capital Services/ Employee	No of Employees	R&D Capital/ Employee
Levels				
Large Sample	100	26	7,950	16
Long Sample	96	26	9,300	10

Note: Any monetary value above is in £1000.

4.4 Comparison of the Five Broader Groups

Table 7.10 presents descriptive statistics for the five broader groups of the main research sample. It can be seen that the R&D-intensity of the mechanical machinery and 'remaining' industries is low (1.7 and 1.2 percent respectively). It is higher, however, for the transportation firms (3.4 percent) and even higher for chemicals and electronics firms (5.0 and 6.9 percent respectively). This trend is also reflected by the 'R&D capital per employee' variable; the mean value starts at £5000 per employee for the 'remaining' group, and reaches £26,000 per employee in the case of chemical firms. It should also be noted, that in most cases the R&D-Intensities of our sub-samples do not vary significantly from the industry-level R&D-intensities reported by the UK Office of National Statistics (ONS, 2000). Table 7.10 also provides information regarding the average size of the firms within each group. The average size of the electrical and electronics firms is relatively small with a mean number of employees of about 2598. By contrast, the average size of the firms in other groups is much larger, rising to a mean number of employees of approximately 14,000 in the last group.

Table 7.10 Descriptive statistics for the five main sectors (mean values)

	Sales / Employee	Capital Services / Employee	No of Employees	R&D Capital / Employee	R&D/ Sales
Levels					
Chemicals	131	38	11,971	26	5.0%
Mechanical Machinery	85	19	5,836	6	1.7%
Electrical and Electronics	96	20	2,598	22	6.9%
Transportation	105	22	16,296	14	3.4%
Remaining	98	42	14,062	5	1.2%

Note: Any monetary value above is in £1000.

The mean capital services per employee also follow a similar pattern, being about £20,000 per employee for the industries of mechanical machinery, electrical/electronics and transportation but about double that for the chemicals and 'remaining' groups. The level of labour productivity, measured as sales per employee, is again different for the five groups lying between £85,000 and £131,000 per employee.

4.5 Comparison of Low/High Technology and Smaller/Larger Firms

Table 7.11 identifies some peculiarities of the data that arise when the sample is divided into low and high tech firms or smaller and larger firms. Starting with the productivity of low- and high-tech firms (first column) there are some differences in terms of levels. The average sales per employee for high-tech firms is approximately £102,000 whereas the corresponding average sales for low-tech firms is lower at £98,000. The levels of the capital services per employee are similar for the two samples. However, there is a substantial difference in terms of R&D capital per employee which is £23,000 for the high-tech firms, yet only £6000 for the low-tech firms.

Similarly, the R&D-intensity of the two samples also varies dramatically, being 6.1 percent for high-tech sample but only 1.6 percent for the low-tech sample. As for the smaller-firms and larger-firms sub-samples, the levels of 'sales per employee' differ significantly, being £94,000 and £106,000 respectively. The mean level of R&D capital per employee and R&D-intensity differ too. The high R&D-intensity of smaller firms can be explained by the fact that even when a smaller firm invests in small R&D projects, the minimum required investment is still a high proportion of its sales, therefore increasing its R&D-intensiveness (Mansfield, 1968a).

Table 7.11 Descriptive statistics for high/low-tech and large/small firms

	Sales/ Empl.	Capital Services/ Empl.	No of Empl.	R&D Capital / Empl.	R&D / Sales
Levels					
High-tech firms	102	26	7,360	23	6.1%
Low-tech firms	98	25	8,757	6	1.6%
Smaller firms	94	24	599	19	5.9%
Larger firms	106	27	14,070	14	2.9%

Note: Any monetary value above is in £1000.

4.6 Investigating R&D-intensity over Time

It is also important to explore whether or not the R&D-intensity of the firms has changed over time. Table 7.12 presents the R&D-intensities over different periods of time, and also for each industry, comparing low- with high-tech firms, and smaller with larger firms. As the first row of this table indicates, there is a tendency for the whole sample to become more R&D-intensive, increasing from an average of 3.9 percent between 1995 and 1998, to an average of 4.5 percent between 1999 and 2002.

The next five rows of Table 7.12, which present the R&D-intensity for different industries, shed more light on this change. The chemical, electrical/electronics and transportation industries all became more R&D-intensive after 1998 (from 4.5 to 5.5 percent, from 6.3 to 7.5 percent and from 3 to 3.8 percent respectively). Similarly, the mechanical machinery industry increased its R&D-intensity from 1.6 to 1.8 percent. This pattern is also reflected in the difference between high- and low-tech firms (rows seven and eight). The R&D-intensity of high-tech firms increased from 5.6 percent in the first time-period to 6.6 percent in the second one. The R&D-intensity of low-tech firms increased slightly from 1.5 to 1.7 percent. Similarly, both smaller- and larger-firms samples became more R&D-intensive, from 5.4 to 6.4 and from 2.6 to 3.2 percent respectively.

Table 7.12 R&D-intensity over time

	1995-2002	1995-1998	1999-2002
Whole sample	4.2%	3.9%	4.5%
Chemicals	5.0%	4.5%	5.5%
Mechanical machinery	1.7%	1.6%	1.8%
Electrical and electronics	6.9%	6.3%	7.5%
Transportation	3.4%	3.0%	3.8%
Remaining	1.2%	1.2%	1.2%
High-tech firms	6.1%	5.6%	6.6%
Low-tech firms	1.6%	1.5%	1.7%
Smaller firms	5.9%	5.4%	6.4%
Larger firms	2.9%	2.6%	3.2%

5. SUMMARY

This chapter describes the research data and explains how the final variables were constructed. The first section presents the sources of the data and describes the two samples of the study: the 'Large' and the 'Long' samples. The 'Large' sample includes 107 UK manufacturing MNEs, and covers the period between 1995 and 2002. It may be considered as representative of the UK R&D manufacturing sector as it covers 77 percent of the total UK R&D. This is the main research sample and is used to answer the majority of the research questions. The 'Long' sample is composed of 84 UK manufacturing MNEs and accounts for approximately 48 percent of the total UK R&D. This sample covers a longer time period (1989 to 2002) and for that reason will be used to explore the time lag structure of R&D.

The first section also discussed a number of issues associated with the quality of the research data. The most important are the problem of industrial classification and the accounting treatment of R&D expenditures. The classification of firms in sectors of economy hides pitfalls that can distort the estimates as MNEs are either diversified or change their main field of business over time. Two questions were answered in order to investigate the accounting problem of R&D: first, what factors influence a firm's decision whether to disclose its R&D expenditure? and second, assuming that a firm decides to disclose its R&D expenditure, what factors affect how much R&D this firm will report? Both issues are discussed in detail.

The second section of this chapter described how the main variables of the study were constructed. Lacking direct measures of the variables of interest, some proxies must be used to represent Output (Q), Capital (K), Labour (L) and R&D capital. For that reason, several proxy-variables were constructed from the raw data. However, many problems arise from the fact that proxies do not always represent accurately what they purport to measure (Griliches, 1984). Another practical problem also discussed is that research employees and research equipment are counted twice, once in the conventional inputs of Capital (K) and Labour (L) and again in the input of R&D capital (Schankerman, 1981). A further problem is that of aggregation. Although this study is based on firm-level data and consequently many errors which come from aggregation are avoided, as discussed earlier, a degree of aggregation still remains.

The third section of this chapter was devoted to the issues of deflation. It described the deflation of the research data and explained how an inappropriate price index can distort the research findings. In the final section of the chapter, the 'Large' sample is split into a number of sub-samples. Initially, it is divided into five broader groups representing different sectors of economy (chemicals, mechanical engineering, electrical/electronics, transportation and 'remaining'). Then, in order to investigate the role of technological opportunities, it is split in technologically advanced and low-tech firms. Finally, to look into the role of firm size, the sample was divided into smaller firms and larger firms. After further cleaning of the data, the last section provides some descriptive statistics that indicate the different paths that the samples have followed through time.

PART III

Empirical Findings

8. The Impact of Scientific Knowledge on the Performance of Multinational Corporations

This chapter empirically examines the impact of scientific knowledge on the economic performance of multinational firms. It also investigates what factors trigger high or low returns to industrial research. The findings indicate that the appropriation of many of the benefits of R&D by the inventor results in the generation of a significant stream of revenues. The chapter also offers new insights on the role of competition, degree of internationalization, firm size and technological opportunities, which in many cases contradict previous studies.

1. INTRODUCTION

As discussed earlier, investments in industrial research and development generate new technological and scientific knowledge. Using this knowledge, multinational corporations develop product and process innovations, and more efficient production techniques. Consequently, they increase their revenues, output and productivity. The empirical literature however, does not always confirm this theoretical prediction. Many econometric studies indicate that the impact of innovation on a firm's productivity performance can be positive, insignificant or even negative. Hence, it is often unclear why some firms profit from their R&D, yet others fail to do so.

This chapter extends prior research by investigating the impact of R&D on the productivity performance of multinational corporations, and by examining a number of factors that may influence a firm's ability to benefit from innovation. Specifically, our analysis focuses on the following factors: (1) competition, (2) degree of internationalization, (3) technological opportunities and (4) firm size. In this chapter, we estimate the effects of R&D (in terms of elasticity), but also its real monetary returns. The benefit of this approach is that it takes into account the cost that each multinational corporation pays for its innovative efforts. In order to estimate these effects accurately, we use the R&D price indices constructed in Chapter 5. We thereby control for the fact that the cost of R&D for some MNEs is higher. Note that parts of this chapter are in part based on the study of Kafouros (2005), which is published in the Journal of Economics of Innovation and New Technology (http://www.informaworld.com).

2. MAIN FINDINGS

In order to serve its research objectives and estimate the private returns to R&D, this chapter employs the sample of 107 multinational corporations (described in Chapter 7). The findings that the next sections report have resulted from the model described in Chapter 6 and the method of ordinary least squares (OLS). The main equation of the model is reproduced below (in logarithmic form):

$$(q_{it} - l_{it}) = a + a(k_{it} - l_{it}) + \gamma(r_{it} - l_{it}) + (\mu - 1) l_{it} + D_{industry} + D_{time} + \varepsilon_{it} \qquad (8.1)$$

The lower case letters (q, k, l, r) denote the logs of the main variables (output, capital, labour, and scientific knowledge stock), whereas α, and γ are the elasticities of output with respect to capital and scientific knowledge respectively. The term a is the residual of the Cobb-Douglas function and ε_{it} stands for the disturbance term (for more details see Chapter 6).

2.1 Cross Sectional Results

Table 8.1 presents the main research findings. These are obtained from the cross-sectional dimension of the data. Model 1 presents the findings when the constant returns to scale (CRS) assumption is not imposed and time and industry dummies are included. The elasticity of capital is 0.20. This finding suggests that when a firm increases its capital per employee by 1 percent (with all the other inputs held constant), its labour productivity will be increased by 0.20 percent. The fact that the standard error of this coefficient is 0.02 indicates that the impact of ordinary capital on labour productivity is statistically significant at the 0.1 percent level of significance.

The elasticity of capital is also consistent with the findings of published studies. Dilling-Hansen et al. (2000) found the elasticity of capital to be 0.17 for Denmark; Hall and Mairesse (1995) found an elasticity of 0.18 for France, and Griliches (1986) found the corresponding elasticity for the US to be 0.22. The results of Harhoff (1998) were slightly higher, at 0.24 for Germany. As for the elasticity of labour, it is 0.03 at the 0.1 percent level of significance. As it measures the departure from constant returns to scale, this finding suggests that the scale factor (i.e. the sum of elasticities of capital, labour and R&D capital) is 1.03, implying that the UK manufacturing industry during the 1995-2002 period experienced increasing returns to scale. The R^2 (goodness of fit) is relatively low at 0.37, but is still consistent with that of other studies (Harhoff, 1998; Cuneo and Mairesse, 1984; Sassenou, 1988; Wang and Tsai, 2003), which indicate that it lies between 0.20 and 0.41.

Table 8.1 The impact of scientific-knowledge stock on performance (cross sectional dimension, 107 multinational firms, 1995-2002) [a, b]

	Model 1	Model 2	Model 3	Model 4
Log (K/L)	0.20*** (0.02)	0.24*** (0.02)	0.23*** (0.02)	0.22*** (0.02)
Log L	0.03*** (0.008)	0.04*** (0.007)	-	0.03*** (0.008)
R&D elasticity	0.15*** (0.01)	0.12*** (0.01)	0.14*** (0.01)	0.13*** (0.01)
Control for time	yes	no	yes	yes
Control for industry	yes	no	yes	yes
R^2	0.37 (0.15)	0.35 (0.15)	0.36 (0.15)	0.36 (0.15)

Notes:
[a] The dependent variable is labour productivity.
[b] ns = not significant, * 5% level of significance, ** 1% level of significance, *** 0.1% level of significance, the absence of a star indicates a level of significance of 10%.

The third row of Model 1 reports the elasticity of scientific-knowledge (or R&D capital) stock. Its average impact on corporate performance is positive and statistically significant at the 0.1 percent level. The elasticity of R&D is 0.15, suggesting that when a firm increases its R&D capital per employee by 1 percent (with all other inputs held constant), its labour productivity will be increased by 0.15 percent. The magnitude of the impact of R&D is relatively high, showing that R&D offered a significant contribution to the productivity performance of these firms. The results are highly consistent with the findings for other countries. Sassenou (1988) found the elasticity of R&D for Japan to be 0.10 and Harhoff (1998) found the corresponding elasticity for

Germany to be 0.13. Similarly, Mairesse and Hall (1996) found the impact of R&D on the productivity performance of the French manufacturing sector to be 0.09. The estimates of Adams and Jaffe (1996), Griliches (1980; 1986), Griliches and Mairesse (1984) and Schankerman (1981) are very similar too, as they found that the contribution of R&D to the productivity of the US firms lay between 0.07 and 0.11.

Model 2 examines the impact of dummy variables on the estimated coefficient of R&D. The estimates are to some extent sensitive to the exclusion of dummies. By including no dummies at all, the coefficient of R&D becomes 0.12. The fact that the inclusion of dummies does not decrease the R&D elasticity but increases it is surprising and not consistent with the majority of studies. However, analogous phenomena have been observed in studies that use sales rather than value added (e.g. Harhoff, 1998). This phenomenon also relates to the argument of Mairesse and Sassenou (1991) that industry dummies might not always be representative proxies of the real omitted variables and thus might increase (rather than decrease) the bias. Model 3 reports the results when the CRS assumption is imposed (the elasticity of labour is not reported as labour is not included in the production function). In contrast with the estimates from other studies, which are very sensitive to the CRS assumption, we find that the elasticity of R&D remains relatively stable when the CRS assumption is imposed.

We also investigated the sensitivity of the findings to a change in the R&D price index. As discussed in Chapter 5, because official R&D price indices do not exist, most published studies use the GDP deflator to convert R&D expenditures to constant prices. Hence, they implicitly assume that the costs of R&D inputs are similar across firms. This approach, however, does not allow the accurate measurement of R&D spending. Considerable empirical evidence suggests that the costs of R&D inputs do not follow the path of prices within the economy as a whole (Cameron, 1996). In such cases, inaccurate price indices can lead to biases. Model 4 presents the results obtained by using the GDP price index (rather than the R&D price indices of Chapter 5). The analysis provides support to previous arguments. As the estimates indicate, the elasticity of R&D decreased from 0.15 to 0.13. The implications of these findings are important as they suggest that the results of the studies that use the GDP deflator could be biased downward, underestimating the consequences of industrial research for corporate performance.

Appendix A investigates how sensitive the main findings are to the use of different deflators, variable definitions, and depreciation rates. Additionally, given that the above estimates are based on the ordinary least squares method, a number of econometric assumptions are required in order to confirm that these findings are unbiased and robust. Appendix B investigates the extent to which the findings may be biased by problems such as departures from normality, heteroscedasticity and serial correlation.

2.2 Time Series Results

An important econometric problem that may lead to inconsistent estimates is that of simultaneity. It is engendered by the fact that inputs are not always exogenously determined as they should be, but there is a degree of feedback from output to input. This occurs when output is determined by inputs, and equally, some inputs are determined by output (Gujarati, 1995). For instance, although corporate performance depends on past R&D, R&D also depends on past performance. In such cases, referring to the so-called 'reversed causality' problem, we may end up estimating the impact of performance on R&D expenditure rather than the opposite (Griliches, 1979). As Griliches (1986) suggests, a simple – but effective – way to remedy simultaneity is to focus not on the levels of the variables but on their differences. The closer the estimates of the time-series dimension are to the estimates of the cross-sectional dimension, the lower will be the problem of simultaneity. Great differences between the two types of estimates signify that simultaneity is influencing the results. One solution to this can be provided by the so-called simultaneous equation and instrumental variables models, such as the Two Stage Least Squares (2SLS) and the Reduced Form (RF).

These models try to reduce simultaneity by including more than one equation in the system. By using such models, however, three other problems arise. Firstly, although they can diminish simultaneity, if there is no simultaneity then the estimates become less efficient, having larger variance (Gujarati, 1995). Secondly, as Griliches (1986) argues, these methods do not solve the problem but merely shift it to the validity and exogeneity of external instruments. As he suggests, it is difficult to construct any valid instrument and perhaps even more difficult to find good quality data to support these instruments. Thirdly, in practice the findings of studies that used the 2SLS or the RF method (Cuneo and Mairesse, 1984; Griliches, 1980; Sassenou, 1988) are only marginally better than those obtained from the ordinary least squares method (Mairesse and Sassenou, 1991).

Because of the reasons mentioned above, we will try to address the simultaneity problem by focusing on the differences of the variables (time-series regression). The comparison of the cross-sectional and time series dimension of the data can indicate whether simultaneity exists or not. If not, then the two estimates should be very close. As Hall and Mairesse (1995) emphasize, the simultaneity bias can affect the cross-sectional R&D elasticity greatly, but the corresponding time-series elasticity only slightly. Generally, as discussed in the previous chapters, the disturbances in the cross-sectional dimension are different from disturbances in the time-series dimension. Table 8.2 presents the findings obtained from the time-series dimension of the data (see Chapter 6).

The elasticity of ordinary capital decreased to 0.15 (from 0.20 in the cross-sectional case) whilst the coefficient of labour became statistically insignificant, implying constant returns to scale. Once again, the elasticity of R&D was positive and highly significant, confirming the important contribution of industrial research to corporate performance. The fact that it is lower than the elasticity obtained from the cross-sectional dimension of the data (0.13 instead of 0.15) is consistent with the findings of other studies that indicate that the coefficient of R&D is attenuated when the time-series dimension is used.

Table 8.2 The impact of scientific-knowledge stock on performance (time-series dimension, 107 multinational firms, 1995-2002) [a, b]

	Model 1
Log (K/L)	0.15*** (0.02)
Log L	-0.04[ns] (0.04)
R&D elasticity	0.13*** (0.04)
Control for time	yes
Control for industry	yes
R^2	0.20 (0.07)

Notes:
[a] The dependent variable is labour productivity differences.
[b] ns = not significant, * 5% level of significance, ** 1% level of significance, *** 0.1% level of significance, the absence of a star indicates a level of significance of 10%.

The R&D elasticity of 0.13 for the UK appears to be higher than that of other countries. Sassenou (1988) finds that it is negative (-0.01) for Japan; Harhoff (1998) finds that the corresponding elasticity for Germany is 0.08. Hall and Mairesse (1995) find that the impact of R&D on productivity growth of the French manufacturing sector is 0.10. The estimates of Minasian (1969) and Griliches (1980; 1986) are similar. They find that the contribution of R&D to the productivity growth of the US firms lies between 0.08 and 0.12. The fact that the cross-sectional and time-series R&D elasticities are close indicates that there is no severe bias arising from problems such as simultaneity. Nevertheless, in order to ensure that the findings are robust, many econometric tests were carried out. Specifically, it was examined whether there were problems of heteroscedasticity, serial correlation and normality, by carrying out the 'white' heteroscedasticity, Durbin-Watson and Jarque and Bera tests respectively. These tests indicated that there was no evidence of such problems.

2.3 Rate of Return Results

Table 8.3 presents the estimates obtained using the 'rate of return' econometric specification. These estimates are based on the two-year growth rates of each variable because, as has been emphasized (Mairesse and Sassenou, 1991), the one year growth rates tend to be affected by extreme short-term variations of the variables. Indeed, it was observed that the R&D intensity of the firms of the sample varied significantly from year to year. Thus two-year growth rates have been used to average out such extreme variations. The first column of Table 8.3 reports the gross returns to R&D. The rate of return to R&D is 0.23 (at the 0.1 percent level of significance), implying that industrial research generates a significant stream of revenues.

Table 8.3 The rate of return to scientific-knowledge stock [a, b]

	Gross returns	Net returns
Log (K/L)	0.08*** (0.02)	0.10*** (0.03)
Log L	- 0.09*** (0.02)	- 0.13*** (0.02)
Rate of return to R&D	0.23*** (0.04)	0.40*** (0.07)
Control for time	yes	yes
Control for industry	yes	yes
R^2	0.22 (0.07)	0.22 (0.08)

Notes:
[a] The dependent variable is labour productivity differences.
[b] ns = not significant, * 5% level of significance, ** 1% level of significance, *** 0.1% level of significance, the absence of a star indicates a level of significance of 10%.

The estimates of Table 8.3 are comparable to those of Wakelin (2001). The researcher found the returns to R&D to be 0.29. It is also noteworthy that the results were similar when the rate of return to R&D was re-estimated using four year growth rates. Rather like the cross-sectional and time-series findings, the findings in Table 8.3 indicate once again that R&D contributed significantly to firms' productivity performance. Griliches and Mairesse (1990), Link (1982), Minasian (1962) and Mansfield (1980), using similar specifications to those we use, found that the returns to R&D for the US lie between 0.25 and 0.31. Harhoff (1998) found the returns to R&D for

Germany to be 0.22, whist Griliches and Mairesse (1983) found the corresponding returns for French firms to be 0.31. Similar estimates have been found for Japan, with the results of Griliches and Mairesse (1990) and Odagiri (1983) suggesting that the returns to R&D for Japanese firms lie between 0.26 and 0.30. Nevertheless, Sassenou (1988) also used a sample of Japanese firms and found that they were quite a lot higher than this at 0.69.

We also investigated what happens when the returns to R&D are estimated more correctly by using R&D capital (rather than R&D expenditure). This issue relates to the discussion of Chapter 6 concerning gross and net returns to R&D. In order to avoid the measurement of R&D capital and simplify the 'rate of return' specification, researchers make the implausible assumption that investments in R&D do not depreciate and that the difference of R&D capital (ΔR) is equal to the current R&D investment (RD). Thus, the rate of returns (0.23) that the first column reports is the return to gross R&D. As the association between net and gross returns to R&D has been controversial, it seems worthwhile to estimate the net returns to R&D. As Harhoff (1998) emphasizes, there are two arguments. If the estimated net returns are equal to the gross returns minus the depreciation, net returns should be lower than gross returns. On the other hand, because the gross flow of R&D is much higher than net R&D, the coefficient of net rate of return should be considerably higher than that of gross (Hall and Mairesse, 1995). As we have constructed the stock of R&D capital, we estimated the net returns to R&D using the difference of R&D capital (ΔR) (instead of the current R&D investment), thereby investigating the above arguments empirically.

The second column of Table 8.3 reports the estimates. The net return to R&D increased significantly from 0.23 to 0.40, supporting the argument of Hall and Mairesse (1995). The implication of this finding is significant as it implies that the real contribution of R&D to productivity is significantly higher than most past studies have found through estimating the gross returns to R&D. The validity of this finding is further confirmed by the estimates of two other studies which estimate both the gross and net returns to R&D. Goto and Suzuki (1989) find that the net returns to R&D for most of the Japanese industries examined are higher than their gross returns. Similarly, Harhoff (1998) finds that the net returns to R&D for the German manufacturing sector are dramatically higher than gross returns, at 0.86 compared to 0.22.

3. THE ROLE OF COMPETITION

Chapter 3 demonstrated that competition plays an important role in the appropriation of the benefits of industrial research. Although the relationship between competitive conditions and innovation has attracted a lot of interest, it is still a subject for debate. On the one hand, Schumpeter (1950) argued that oligopolistic and monopolistic markets promote R&D because they provide profitable innovative opportunities. In contrast, many other researchers, such as Arrow (1962), have emphasized that markets with the characteristics of perfect competition provide more incentives to innovate because they allow an inventor to license his innovations to many firms.

Other scholars have argued that innovation may allow an organization to gain a better competitive position in relation to its rivals (Aghion et al., 2001). However, even though MNEs innovate in order to avoid competitive pressures, as shown in Chapter 3, when they all invest in innovation, some of the value of such investments is forwarded to other firms (Porter, 1980; Chen and Miller, 1994). In other words, even an important innovation may not have a significant effect if competition is high and does not allow a firm to capture its benefits (McGahan and Silverman, 2006). Overall then, theory suggests that the presence of a high level of competition may lead to low returns to a firm's own R&D. In contrast, lower competitive pressure may allow firms to better appropriate the value of R&D.

In order to investigate how competition influences the returns to R&D, we need to measure the competitive pressure that a firm faces. One of the measures of competition adopted here is that of concentration ratio. This is an industry-level proxy that measures the extent to which the largest firms contribute to the activity in an industry (that is, sum of sales for the largest firms over total sales for an industry). We have calculated the concentration ratio for the top 15 firms of each industry of our sample. Due to data constraints, we were able to do this only for the home country (that is the UK) of these multinational firms, rather than for all the countries in which the firms of the sample operate. The concentration ration varies between 10 and 80 percent, depending on the industry involved. Put differently, in some industries in the UK the sales of the top 15 firms accounted for about 10 percent of the total industry sales. By contrast, in high-concentration industries the corresponding figure was 80 percent. The rank order remained similar when we used value added (rather than sales). It also remained similar when we calculated the ratio for the largest five (rather than largest 15) firms of each sector.

Using the median of the concentration ratio (which was approximately 50 percent), we split the sample into lower- and higher-concentration subgroups. Then we re-estimated the model for each sub-sample separately. Table 8.4 reports the results. The first sub-sample (left column) contains industries that tend to have characteristics of perfect competition. The second one (right column) includes industries that tend to have oligopolistic characteristics; that is, the market is dominated by a few firms. The results support the notion that when a market tends to have conditions of perfect-competition, the returns to a firm's own R&D are significantly lower at 0.12 than the economic returns (of 0.19) enjoyed by firms in oligopolistic markets. The results are in line with previous studies that showed that firms in oligopolistic or monopolistic environments can more easily appropriate the benefits of R&D (Kamien and Schwartz, 1982; Tang, 2006). The findings are also consistent with the fact that when markets contain many firms, the likelihood that newly-developed knowledge will be exploited by external agents is higher.

Table 8.4 The effects of competition (as measured by concentration ratio) [a, b]

	Perfect Competition	Oligopoly
Log (K/L)	0.22*** (0.03)	0.20*** (0.05)
Log L	0.03*** (0.009)	0.002^{ns} (0.02)
R&D elasticity	0.12*** (0.02)	0.19*** (0.02)
Control for time	yes	yes
Control for industry	yes	yes
R^2	0.28 (0.13)	0.39 (0.18)

Notes:
[a] The dependent variable is labour productivity.
[b] ns = not significant, * 5% level of significance, ** 1% level of significance, *** 0.1% level of significance, the absence of a star indicates a level of significance of 10%.

The results of Table 8.4 are based on the industry-level measure of 'concentration ratio'. Hence, it is implicitly assumed that all firms within an industry face similar competitive pressure. To investigate if there existed intra-industry differences, we employed a firm-level proxy of competition that takes into account the market share of each firm; that is, the ratio of its sales over the total sales of the industry to which this firm belongs. This measure of competition has been used widely. The larger the market share a firm has, the lower is the competition that it faces. We should note that a limitation of the results relates to the fact that the data include only the UK market, rather than all the markets in other countries. Following the previous approach and using the median of the market share, we split the sample into lower- and higher-market share subgroups. Then, we re-estimated the model for each subgroup separately.

Table 8.5 reports the results, which confirm the findings of Table 8.4. They indicate that market share has a positive association with the returns to R&D. In other words, the lower the competition that a firm faces, the better it can appropriate the benefits of its own R&D. The findings are in line with the results of Greenhalgh and Rogers (2006) who found that a higher market share increases the market valuation of patent activity. The results also support Tang (2006) who argued that firms with significant market power can better finance their R&D activities because of the profits arising from such power.

Table 8.5 The effects of competition (as measured by market share) [a, b]

	High competition	Low competition
Log (K/L)	0.27*** (0.04)	0.15*** (0.03)
Log L	-0.007[ns] (0.02)	-0.01[ns] (0.01)
R&D elasticity	0.07*** (0.02)	0.20*** (0.02)
Control for time	yes	yes
Control for industry	yes	yes
R^2	0.22 (0.17)	0.50 (0.13)

Notes:
[a] The dependent variable is labour productivity.
[b] ns = not significant, * 5% level of significance, ** 1% level of significance, *** 0.1% level of significance, the absence of a star indicates a level of significance of 10%.

4. FIRM SIZE

As discussed in Chapter 3, the parameters that influence the impact of the stock of scientific knowledge can be grouped into two categories. The first relates to those variables that influence a firm's innovative capacity; that is, a firm's ability to translate scientific knowledge into new products and processes. The second group refers to those factors that allow a firm to appropriate its stock of scientific knowledge more successfully. The section below discusses how firm size may affect innovative capacity and the appropriability of innovation and, in turn, the impact that scientific knowledge has on the productivity of multinational corporations. We then empirically test this prediction.

4.1 Theoretical Predictions

Many scholars, such as Lichtenberg and Siegel (1991) and Cohen and Klepper (1996) have emphasized that firm size may influence the economic consequences of innovation. On the one hand, a number of theoretical arguments suggest that the process of R&D is not always easy for larger firms. For instance, co-ordination and communication for very large and thus decentralized firms is difficult, costly and time-consuming, while the infrequent face-to-face contact slows down the knowledge-creation process. In contrast, many other theoretical predictions suggest the opposite. Larger firms can build on or imitate technologies, ideas and research findings from several countries and from a broader group of scientists (Kotabe et al., 2002; Kafouros, 2005; 2006). Their diversity and the different backgrounds of R&D employees may also increase the creativity of research teams, which can access a large reservoir of knowledge created in different countries, and collect and circulate information concerning recently-registered patents and scientific and technological advances. Another argument involves the cost of innovation, which tends to be lower for very large firms that can either obtain loans more readily and at preferential rates (Mansfield, 1968a) or fund R&D using their own money (Schumpeter, 1950). Due to financial constraints, small firms cannot easily undertake long-term projects. This is also confirmed by many empirical studies which showed that because small firms cannot wait a long time for the payoff, their strategy tends to place emphasis upon short-term incremental (rather than radical) innovations (Pavitt et al., 1987; Piergiovanni et al., 1997).

A number of other theoretical arguments and scattered pieces of evidence indicate that firm size allows an organization to better exploit and appropriate the fruits of innovation as it is associated with a larger market share and thus sufficient control of the market (Schumpeter, 1950). Larger firms also benefit from economies of scale as they internalize many activities, incorporate their developments in many products, and transfer their process innovations to many plants (Cohen and Klepper, 1996; Kotabe et al., 2002). As Mansfield (1968a, p.108-110) argued, 'projects must be carried out on large enough scale so that successes and failures can in some sense balance out'. In a similar way, the results of R&D are more likely to be useful for larger firms because of their greater diversity. This relates to the work of Nelson (1959) who suggested that diversified firms have more opportunities to exploit the unpredictable outcomes of R&D.

Even though the previous arguments suggest that firm size has a positive impact on the economic payoff of innovation, previous empirical findings are inconsistent with theory. Many studies found that a positive relationship between firm size and the returns to R&D (Link, 1981; Lichtenberg and Siegel, 1991; Cohen and Klepper, 1996). Other studies however (Griliches, 1980; Wang and Tsai, 2003) found that firm size does not play an important role.

4.2 Empirical Results

In order to test the above theoretical predictions and investigate the relationship between firm size and the effects of industrial research, the sample was divided into smaller and larger firms and the model was re-estimated. Table 8.6 presents the findings. The results suggest that whilst the effect of R&D on the productivity of larger firms is very high at 0.18, the corresponding effect is considerably lower for smaller firms at 0.10. These findings confirm the Schumpeterian hypothesis suggesting that the impact of R&D is much higher on the productivity performance of larger firms.

Table 8.6 Results for firm size [a, b]

	Larger firms (59 Firms)	Smaller firms (48 Firms)
Log (K/L)	0.23*** (0.03)	0.20*** (0.04)
Log L	-0.02[ns] (0.01)	0.04* (0.02)
R&D elasticity	0.18*** (0.02)	0.10*** (0.02)
Control for time	yes	yes
Control for industry	yes	yes
R^2	0.51 (0.14)	0.23 (0.17)

Notes:
[a] The dependent variable is labour productivity differences.
[b] ns = not significant, * 5% level of significance, ** 1% level of significance, *** 0.1% level of significance, the absence of a star indicates a level of significance of 10%.

The findings support the notion that larger companies may be better equipped to exploit their new products and technologies, as they can offer them to a large number of potential buyers (Lu and Beamish, 2004). The results are also consistent with the fact that larger firms afford to have staff working on the patenting of their inventions, which allows them to protect their findings more efficiently. This discrepancy between larger and smaller firms was not anticipated as it was thought that sample-selection bias might be different for the two sub-samples. The smaller firms that reported their R&D expenditure might be very successful and consequently, the impact of R&D might be similar to the impact on larger firms. Contrary to our expectations however, the research findings suggest the opposite.

5. TECHNOLOGICAL OPPORTUNITIES

As discussed earlier, the returns to innovation depend on a firm's innovative capacity as well as on a firm's ability to exploit, protect and appropriate its technologies successfully. Another factor that may affect these two parameters relates to the technological opportunities that a firm faces. The section below theoretically investigates and empirically tests the relationship between technological opportunities and the returns to R&D.

5.1 Theoretical Predictions

It has been suggested that a firm's innovative capacity depends on the technological opportunities that it faces. If this assumption holds, then the effects of innovation should be significantly higher for firms belonging to high-tech industries (for example, aerospace, computing and pharmaceuticals). Consistent with this view, Nelson (1982, p.454) pointed out that 'technological advance proceeds much more rapidly in areas where knowledge is strong than where it is weak'. A large body of literature suggests that high-tech – and thus R&D-intensive – firms may be more capable of acquiring, assimilating and exploiting external knowledge (Cohen and Levinthal, 1990). High-tech firms are also significantly affected by knowledge spillovers. Clark and Griliches (1984) argued that whilst many organizations use techniques where the possibility of new technical understanding is limited, others participate in sectors where scientific knowledge is rich and growing. Firms that operate in R&D-intensive industries can also acquire knowledge from a larger knowledge reservoir.

Another explanation may be associated with dynamic capabilities. The high R&D-intensity of high-tech firms might improve their dynamic capabilities which, in turn, further increase their innovative capacity which is subsequently reflected in higher returns to R&D. Many econometric studies provide support to the above propositions, showing that the contribution of R&D to the economic performance of high-tech firms is positive (Griliches and Mairesse, 1984; Hambrick and Macmillan, 1985; Harhoff, 1998). As we have previously emphasized, however, the effects of industrial research depend not only on a firm's innovative capacity but also on its ability to effectively appropriate the benefits of R&D. As high-tech products are withdrawn from the market quickly, they only contribute to a firm's performance for a limited period. This suggests that low-tech (rather than high-tech) MNEs are better able to profit from R&D. Indeed, because their products' life cycle is short, technologically sophisticated firms focus on short-term innovations, the returns of which tend to decline rapidly. High tech firms also experience high depreciation rates of their stock of scientific knowledge. Ravenscraft and Scherer (1982) showed that technologically dynamic markets tend to erode the returns to R&D rapidly. This is in line with the fact that technologically advanced firms face strong competition, which is generated by their high-tech and technologically capable rivals. Hence, previous theory does not clearly indicate how technological opportunities may influence the effects of R&D.

5.2 Empirical Results

In order to investigate the role of technological opportunities, following the usual practice (e.g. Griliches and Mairesse, 1984; Harhoff, 1998), the sample was divided into low- and high-tech firms. Then, the model was re-estimated for each sub-sample separately. Table 8.7 presents the findings.

Table 8.7 Results for technological opportunities [a, b]

	High-tech firms (63)	Low-tech firms (44)
Log (K/L)	0.25*** (0.03)	0.15*** (0.02)
Log L	0.02* (0.01)	0.03*** (0.009)
R&D elasticity	0.16*** (0.02)	0.09*** (0.01)
Control for time	yes	yes
Control for industry	yes	yes
R^2	0.41 (0.17)	0.61 (0.10)

Notes:
[a] The dependent variable is labour productivity differences.
[b] ns = not significant, * 5% level of significance, ** 1% level of significance, *** 0.1% level of significance, the absence of a star indicates a level of significance of 10%.

The returns to R&D for technologically advanced firms are significantly higher than the corresponding returns for low-tech firms. Specifically, the coefficient of R&D for high-tech firms is 0.15 whereas the corresponding coefficient for low-tech firms is only 0.09, implying that R&D is particularly important for the productivity performance of technologically advanced firms. The findings of Table 8.7 are also in line with the findings of firm-level studies for other countries. Harhoff (1998) reports that although the R&D elasticity for high-tech German firms is 0.16 it is only 0.09 for low-tech firms. Wang and Tsai (2003) find similar results for Japan, with 0.30 for technologically advanced firms and only 0.07 for low-tech ones. Griliches and Mairesse (1984) find that the impact of R&D on productivity is always higher for high-tech US industries.

6. THE FINDINGS FOR DIFFERENT INDUSTRIES

The estimates of Table 8.1 have been computed assuming that all sectors of the economy experience a similar production function. Nevertheless, if we take into account that the technological infrastructure and the production techniques vary widely across industries, this assumption appears implausible. For that reason, we estimate the different impacts of R&D on the productivity performance of different industries by regressing the model for each of the four broader groups separately (see Section 4.4 in Chapter 7). The first four columns of Table 8.8 present the cross-sectional estimates for the chemical, mechanical, electrical/electronics and transportation industries respectively. The fifth column reports the estimates for the remaining industries (e.g. textiles, paper and printing, rubber and plastics). The statistical cost we pay for dividing the research sample into smaller sub-samples is the higher standard errors of both ordinary and R&D capital which leads to less reliable estimates. Nevertheless, many estimates are still statistically significant at the 0.1 percent level.

As anticipated, the effects of R&D vary considerably depending on the industry. However, they remain positive and high for most of them. The elasticity of R&D for chemicals and pharmaceuticals is higher than the average elasticity of the UK manufacturing sector (0.19 instead of 0.15). The effects of R&D appear to be equally high for the transportation sector (0.17). Although this high R&D elasticity for the transportation sector was not expected, it might be explained by the fact that aerospace industry is well funded by the UK government (Van Reenen, 1997). By contrast, the corresponding impact on the productivity of machinery and mechanical engineering industries is lower at 0.13. Interestingly, the elasticity of R&D for the remaining industries is statistically insignificant implying that R&D

does not contribute to their productivity performance. This finding was not anticipated as we believed that the sample selection bias for firms that do not spend a lot on R&D would vary. In other words, we expected that non R&D-intensive firms such as metal and plastic manufacturers that reported their R&D spending would be 'success stories', so the estimated impact of R&D would be relatively high. Although the above findings imply the opposite, it is difficult to know whether the statistically insignificant R&D elasticity of remaining industries is 'real' or simply arises because of the aggregation of heterogeneous industries.

Table 8.8 Results for different industries [b, c]

Industries: [a]	1	2	3	4	5
Log (K/L)	0.25** (0.07)	0.04^{ns} (0.03)	0.27*** (0.05)	-0.04^{ns} (0.06)	0.36*** (0.04)
Log L	0.04* (0.02)	0.03*** (0.008)	0.008^{ns} (0.02)	-0.03^{ns} (0.03)	0.04^{ns} (0.01)
R&D elasticity	0.19*** (0.03)	0.13*** (0.01)	0.14*** (0.03)	0.17*** (0.04)	-0.02^{ns} (0.04)
Control for time	yes	yes	yes	yes	yes
R^2	0.44 (0.17)	0.38 (0.07)	0.29 (0.19)	0.32 (0.11)	0.60 (0.10)

Notes:
[a] 1.Chemicals, 2.Machinery and mechanical engineering, 3.Electrical and electronics, 4.Transportation, 5.Remaining industries.
[b] The dependent variable is labour productivity differences.
[c] ns = not significant, * 5% level of significance, ** 1% level of significance, *** 0.1% level of significance, the absence of a star indicates a level of significance of 10%.

All the above findings, with the exception those for the remaining industries, are consistent with the findings for other countries. Adams and Jaffe (1996) find that the impact of R&D on productivity is higher for US drug and agricultural chemical industries. Odagiri (1983) finds that the impact of R&D is higher for chemical and electrical Japanese firms. The research findings are also consistent with industrial practice. They can explain the decisions of managers of chemical and pharmaceutical firms to invest heavily in R&D as well as the decisions of managers of mineral, plastic and metal manufacturers to keep R&D investments at relatively low levels.

But why is the impact of R&D on the productivity performance of some industries such as chemicals higher than that of industries like mechanical engineering? One explanation for these differences relates to the fact that the output of some industries might be more accurately measured than that of others. The productivity growth of poorly measured industries might be low and, in consequence, the impact of R&D underestimated. A similar distortion could come from the different amount of intermediate materials that each industry uses. The use of value added would measure output in a more comparable way (Brynjolfsson and Hitt, 2000), giving greater precision in estimating the impact of R&D and thereby allowing a better comparison of different industries. As was noted earlier, however, there are no data on value added.

There is a plethora of additional factors that can differentiate industries with high returns to R&D from low performers. One factor relates to products life-cycle. R&D is more important for firms whose products have a short life cycle and thus are withdrawn from the market very quickly. This argument is consistent with some of the research findings which indicate that the impact of R&D is lower for mechanical engineering and metal manufacturing firms (whose products usually have a relatively long life cycle). The lower elasticity of R&D for the mechanical engineering industry can also be explained by their different types of R&D investment. As the life cycle of mechanical engineering products is often long, there is no need to develop new products continually. Hence, these firms could possibly invest more in process R&D to reduce their production costs and in consequence, decrease their selling prices and increase sales.

But if this argument holds, then why does their R&D elasticity appear to be lower than that of other sectors? As discussed in previous chapters, one possible explanation is that the reduction of selling prices may not be proportional to the reduction of production costs. In that case, some of the impact of R&D is forwarded to profits, and thus the impact of R&D on productivity appears to be lower. Another explanation relates to the time lag of R&D which presumably varies from industry to industry. The estimates of Table 8.8 reflect the immediate impact of R&D on productivity performance, thus they may not provide any insight into what will happen a few years after the initial investment in R&D (the next chapter investigates this).

The magnitude of the impact of R&D on productivity might also be associated with R&D-intensity. As the research findings of Table 8.8 indicate, the impact of R&D is high for R&D-intensive industries such as chemical and electrical/electronics, and lower for the non R&D-intensive industries such as mechanical engineering, metal manufacturing and plastics. The R&D-intensity of a firm might not have an immediate impact on its productivity but it can influence other organizational factors. High R&D-

intensity, for example, could be translated into a higher ratio of 'scientists and technologists' over 'ordinary employees', thus making the entire organization more innovative (Kafouros, 2006). High R&D-intensity could also be associated with better dynamic capabilities. According to the relevant literature (Eisenhardt and Martin, 2000; Teece et al., 1997) the mechanisms underlying strategic processes like product development increase a firm's dynamic capabilities. This in turn provides a dynamic environment of knowledge-creation. Moreover, where the potential for innovation is high, firms may differ in their ability to exploit those opportunities because of differences in management skills and other organizational differences.

Another significant factor responsible for the variation of R&D effects might be the different appropriability conditions across industries. Competition might be lower in some industries enabling some firms to appropriate more benefits from R&D. It is difficult, however, to accept as true that the competition, say, in the industry of mechanical machinery (in which the estimated R&D elasticity is 0.13) is higher than that in industries such as chemicals and pharmaceuticals (in which the estimated R&D elasticity is 0.19). Nevertheless, the extent to which a firm can appropriate its research findings also depends on the concentration of the industry (Schumpeter, 1950). As the findings of Section 3 indicated, a firm can more easily appropriate the benefits of R&D if it belongs to an industry comprising a few firms. In other cases, firms may be more able to appropriate their research findings simply because patent law is more effective in their industry. Nevertheless, this argument is speculative as there is no evidence to support it.

7. INTERNATIONALIZATION AND R&D

The relationship between innovation and productivity performance becomes more complex if we take into account that this book examines the performance of multinational corporations which operate, sell and develop their products and processes in many different locations around the globe. As discussed in Chapter 3, the degree of a firm's internationalization plays a crucial role. Multinational corporations have a number of firm-specific characteristics that allow them to develop new technologies successfully, and better exploit and appropriate the benefits of innovation. On the other hand however, a greater degree of internationalization increases substantially coordination, communication and control costs.

In order to examine empirically the impact of internationalization on the economic payoff from innovation, we collected data concerning the internationalization of the multinational corporations of our sample.

Following the majority of previous studies (Grant, 1987; Kotabe et al., 2002), we measure a firm's level of internationalization by using the ratio of foreign sales to total sales. Even though this proxy does not capture the internationalization of a firm's R&D network, earlier studies (von Zedtwitz and Gassmann, 2002) indicated that the degree of internationalization of sales tends to be correlated with that of R&D network. Using the median of the data, we split the sample into firms with a higher and lower degree of internationalization, and estimated the model for each subgroup separately. Table 8.9 reports the results.

Table 8.9 Internationalization and R&D

	Low internationalization	High internationalization
Log (K/L)	0.27*** (0.05)	0.18*** (0.02)
Log L	0.03^{ns} (0.02)	0.05*** (0.007)
R&D elasticity	0.08*** (0.03)	0.18*** (0.01)
Control for time	yes	yes
Control for industry	yes	yes
R^2	0.22 (0.19)	0.54 (0.12)

As the findings indicate, the impact of innovation on performance differs significantly across the two groups of firms. The coefficient of R&D for the firms with lower degree of internationalization is only 0.08. It seems that because their innovations are not marketed in many countries, the significant costs associated with the development of new technologies outweigh the potential benefits. In contrast, the corresponding coefficient for the multinational corporations with greater degree of internationalization is considerably higher at 0.18. These findings provide strong support to the arguments discussed in Chapter 3, and confirm that internationalization is a firm-specific characteristic that affects the payoff from innovation, and that allows these firms to profit from innovation.

8. ADDITIONAL RESULTS

Following similar published studies, the previous sections of this chapter reported the elasticity of R&D for different types of firms and examined a number of factors that may influence the returns to R&D. Using the estimated elasticities from the previous sections, we estimate the monetary returns to the stock of scientific knowledge. The labour productivity of the multinational corporations of the sample is on average £100,000, whereas the value of their tangible assets per employee is approximately £26,000. According to the estimates of Table 8.1, a 1 percent increase of ordinary capital per employee (which is £260) leads to a 0.20 percent increase of revenues per employee (which is £200). This means that for every additional pound of fixed assets per employee that a firm spends, its labour productivity will increase by 77 pence. Similar calculations indicated that for every pound that a firm invests in R&D, labour productivity performance will increase by 94 pence. These findings indicate that the gross returns to investments in innovation are higher than the returns to other investments in tangible assets (94 pence per pound instead of 77 pence per pound). We have also calculated the monetary returns for the higher- and lower-internationalization firms, broader sectors, larger, smaller, high- and low-tech firms. Table 8.10 presents the findings. Unfortunately, the statistically insignificant coefficient of ordinary capital for the industries of mechanical engineering and transportation did not allow us to estimate its returns.

Table 8.10 Returns to tangible assets and R&D

	Returns to tangible assets	Returns to R&D
High internationalization firms	0.68	1.27
Low internationalization firms	1.19	0.41
Larger firms	0.9	1.36
Smaller firms	0.78	0.5
High-tech firms	0.98	0.66
Low-tech firms	0.59	1.46
Chemicals	0.86	0.96
Machinery and mechanical engineering	-	1.83
Electrical and electronics	1.29	0.61
Transportation	-	1.27

Table 8.10 provides the opportunity to compare the impacts of R&D with the impacts of tangible assets. For example, for every additional pound of tangible assets that a highly internationalized firm spends, its productivity will increase by 68 pence per year, whilst every additional pound of R&D-

Capital will lead to a productivity increase of 127 pence. As Table 8.10 indicates, in many cases the returns to R&D are higher than those to ordinary capital. Particularly for low-tech firms, the difference is remarkable. The findings of this section concerning the impact of firm size are consistent with those presented in Section 4, confirming that the impact of R&D on the productivity of smaller firms is low. Nevertheless, although the results of Section 6 show that the elasticity of R&D for mechanical engineering firms is relatively low, Table 8.10 indicates that their returns to R&D are high. Similarly, although the findings of Section 5 confirm many previous studies, showing that the stock of scientific knowledge is important for technologically dynamic industries, the results of table 8.10 indicate the opposite. The explanation for this relates to the discussion of Chapter 5 and to the fact that the costs for R&D varies across firms. For instance, as low-tech firms are not R&D-intensive, the money they invest in order to increase their knowledge stock by 1 percent is less than the investment that other more R&D-intensive firms have to pay in order to do so. For this reason, even though the coefficient of R&D is low, the monetary returns for R&D are higher.

9. LIMITATIONS

The findings are subject to a variety of limitations. One main limitation is the fact that the use of firm-level data does not allow us to investigate the social returns to R&D. Nevertheless, the externalities and returns that spill over to other firms will be explored in the next chapters. A second limitation is that although the majority of R&D studies (including the current research) use sales as a measure of output, they may not capture immeasurable improvements of output such as better quality or increased product variety. Similarly, output price indices do not fully account for improvements in output (Griliches, 1979). As a result, the estimated contribution of R&D to firms' performance is likely to be underestimated. An additional downward bias may arise from the fact that the materials used in the production are not included in the model.

Furthermore, R&D capital cannot adequately capture the stock of scientific knowledge within a firm. R&D expenditure can only represent the formal research effort. However, scientific knowledge is also determined by many other sources of knowledge such as informal research and the knowledge produced from 'learning by doing'. Additional limitations relate to the productivity framework used here. First, it is not clear that knowledge is separable in the production function (Cameron, 2000) and second, when certain restrictive conditions of the framework are not met, further biases may be engendered (Basu and Fernald, 1997). Similarly, the productivity framework adopted here is based on a number of simplified assumptions (e.g. that technical change is neutral and that the production function is Cobb-Douglas) that may bias the results.

Additionally, many MNEs are diversified and thus produce a wide variety of products. In other cases they change their main field of business over time. One may therefore end up aggregating dissimilar firms. This problem affects the extent to which we can estimate the coefficients accurately and is magnified when examining industries such as mechanical manufacturing firms which may be involved, for example, with metal manufacturing. R&D is also in itself aggregated in terms of composition. Reported R&D expenditure is the sum of different R&D activities, such as basic and applied R&D, product and process R&D, short-term and long-term projects as well as small and large projects (Mansfield, 1984). Thus, we actually estimate the average impact of all the different types of industrial research. More detailed data may allow us in the future to estimate, for example, the returns to basic research or those to process R&D. Moreover, even though proxies such as 'concentration ratio' and 'market share' have been used widely by previous studies, they do not measure accurately the level of competition. Therefore, other factors that influence competitive conditions should be employed in the future. These may include, for example, the time needed by rivals to imitate a firm's innovation (Levin et al., 1987).

Furthermore, the variable of 'number of employees' used here as labour input does not take into account the heterogeneity of employees in terms for example, of their education and skills. Similarly, the R&D included in the model is a simplified representation of R&D activity, i.e. research is undertaken by a singe agent who finances the project and is at the same time the creator, owner and user of the innovation. However, as Baussola (1999) emphasizes, R&D activity takes place either within firms, or through contractual agreement between firms. A final limitation to the study relates to the quality of the data and the accounting treatment of R&D. Because these data are collected from firms' financial statements, the accounting treatment of R&D expenditures determines the quality of data. As the reporting of R&D remains, at least to some extent, voluntary (Stoneman and Toivanen, 2001), some potential selectivity bias may occur.

10. CONCLUSION

Using a firm-level dataset of multinational corporations, this chapter estimates the effects of R&D for the firms of a country (UK) whose productivity level, however measured, is lower than that of many other industrialized countries (HM Treasury, 2003). This research extends previous studies by examining the conditions under which MNEs profit from innovation. The findings may improve the academic and managerial understanding of the relationship between R&D and corporate performance. Firstly, they indicate that, on average, the impact of the stock of scientific-knowledge on productivity performance is positive and high. A number of econometric tests, the calculation of the results using different econometric specifications, and a sensitivity analysis (see Appendix A and B) indicate that the findings are robust and unbiased.

It was also found that the real monetary returns to R&D are usually higher than that to investments in tangible assets. This finding is significant for firms' economic performance and competitiveness, implying that UK manufacturing firms could have generated a higher output per employee if had they invested more in R&D. Another important finding is that the results of the regression analysis do not always confirm the results for the monetary returns to R&D (which take into account the role of cost). This result has important implications for academic research as it shows that when the cost of R&D is ignored, the interpretation of the results may be misleading. However, one should be very careful when interpreting the above findings. They do not necessarily imply that a firm can increase its productivity and economic performance by simply investing in R&D (Frohman, 1982). Those firms that experience high returns to R&D may differ from other firms in ways which cannot be fully remedied in this way. The organizational culture, managerial qualities and the ability of some MNEs to translate their inventions to commercially successful products, for example, may be the complementary factors that allow them to benefit from innovation (Teece et al., 1997). Current methodology may not capture the value hidden in R&D. The mechanisms underlying R&D do not just favour productivity performance, but can also improve the capability of firms to collect, assimilate and exploit knowledge (Cohen and Levinthal, 1990), facilitate business reengineering and increase profitability.

This chapter has demonstrated that another key factor that explains variations in the economic returns to R&D is that of competition. Utilising both industry- and firm-level data, the results showed that the payoff for firms' own R&D was lower when they participated in environments of perfect-competition and generally when they face intense competition. In this chapter, we also suggested that another significant firm-specific factor that allows companies to improve performance through innovation is that of internationalization. The evidence indicated that the returns to innovation are significantly higher for those firms that extend their activities in many markets, thereby confirming the critical role of internationalization in reaping rewards from innovation. This finding has implications for empirical research as it implies that econometric models that do not incorporate for the effects of internationalization may yield biased results concerning the consequences of innovation for firms' economic performance.

The analyses employed in this chapter may also improve our knowledge concerning the role of firm size. Our findings contradict some past studies which indicated that firm size does not influence the economic impacts of R&D (Griliches, 1980; Wang and Tsai, 2003). The analysis demonstrates that the returns to R&D for larger firms are significantly higher than the corresponding returns for smaller firms. When smaller firms innovate, they tend to be R&D intensive. This means that the money they invest in R&D is proportionally more than the money that large firms spend. In other words, even though past regression results indicate that the coefficient of R&D is high for smaller firms, when the costs of these investments are taken into account, the monetary returns to the R&D efforts of such firms are lower.

Another interesting finding relates to the role of technological opportunities. In contrast to past studies, we found that the economic payoff for R&D is in fact higher for low-tech multinational corporations. This implies that previous research underestimated the importance of the stock of scientific knowledge for the productivity of low-tech firms. In addition, it indicates that scientific achievement and technological potential does not always ensure high productivity performance and economic payoff. The findings also provide support to several studies which indicated that external innovations and technologically superior rivals can reduce a firm's economic performance (Aitken and Harrison, 1999; McGahan and Silverman, 2006).

An implication of the findings for academic research is that future predictions about the impacts of R&D on productivity performance should take into account and control for several factors such as the degree of internationalization, firm size, competitive pressures, sector and the technological opportunities that a multinational corporation faces. The findings of this chapter can also provide an insight to policy makers concerning the role of innovation, suggesting that productivity growth can be significantly accelerated by increasing the spending on R&D. Thus the government should formulate policies that will increase incentives, such as R&D tax credits and R&D-subsidies, thereby encouraging firms to become more innovative and engage in industrial research. As policy makers would want to distribute these incentives as efficiently as possible, the findings may help to identify the types of firms that should be given aid. In order to encourage firms to innovate, policy makers should ensure that the private returns to innovation are positive. As the findings of this research show, however, this does not appear to be the case for smaller firms. This suggests that the government should assist such firms to increase their innovative capacity and better appropriate the benefits of R&D.

The research undertaken in this chapter can be extended in many ways. Future research can estimate the returns to specific types of investments in innovation, such as process and product R&D, or outsourced R&D. A second opportunity for future research relates to the discussion of Chapter 3 and the fact that R&D is often used as a defense mechanism, rather than a competitive weapon. The econometric framework employed in this (and previous) research takes into account only the level of a firm's own stock of scientific knowledge. Nevertheless, the economic consequences of such effects also depend on rivals' stock of scientific knowledge. If all the firms within an industry were to undertake the same R&D, its impact on productivity would be negligible. So what is important is not only a firm's level of R&D, but also the difference of this level from the average level of its competitors. It would thus be of value to develop a methodology which considers R&D as a competitive weapon and which investigates the circumstances under which the returns to R&D are maximized.

APPENDIX A – SENSITIVITY ANALYSIS

This section investigates how sensitive the main findings are to the use of (1) other deflators, (2) different definitions of capital and labour and (3) alternative depreciation rates for R&D capital. Table 8.11 compares the main findings (first row) with the estimates obtained using four alternative deflators of output and capital. The first alternative uses the GDP price index to deflate output (instead of using a 2-digit price index on which the main findings are based). The second alternative uses a manufacturing output price index (PLLU), whilst the third one is based on an output price index (PLLV) designed for all manufacturing products excluding food, beverages, tobacco and petrol. Finally, the estimates of the fifth row are based on an alternative fixed capital deflator (YBFU). All the above price indices were provided by the office for national statistics. The estimates in all cases are similar to the main findings. It is surprising how insensitive the elasticity of R&D is to the use of different deflators. One might expect, for example, that as the GDP price index is a crude way of deflating the manufacturing output, it would affect the estimates significantly. Nevertheless the findings suggest the opposite.

We have also investigated the sensitivity of the main findings to changes in the definitions of capital and labour inputs. Table 8.12 compares the main cross-sectional findings of the first row to three alternatives. First, we re-estimate the elasticity of R&D when the gross fixed capital stock is used (instead of the capital services on which the main findings are based). The second alternative uses as capital input, the net fixed capital stock. Finally the third alternative is based on a measure of labour services (see Section 2.3. in Chapter 7), rather than using the number of employees as labour input.

Table 8.11 Findings estimated using different output deflators [d]

	Log (K/L)	Log L	R&D	R^2
Main findings	0.20*** (0.02)	0.03*** (0.007)	0.15*** (0.01)	0.37 (0.15)
GDP output deflator	0.17*** (0.03)	0.03*** (0.007)	0.15*** (0.01)	0.34 (0.15)
PLLU[a] output deflator	0.17*** (0.03)	0.03*** (0.008)	0.15*** (0.01)	0.34 (0.15)
PLLV[b] output deflator	0.17*** (0.03)	0.03*** (0.007)	0.15*** (0.01)	0.34 (0.15)
YBFU[c] fixed capital deflator	0.16*** (0.02)	0.03*** (0.007)	0.15*** (0.01)	0.34 (0.15)

Notes:
[a] PLLU is an output deflator for all manufacturing products. This deflator was provided by the UK office for national statistics.
[b] PLLV is an output deflator for all manufacturing products, excluding food, beverages, tobacco and petrol. This deflator was provided by the UK office for national statistics.
[c] YBFU is an alternative fixed capital deflator. This deflator was provided by the UK office for national statistics.
[d] ns = not significant, * 5% level of significance, ** 1% level of significance, *** 0.1% level of significance, the absence of a star indicates a level of significance of 10%.

As the second and third rows indicate, the elasticity of R&D is fairly stable when a different definition for capital input is used. The goodness of fit remains similar, whilst the elasticity of ordinary capital is slightly higher when the gross fixed capital stock is used and significantly lower in the case of net fixed capital stock. The findings are relatively insensitive when the measure of labour services is used. The elasticity of ordinary capital is lower but that of R&D remains approximately the same. The goodness of fit is slightly decreased from 0.37 to 0.35, indicating that the use of the alternative labour input does not change the findings. The R&D coefficient of 0.15 of Table 8.1 is based on the assumption that R&D capital depreciates at a rate of 20 percent per year. However, as discussed in previous chapters, there is some evidence suggesting that the rate of depreciation of R&D varies from 15 to 25 percent (Goto and Suzuki, 1989; Pakes and Schankerman, 1984).

Table 8.12 Findings estimated using different capital and labour definitions

	Log (K/L)	Log L	R&D Elasticity	R^2
Main findings	0.20*** (0.02)	0.03*** (0.007)	0.15*** (0.01)	0.37 (0.15)
Gross fixed capital stock	0.21*** (0.03)	0.02*** (0.008)	0.14*** (0.01)	0.36 (0.15)
Net fixed capital stock	0.13*** (0.02)	0.02*** (0.007)	0.16*** (0.01)	0.34 (0.15)
Labour services	0.16*** (0.03)	0.03*** (0.007)	0.14*** (0.01)	0.35 (0.15)

Notes: ns = not significant, * 5% level of significance, ** 1% level of significance, *** 0.1% level of significance, the absence of a star indicates a level of significance of 10%.

Table 8.13 Findings estimated using different rates of R&D depreciation

	Log (K/L)	Log L	R&D Elasticity	R^2
Main findings (20%)	0.20*** (0.02)	0.03*** (0.007)	0.15*** (0.01)	0.37 (0.15)
15% depreciation rate	0.20*** (0.02)	0.03*** (0.007)	0.14*** (0.01)	0.37 (0.15)
25% depreciation rate	0.20*** (0.02)	0.03*** (0.007)	0.15*** (0.01)	0.37 (0.15)

Notes: ns = not significant, * 5% level of significance, ** 1% level of significance, *** 0.1% level of significance, the absence of a star indicates a level of significance of 10%.

We have investigated the sensitivity of the R&D coefficient to changes in the depreciation rate of R&D capital. The second and third row of Table 8.13 presents the findings when 15 and 25 percent rates of depreciation are used. It may be noted that the coefficient of R&D remains approximately the same. Similarly the elasticity of ordinary capital as well as the goodness of fit remain quite stable. These findings are consistent with those of other studies that also found the coefficient of R&D to be insensitive to the R&D capital depreciation rate (Hall and Mairesse, 1995; Kafouros, 2005).

APPENDIX B – ECONOMETRIC PROBLEMS AND TESTS

Given that the research findings are based on the OLS method, a number of econometric assumptions should be tested in order to investigate the extent to which the findings are unbiased and consistent. The first important assumption is that of 'normality' which states that the residuals must be normally distributed. In order to investigate whether they are normally distributed, we conducted the so-called Jarque and Bera test, which examines both the skewness and kurtosis of residuals (for more details on this test see Bera and Jarque, 1981). The null hypothesis, that the residuals were normally distributed, was not rejected at the 1 percent confidence level.

Additionally, the variance of the disturbances must be equal (homoscedastic). However, this assumption is difficult to fulfil in a function such as the Cobb-Douglas because in addition to the three inputs of our model, other unobservable factors, such as managerial efficiency, that are likely to affect a firm's productivity are included in the error term. As these factors vary across firms, the variance of the error terms may be heteroscedastic (Griliches, 1984). The consequence of heteroscedasticity is that although the OLS estimator remains unbiased, it is no longer 'best' (it no longer has minimum variance). In order to investigate the problem of heteroscedasticity, a 'white' heteroscedasticity test (Koenker, 1981) as well as the Goldfeld-Quandt test was conducted. We found no evidence of heteroscedasticity. Similarly, we found no evidence of serial correlation.

Another assumption of the classical linear regression model is that there is not multicollinearity among the explanatory variables, otherwise there are large standard errors and it becomes difficult to calculate accurately the contribution of each input (Berndt, 1991). The problem of multicollinearity arises because the variables are collinear. For example, when a firm hires more employees, it usually invests in more equipment too. But what can be done in order to reduce multicollinearity? Given that the main source of multicollinearity is the limited range of the values taken (Gujarati, 1995), the fact that we use firm-level data (instead of macro-level data) reduces multicollinearity. However, even at the firm-level, some multicollinearity problems may arise if the sample is divided into more homogeneous sub-samples. If these sub-samples are, for example, composed of firms of the same industry, the range of values is more limited and therefore standard errors tend to be larger. Whilst a sample of dissimilar firms reduces multicollinearity, this introduces a conceptual problem through the aggregation of different production methods.

Another way to reduce multicollinearity is to use as many observations as possible (Gujarati, 1995). Given that the approximately 1000 observations of the sample provide a lot of variability, multicollinearity is expected to be relatively low. The rule of thumb in order to detect multicollinearity is to check the goodness of fit and the t-ratios. If R^2 is very high and at the same time the t-ratios are very low, then it is very likely that some variables are collinear. Given that all the coefficients of our model are statistically significant with very low standard errors, and R^2 is relatively low, multicollinearity should not be a problem. However, the problem cannot be eliminated. As Gujarati (1995) emphasizes, that many of our explanatory variables are collinear is 'a fact of life'.

9. The Effects of Innovation Over Time

Analysing a sample of 84 UK multinational firms, this chapter investigates how rapidly the returns to R&D decay, and after how many years they are maximized. Given that both the decay and maximization of the impacts of R&D are likely to be influenced by the degree of a firm's internationalization and by other industry idiosyncrasies, we estimate the results for a number of sectors and sub-samples separately.

1. INTRODUCTION

The previous chapter investigated the impact of the stock of scientific knowledge on corporate performance. As many studies have emphasized, time is needed in order to complete a project, to introduce its outputs to the market, and to gain a market share. If this argument is valid, then the impact of knowledge stock on productivity and on other measures of performance may not be maximized immediately (as was implicitly assumed in the previous chapter). Hence, there may be a time lag between investment in R&D and the maximization of its impact on productivity (henceforth 'R&D lag'). Nevertheless, it has also been argued that a firm's stock of R&D capital includes not only new research projects but also projects that may have started several years earlier (Griliches, 1979). This suggests that because firms have in their R&D portfolio projects that are at different 'stages of fruition' (some of them not far from completion), the impact of R&D on performance may appear to be immediate. The first aim of this chapter is to examine empirically the time lag between R&D investments and their effects on the productivity performance of a sample of MNEs. It should be emphasized that even though these issues have been a point of debate at the conceptual level, there has been little empirical research undertaken in this area.

The second objective of this chapter relates to the fact that once a new technology is introduced to a market, other firms will imitate it. Hence, the returns to R&D will sooner or later start to decay. This issue becomes even more complicated when we take into account the fact that as the internationalization of multinational corporations varies, their technologies and products are diffused and imitated at a different rate. Using the econometric framework presented in Chapter 6, we try to investigate how rapidly the economic payoff of industrial research decays. To do so more accurately, our analysis takes into account variation in the results, dependent on the industry involved and a firm's degree of internationalization. This chapter is organized as follows. We start by reviewing past findings. Then the findings are presented, followed by a discussion regarding the limitations of the study. Finally, the conclusions which may be drawn are outlined in the last section.

2. PAST FINDINGS AND FRAMEWORK

Unfortunately, even though the lag structure of industrial R&D has attracted theoretical interest, the empirical findings are limited. Indeed, there are only a few studies which tried to estimate the lag of R&D. The starting point of our analysis is that there are two types of R&D lags (see Pakes and Schankerman, 1984): the 'gestation lag' (that is, the time between project inception and project completion); and the 'application lag' (the time between the project completion and its commercial application).

One of the first studies that examined the time lag structure of industrial research is that of Mansfield (1968b). Analysing data from personal interviews with R&D employees, he found that the application lag of R&D is approximately six months. Another study that provides evidence regarding the application lag of R&D is that of Pakes and Schankerman (1984). The researchers found that this lag is often only three months, showing that it may be particularly short. Pakes and Schankerman (1984) also estimated the gestation lag of R&D. Their results showed that this lag is often between nine months and one year. Based on these findings, we may conclude that the total R&D lag (gestation lag plus application lag) could be as short as a year.

Using a different approach, Branstetter and Sakakibara (2002) examined the time path of the benefits of research consortia and showed that this lag was longer. Specifically, their analysis indicated that the patenting activity of these consortia was maximized when a three year lag variable was used. Other researchers investigated the time lag structure between R&D and profitability (rather than between R&D and productivity). One of those studies is that of Ravenscraft and Scherer (1982). Their results demonstrated that the time lag between R&D investments and their effects on profitability of US firms was about four years. These results are also supported by more recent studies. Lev and Sougiannis (1996) found that the value found in R&D is usually maximized in two or three years. However, the researchers have also emphasized that this lag depends on the industry involved. Specifically, they demonstrated that the average life of R&D for chemicals and pharmaceuticals can be up to nine years, thereby suggesting that the effects of R&D may decay slowly.

Similarly, the lag of R&D may also depend on the type of innovation. For instance, when firms focus on process innovation, for a whole host of plausible reasons (such as time to build new plants and re-train the workforce) it is reasonable that the time lag of R&D will be longer. Similarly, the rate of decay of R&D may be lower when firms invest in process R&D. Process innovations cannot be imitated as easily as the outcomes of product R&D. As such, firms that invest in process R&D may be able to appropriate their own research findings for a longer time period.

There are two major methods which can be used to estimate the lag of R&D. The first is based on interviews with R&D project evaluation staff (as utilized by Mansfield, 1968b). The second method is similar to that of Griliches and Mairesse (1984) who investigated the lag of R&D by using the Cobb-Douglas framework. Because data from interviews with R&D employees were not available, the second method was employed. The easiest way to investigate the lag of R&D using the Cobb-Douglas production function is to use the rate of return approach (see Chapter 6). The only difference is that the R&D intensity $(RD/Q)_{it}$ should be substituted with its lagged measures $(RD/Q)_{it-1}$, $(RD/Q)_{it-2}$, $(RD/Q)_{it-3}$ and so on. Hence, it is possible to estimate the effects of the R&D investments made some years earlier, rather than the impact of current R&D.

This approach, however, has a major drawback. Current and past R&D intensities should be simultaneously added in the model; otherwise a bias will be generated because of the interrelation of the variables. Nevertheless, when they are all added in the model simultaneously, severe multicollinearity problems do not allow us to estimate the model (many of the coefficients of R&D become negative). One way to deal with this problem is to estimate several equations (one for each lagged year). But in that case, the estimates will be biased due to the omitted variables. For that reason, in order to assess the time lag structure of R&D, the approach described in Chapter 6 is employed here (this uses lagged measures of R&D capital, rather than R&D intensities).

A set of observations spanning eight years, as used in the previous chapter, is not long enough to investigate the lag structure of R&D. For that reason, the 'long' sample of 14 years (1989-2002) is used in this chapter to estimate the lag structure of R&D (a description of this dataset can be found in Chapter 7). The 14 year dataset allows us to calculate up to 13 lagged years. Nevertheless, in order to include a sufficient number of observations in the regression, we preferred to estimate up to six lagged years. We should also note that our model controls for time effects. This is particularly important as the time lag of R&D may change over time (for instance, the development time in the automotive industry was 60 months in the early 1990s but only 18 months in the early 2000s; Advanced Manufacturing, 2001).

3. MAIN RESULTS

Table 9.1 presents the main findings for the main lagged R&D capital. As noted earlier, the 'long' research sample of 14 years (1989-2002) is used here (see Chapter 7). The results have been obtained by using the method of ordinary least squares. In order to avoid multicollinearity problems, we have estimated several regressions (one for each lag). However, there is no omitted-variables bias as both current and past expenditures are included in the model. All the findings reported in this chapter are based on the cross-sectional dimension of the data.

The first row of Table 9.1 reports the elasticity of R&D excluding any lag (hence, it is assumed that the impact of R&D on firm performance is maximized immediately). The remaining six rows present the elasticity of R&D for up to six lagged years. That is, the performance implications of R&D when it is assumed that its impact is maximized one, two, ... six years after the investment has been made. The analysis delivers a number of interesting findings. Consistent with the results presented in the previous chapter (using the 'large' sample), the findings of Table 9.1 indicate that the impact of the stock of scientific knowledge on the performance of UK multinational corporations is economically and statistically significant.

The elasticity of R&D is 0.14, which is very close to the elasticity of 0.15 obtained using our larger sample in Chapter 8. In other words, the results show that when a firm increases its R&D capital per employee by 1 percent, its productivity will be increased by 0.14 percent. The results of Table 9.1 also shed light on the rate of decay of R&D, as well as on the time that R&D effects need in order to be maximized. Starting from the latter, it may be observed that (on average) the impact of R&D on productivity performance is maximized after one year (rather than immediately). The finding is consistent with the results of several studies.

As discussed earlier, Mansfield (1968b) found that the application lag was as short as six months, whereas Pakes and Schankerman (1984) found that the lag of R&D could be approximately a year. Griliches and Mairesse (1984), using a method similar to the method employed here, estimated the total lag of R&D, and found evidence that it is indeed very short. The findings of the researchers indicated an immediate effect on firm performance, which then drops sharply, before remaining constant throughout the rest of the period. Even though the findings of other studies (examining the association between profitability and R&D) found that the time lag was significantly longer (Ravenscraft and Scherer, 1982), this does not mean that their results contradict the analysis of the current research. The writing-off of complementary investments (such as marketing) will take at least one or two years, so the time lag between R&D and profits is longer than that between R&D and firm performance.

Table 9.1 The time lag of the effects of R&D [a, b, c]

	Log (K/L)	Log L	R&D elasticity	Control for time	Control for industry	R^2
Lag0	0.21*** (0.02)	0.00ns (0.01)	0.14*** (0.01)	yes	yes	0.44 (0.12)
Lag1	0.21*** (0.02)	0.00ns (0.01)	0.15*** (0.01)	yes	yes	0.44 (0.12)
Lag2	0.21*** (0.02)	0.00ns (0.01)	0.13*** (0.01)	yes	yes	0.44 (0.12)
Lag3	0.21*** (0.02)	0.00ns (0.01)	0.13*** (0.01)	yes	yes	0.44 (0.12)
Lag4	0.21*** (0.02)	0.00ns (0.01)	0.13*** (0.01)	yes	yes	0.44 (0.12)
Lag5	0.21*** (0.02)	0.00ns (0.01)	0.13*** (0.01)	yes	yes	0.43 (0.12)
Lag6	0.22*** (0.02)	0.00ns (0.01)	0.12*** (0.01)	yes	yes	0.43 (0.13)

Notes:
[a] The dependent variable is labour productivity. Both the effect and depreciation rate is set at 20%.
[b] ns = not significant, * 5% level of significance, ** 1% level of significance, *** 0.1% level of significance, the absence of a star indicates a level of significance of 10%.
[c] We also estimated the results using an effect rate of 30 and 40% (rather than 20%). These findings were qualitatively similar to those obtained using the rate of 20%.

The findings presented in Table 9.1 may also shed light on how rapidly the returns to R&D decay. Interestingly, its rate of return does not decay as rapidly as might be expected. The elasticity of the R&D that had been undertaken six years ago is statistically significant and relatively high. Hence, despite the problems associated with the appropriability of the benefits of innovation, investments in industrial research may generate substantial increases in performance for a long period of time. These results are consistent with previous results that showed that the useful life of R&D can be up to nine years (Lev and Sougiannis, 1996).

Table 9.2 *The time lag of R&D for firms with low degree of internationalization* [a, b, c]

	Log (K/L)	Log L	R&D elasticity	R^2
Lag0	0.14***	0.02ns	0.10***	0.35
	(0.04)	(0.02)	(0.03)	(0.14)
Lag1	0.14***	0.02ns	0.10***	0.35
	(0.04)	(0.02)	(0.03)	(0.14)
Lag2	0.15***	0.02ns	0.10***	0.35
	(0.04)	(0.02)	(0.03)	(0.14)
Lag3	0.14***	0.02ns	0.10***	0.35
	(0.04)	(0.02)	(0.03)	(0.14)
Lag4	0.14***	0.02ns	0.10***	0.35
	(0.04)	(0.02)	(0.03)	(0.14)
Lag5	0.14***	0.02ns	0.10***	0.35
	(0.04)	(0.02)	(0.03)	(0.14)
Lag6	0.14***	0.02ns	0.09***	0.35
	(0.04)	(0.02)	(0.03)	(0.14)

Notes:
[a] The dependent variable is labour productivity.
[b] ns = not significant, * 5% level of significance, ** 1% level of significance, *** 0.1% level of significance, the absence of a star indicates a level of significance of 10%.
[c] Control variables for time, industry and size have been included in the regression.

One factor that may influence the decay of the returns to R&D is a firm's degree of internationalization. On the one hand, it can be argued that the companies which are more international can progressively market their new products to many countries. As such, they can benefit from the value of R&D for a longer period. However, a higher degree of internationalization also implies that these firms are more decentralized. This, in turn, increases the risk of knowledge leakage from poorly-controlled departments (Fisch, 2003). In such cases, the rate of decay of the returns to R&D will be higher. To test empirically these predictions, we divided the data into two sub-samples of higher- and lower-degree of internationalization (separating higher and lower at the median). We then estimated the model for each sub-sample separately. Tables 9.2 and 9.3 present the recalculated results.

Table 9.3 The time lag of R&D for firms with high degree of internationalization [a, b, c]

	Log (K/L)	Log L	R&D elasticity	R^2
Lag0	0.25*** (0.03)	0.01ns (0.01)	0.16*** (0.01)	0.57 (0.11)
Lag1	0.26*** (0.03)	0.01ns (0.01)	0.17*** (0.01)	0.57 (0.11)
Lag2	0.25*** (0.03)	0.01ns (0.01)	0.15*** (0.01)	0.56 (0.11)
Lag3	0.26*** (0.03)	0.01ns (0.01)	0.15*** (0.01)	0.56 (0.11)
Lag4	0.27*** (0.03)	0.01ns (0.01)	0.14*** (0.01)	0.55 (0.11)
Lag5	0.27*** (0.03)	0.01ns (0.01)	0.13*** (0.01)	0.54 (0.11)
Lag6	0.27*** (0.03)	0.01ns (0.01)	0.12*** (0.01)	0.53 (0.11)

Notes:
[a] The dependent variable is labour productivity.
[b] ns = not significant, * 5% level of significance, ** 1% level of significance, *** 0.1% level of significance, the absence of a star indicates a level of significance of 10%.
[c] Control variables for time, industry and size have been included in the regression.

As we can observe from the tables, whilst the economic payoff of R&D for the firms with a lower degree of internationalization is maximized immediately, the corresponding return for the more highly internationalized firms is maximized when the assumed peak is one year after the investment in R&D. Hence, it appears that the less international firms are capable of marketing their technological discoveries very quickly. Furthermore, interesting differences can be observed concerning the decay of the economic payoff of R&D. In contrast to our expectations, the results indicate that the returns to R&D decay very slowly for less international firms. Even in the case of more international companies, however, the findings show that the return to industrial research does not decay as rapidly as might be expected, showing that a significant proportion of the value of R&D is appropriated by the innovator over a long period.

4. ADDITIONAL RESULTS

Imposing the same peak for all firms, the findings of the previous section have implicitly assumed that all firms in the sample have similar characteristics. As discussed previously, however, considerable pieces of evidence indicate that innovative capacity and R&D strategies vary widely across the sectors of the economy. Similarly, the technological infrastructure, the type of industrial research (e.g. process and product R&D), the life cycles of products and the production techniques may also be significantly different across firms. Indeed, our earlier findings confirmed these arguments. This section examines the extent to which the lag structure of R&D is influenced by industry-specific idiosyncrasies. In order to do so, following the approach adopted previously, we estimate the model for four main industries separately (definitions and descriptive statistics are included in Chapter 7). The tables below (9.4, 9.5, 9.6 and 9.7) present the findings for the following industries: (1) chemicals and pharmaceuticals, (2) machinery and mechanical engineering, (3) electrical and electronics and (4) transportation.

Table 9.4 The time lag of R&D (chemicals and pharmaceuticals) [a, b, c]

	Log (K/L)	Log L	R&D elasticity	Control for time	R^2
Lag0	0.22*** (0.05)	0.00ns (0.01)	0.22*** (0.02)	yes	0.62 (0.11)
Lag1	0.22*** (0.05)	0.00ns (0.01)	0.23*** (0.02)	yes	0.62 (0.11)
Lag2	0.22*** (0.05)	0.00ns (0.01)	0.23*** (0.03)	yes	0.62 (0.11)
Lag3	0.22*** (0.06)	0.00ns (0.01)	0.22*** (0.03)	yes	0.61 (0.11)
Lag4	0.22*** (0.06)	0.00ns (0.01)	0.21*** (0.03)	yes	0.58 (0.11)

| Lag5 | 0.21*** (0.06) | 0.00ns (0.01) | 0.21*** (0.03) | yes | 0.56 (0.11) |
| Lag6 | 0.22*** (0.06) | 0.00ns (0.01) | 0.20*** (0.03) | yes | 0.55 (0.11) |

Notes:
[a] The dependent variable is labour productivity.
[b] ns = not significant, * 5% level of significance, ** 1% level of significance, *** 0.1% level of significance, the absence of a star indicates a level of significance of 10%.
[c] Control variables for time and firm size have been included in the regression.

Table 9.5 The time lag of R&D (machinery and mechanical engineering) [a, b, c]

	Log (K/L)	Log L	R&D elasticity	Control for time	R^2
Lag0	0.05 (0.03)	0.03*** (0.01)	0.13*** (0.01)	yes	0.35 (0.07)
Lag1	0.05 (0.03)	0.03*** (0.01)	0.13*** (0.01)	yes	0.34 (0.07)
Lag2	0.06 (0.03)	0.03*** (0.01)	0.12*** (0.01)	yes	0.32 (0.07)
Lag3	0.06 (0.03)	0.03*** (0.01)	0.12*** (0.01)	yes	0.32 (0.07)
Lag4	0.06 (0.03)	0.03*** (0.01)	0.11*** (0.01)	yes	0.31 (0.07)
Lag5	0.06* (0.03)	0.03*** (0.01)	0.11*** (0.01)	yes	0.30 (0.07)
Lag6	0.07* (0.03)	0.03*** (0.01)	0.10*** (0.01)	yes	0.28 (0.07)

Notes:
[a] The dependent variable is labour productivity.
[b] ns = not significant, * 5% level of significance, ** 1% level of significance, *** 0.1% level of significance, the absence of a star indicates a level of significance of 10%.
[c] Control variables for time and firm size have been included in the regression.

As was expected, the time lag between R&D and firm performance for some firms is longer than for others. Specifically, the results indicate that the economic payoff of R&D for chemicals and pharmaceuticals as well as for electrical and electronics firms is maximized when we assume that the peak of its contribution is one year after the investment has been made. Our results are reasonably similar to those of Lev and Sougiannis (1996) who found that the lag for the computing, electrical, electronics and other industries was two years. By contrast, as Table 9.7 indicates, the time lag for the transportation industry appears to be significantly longer than that for other firms.

Table 9.6 The time lag of R&D (electrical and electronics) [a, b, c]

	Log (K/L)	Log L	R&D elasticity	Control for time	R^2
Lag0	0.26*** (0.04)	0.03** (0.01)	0.20*** (0.03)	yes	0.56 (0.12)
Lag1	0.26*** (0.04)	0.03** (0.01)	0.21*** (0.03)	yes	0.56 (0.12)
Lag2	0.26*** (0.04)	0.03** (0.01)	0.19*** (0.03)	yes	0.56 (0.12)
Lag3	0.27*** (0.04)	0.03** (0.01)	0.19*** (0.03)	yes	0.56 (0.12)
Lag4	0.27*** (0.04)	0.04*** (0.01)	0.19*** (0.03)	yes	0.56 (0.12)
Lag5	0.27*** (0.04)	0.04*** (0.01)	0.18*** (0.03)	yes	0.55 (0.12)
Lag6	0.27*** (0.04)	0.04*** (0.01)	0.17*** (0.03)	yes	0.55 (0.12)

Notes:
[a] The dependent variable is labour productivity.
[b] ns = not significant, * 5% level of significance, ** 1% level of significance, *** 0.1% level of significance, the absence of a star indicates a level of significance of 10%.
[c] Control variables for time and firm size have been included in the regression.

The impact of R&D is maximized when the assumed peak is four years after the investment has been made. These findings are consistent with the strategic R&D behavior of firms. Whilst many organizations focus on short-term research projects and on incremental (rather than radical) innovations, other multinational corporations prefer to place emphasis on long-term projects of basic research. The results confirm that the payoff of R&D decays slowly, supporting the notion that the useful life of R&D can be very long. Even when the lag is six years, the coefficient of R&D is positive, high and statistically significant, suggesting that firms benefit from their innovations over a long period of time.

Table 9.7 The time lag of R&D (transportation) [a, b, c]

	Log (K/L)	Log L	R&D elasticity	Control for time	R^2
Lag0	-0.06ns (0.04)	-0.04ns (0.03)	0.14*** (0.04)	yes	0.22 (0.12)
Lag1	-0.06ns (0.04)	-0.04ns (0.03)	0.14*** (0.04)	yes	0.21 (0.12)
Lag2	-0.06ns (0.04)	-0.04ns (0.03)	0.14*** (0.04)	yes	0.22 (0.12)
Lag3	-0.07ns (0.04)	-0.04ns (0.03)	0.15*** (0.04)	yes	0.23 (0.10)
Lag4	-0.08ns (0.06)	-0.05 (0.03)	0.16*** (0.04)	yes	0.24 (0.10)
Lag5	-0.08ns (0.06)	-0.05 (0.03)	0.16*** (0.04)	yes	0.24 (0.10)
Lag6	-0.06ns (0.04)	-0.05 (0.03)	0.16*** (0.04)	yes	0.24 (0.10)

Notes:
[a] The dependent variable is labour productivity.
[b] ns = not significant, * 5% level of significance, ** 1% level of significance, *** 0.1% level of significance, the absence of a star indicates a level of significance of 10%.
[c] Control variables for time and firm size have been included in the regression.

5. LIMITATIONS

One important limitation to the study relates to the fact that as the sample includes multinational corporations, it is likely that some R&D activities were undertaken overseas (rather than in the UK). This may have biased the results because the R&D undertaken overseas might be more (or less) efficient than the R&D undertaken in the UK. Unfortunately, the level of detail of the data does not allow us to test these assumptions. A second limitation is associated with the fact that a firm can undertake different types of industrial R&D. Given that the time lag of basic and process R&D is likely to be longer than that for applied and product R&D, it would be of value to re-estimate the results of the study using detailed data for these different types of investments.

As the decay of the benefits of innovation is linked to the appropriability regime (which may vary across counties), another avenue for future research is to control for factors such as competition and the effective enforcement of intellectual-property rights. Once again, more detailed data are needed in order to examine empirically these effects. Furthermore, it should be noted that the time lag estimated here refer to the relationship between firm productivity performance and R&D capital (rather than R&D expenditure). Because the stock of R&D capital includes current and past investments in R&D, it includes many different projects. Whilst some of these research and development projects are new, other projects may have started several years ago. As such, the results presented earlier do not refer to each R&D project separately but to the stock of R&D capital as a whole.

6. CONCLUSION

Analysing a sample of 84 multinational firms, this chapter examined how rapidly the returns to R&D decay, and after how many years they are maximized. Although this chapter is only a first step towards the examination of the time lag of R&D, as there has been little research about the topic, the empirical findings should be of interest to international-business and technology-management scholars. Nevertheless, the results of this chapter may also be used by innovation strategists in order to forecast and predict the time lag of the impacts that R&D has on firm productivity performance.

Our results indicate that the returns to R&D do not decay as much as might be expected, thereby implying that the average life tends to be long. As the elasticity of R&D does not decline rapidly over time, it suggests that a multinational corporation may experience high returns to its R&D investments for a long period of time. Nevertheless, our analysis also demonstrated that the returns to R&D for certain types of firms decay faster than they do for others. Even though we expected that the returns to R&D will decay slowly for more international firms (because they can market progressively their newly-developed products to many countries), our findings imply the opposite. In fact, the elasticity of R&D was found to decrease more slowly for firms with lower degree of internationalization. Hence, managers of highly internationalized companies should keep in mind that the benefits of reaching a large number of potential buyers are confounded with some negative effects such as a higher depreciation rate of the stock of scientific knowledge.

The findings of this chapter also shed light on the time lag between R&D and the maximization of its effects. The results show that on average this lag is very short. The elasticity of R&D is maximized when we assume that the peak of its contribution is one year after the investment has been made. This finding also reflects the fact that as many research projects aim at the improvement of existing products (which have already gained some market share), the contribution of such investments to firm performance is almost immediate.

The maximization of the effects of R&D, however, differs across firms. We found that whilst the impact of R&D on the productivity of machinery and mechanical engineering firms is maximized immediately, the corresponding impact on the performance of the transportation industry is maximized after four years. The implication of this finding for empirical research is that the stock of R&D Capital (as defined by previous studies) may not be optimal. According to our empirical findings, the time lag of R&D should not be fixed. Instead, it should be set at one year for firms such as chemicals, pharmaceuticals, electrical and electronics, but at four years for firms that belong to the transportation industry.

10. The Role of Knowledge Spillovers

The previous chapters examined the impact of a multinational firm's own R&D activities on its productivity performance. This chapter goes one step further and investigates the effects of the so-called knowledge (or R&D) spillovers. In other words, it examines the extent to which other firms' R&D can influence a firm's productivity. The analysis is based on the dataset described in Chapter 7, composed of 107 multinational companies.

1. INTRODUCTION

A significant advance in traditional growth theory was made by the introduction of knowledge (or R&D) spillovers. The rationale behind these spillovers is that the technology, ideas and scientific knowledge of one firm may be beneficial to other organizations too (Griliches, 1979; Jaffe, 1986; Mansfield, 1968a; Scherer, 1982). Because scientific knowledge can be easily transferred through publications, reverse engineering, trade of goods, exchange of R&D scientists, and R&D collaborations (Geroski, 1995), the benefits of R&D are not wholly captured by the inventor, but may spillover to other firms. These externalities arise primarily because knowledge is considered as a public good, so that the use of knowledge by one firm does not preclude its use by others (Geroski, 1995; Los and Verspagen, 2000). Hence, as firms can often build on external knowledge without having to pay for it, R&D may not only improve the productivity performance of firms that undertake such activities, but can also benefit the productivity of companies of the same industry or even of other industries.

As R&D spillovers may influence firm performance, their evaluation has attracted wide interest. Indeed, there are many industry-level and country-level studies that found that the impact of spillovers on productivity is economically and statistically significant (McVicar, 2002; Sterlacchini, 1989). As emphasized by Los and Verspagen (2000) however, the effects of spillovers at the firm-level remain a less-explored area. This chapter contributes to research by analysing the contribution of R&D spillovers to performance at the firm-level. The investigation of R&D spillovers using firm-level data is very important because as well as the numerous advantages discussed in previous chapters, it will also allow us to estimate the extent to which a firm (rather than an industry) benefits from the technological achievements and research discoveries of other firms. The stress is put on the measurement of both within industry (intra-industry) and between industry (inter-industry) spillovers. In other words, the analysis distinguishes between the R&D undertaken by intra-industry competitors and that undertaken by other (inter-industry) firms.

Our analysis differs in a number of ways from the majority of other studies. First, it employs the R&D price indices constructed in Chapter 5, which will allow us to measure the spillover effects more accurately. Second, we examine whether (and to what extent) a firm's degree of internationalization influences its ability to benefit from knowledge spillovers. Third, in contrast to past studies that measured the spillover pool using only the R&D undertaken by the firms of their sample, our spillover pool includes all private R&D in the population of the UK R&D-performing firms. Fourth, the study employs a number of different methods to weight the usefulness of external R&D to each multinational corporation. These methods allow us to investigate whether the estimates are robust or merely artifacts of one weighting approach.

The measurement of the magnitude and the direction of R&D spillovers within and between industries offers new insights on the role of knowledge spillovers that may advance academic knowledge, and which indicate that their impacts can be either positive or negative. By understanding whether the spillovers from certain industries and types of firms generate greater effects than spillovers from other industries and types of firms, policy makers might be able to eliminate those barriers which prevent the knowledge transmission (Mohnen, 1999). Information regarding which types of firms transmit more knowledge, for example, will facilitate the appropriate distribution of R&D subsidies. The remainder of the chapter proceeds as follows. The findings of several studies are surveyed and discussed in Section 2. Section 3 reviews the methods utilized to measure the contribution of spillovers to a firm's productivity performance. It also describes the econometric framework and the construction of the variables. Section 4 presents and puts the findings in context whilst Section 5 discusses the limitations of the study. Section 6 draws the main conclusions and makes suggestions for future research.

2. PAST FINDINGS

As has been emphasized before (Anon Higon, 2004; Sakurai et al., 1996), comparisons across different studies must be looked at very carefully as they differ not only in terms of data and aggregation level (firm- or industry-level), but also in terms of methodological specifications. Additionally, a few studies, rather than estimating the impact of spillovers on productivity performance (the primal approach), use the so-called dual approach and usually associate R&D spillovers with firms' production costs. On top of that, the proximity method used to weight spillover pools also varies widely. Table 10.1 summarizes the findings of a selection of studies. The first two columns present the study along with information about the sample and country examined. The third column reports what weights were used. The last column presents either the elasticity or the rate of return to R&D spillovers. All the studies in the upper part of Table 10.1 (except the two last ones), use the primal approach (that is, the production function framework) and estimate the impact of spillovers on productivity performance. The last two (Bernstein, 1988; Bernstein and Nadiri, 1989) use the dual approach.

Table 10.1 The effects of spillovers: past findings

Study	Sample	Weights	Elasticity or Rate of Return
Firm-Level Studies			
Primal Approach			
Raut (1995)	192 firms (India)	unweighted sum	0.06-0.36
Antonelli (1994)	92 firms (Italy	unweighted sum	insignificant
Harhoff (2000)	443 firms (Germany)	Position in R&D space	0.02-0.08
Branstetter (1996)	209 US and 205 Japanese firms	Position in patent space	0.7-0.83
Adams and Jaffe (1996)	19561 plants (US)	unweighted sum, patent space	0.08-0.24
Jaffe (1986)	432 US firms	Position in patent space	0.02
Jaffe (1989)	435 US firms	Position in patent space	0.15

Los & Verspagen (2000)	485 US firms	Position in patent space	0.51
Wakelin (2001)	170 UK firms	Innovation Flows	insignificant
Dual Approach			
Bernstein (1988)	680 firms (Canada)	unweighted sum	0.17-0.24
Bernstein & Nadiri (1989)	48 US firms	unweighted sum	0.09-0.16
Industry-Level Studies for the UK			
Geroski (1991)	79 industries (UK)	Innovation Flows	0
Sterlacchini (1989)	15 industries (UK)	Input/ Output Flows	0.10-0.12
Sterlacchini (1989)	15 industries (UK)	Innovation Flows	0.3
McVicar (2002)	7 industries (UK)	FDI Trade Flows	0.07
Anon Higon (2004)	8 industries (UK)	I/O Flows	0.41-0.59

Source: Adapted and extended from Mohnen (1996; 1999), Cincera (1998) and Anon Higon (2004).

The top part of Table 10.1 summarizes the findings of firm-level studies. These can be considered as more comparable to the findings of this book. Because there is only one study for the UK (Wakelin, 2001), the lower part of Table 10.1 reports the estimates of four industry-level UK studies (Geroski, 1991; Sterlacchini, 1989; McVicar, 2002; Anon Higon, 2004). It is worth noting, however, that these studies are even more difficult to compare with the results of this book because first, they used industry-level data and second, some of them such as that of Geroski (1991), investigate the spillover effects of innovations rather than those of R&D.

The studies in this table also vary regarding the weights used to construct the spillover variables. Those of Raut (1995), Antonelli (1994), Adams and Jaffe (1996), Bernstein (1988) and Bernstein and Nadiri (1989) use an unweighted sum of all other firms' R&D, whilst those of Branstetter (1996) and Jaffe (1989) are based on patent data to construct technological

proximity matrices. Sterlacchini (1989) and Anon Higon (2004) have based
their weights on input-output flows. As Table 10.1 indicates, several studies
carried out for countries such as India, Japan, Canada, Germany and the US,
found the spillover effects to be statistically and economically significant.
Their findings indicate a strong and positive correlation between productivity
performance and the spillover variable. The coefficient of these spillovers
(either elasticity or rate of return) usually varies from insignificant to 0.36 but
some extreme values do exist. It is also worth noting that in some cases, the
impact of spillovers on productivity performance is higher than the
corresponding impact of their own R&D. McVicar (2002), for example, used
a sample of seven UK industries and found that while the elasticity of their
own R&D was 0.015, the elasticity of inter-industry spillovers was 0.07.
There are also studies which showed that firms can benefit from spillovers
even when they voluntarily reveal their findings (Harhoff et al., 2003). On
the other hand, many studies have not found any evidence of spillovers at all.
As the table indicates, Antonelli (1994), Wakelin (2001) and Geroski (1991)
found that the impact of spillovers on productivity performance is either
statistically insignificant or approximately zero. Similarly, the study of Bonte
(2004) did not provide strong evidence of productivity-enhancing spillover
effects for German R&D.

By observing Table 10.1 the gaps which motivated this study can be easily
identified. First, the majority of studies rely on data from the 1960s to the late
1980s, leaving the 1990s and the early 2000s unexplored. Therefore, there is
little evidence as to whether the faster circulation of knowledge caused by the
use of IT equipment changed the magnitude of the spillovers effects in the
1990s and early 2000s. Second, although there are many firm-level pieces of
evidence for the US, there is only one for the UK (Wakelin, 2001), and that
one only examines the time period between 1988 and 1992. Thus we do not
know whether the impact of spillovers on the productivity of UK firms is as
high as it is in US firms.

There are also a number of additional issues that are not presented in the
table. First, the magnitude of spillovers effects depends not only on the
technological distance between firms but also on the geographical distance
between them (Acs et al., 1993; Adams and Jaffe, 1996; Audretsch and
Feldman, 1994). Adams and Jaffe (1996) broke down spillovers into two
components, one geographically close to the recipient firm and one that is
more distant, and estimated the impact of each component separately on
productivity. They found that the contribution of parent firm R&D to plant-
level productivity is diminished not only by the technological distance but
also by the geographical distance and between the research lab and the plants.

Second, even when spillovers effects are positive, not all firms are capable
of acquiring and using external knowledge. Many researchers, such as Cohen

and Levinthal (1990) and Mohnen (1999), have emphasized the significance of absorptive capacity. The exploitation of external R&D depends on the firm's own R&D resources. In other words, the capability of capturing spillovers is associated with the prior R&D activity of each firm. Indeed, Harhoff (2000) found evidence which indicates that the extent to which spillovers contribute to a firm's productivity depends on its own R&D capital. Levin et al. (1987) found firms' own research efforts to be an effective way of investigating the rival technologies. Similarly, studies of technological diffusion found that R&D intensive firms adopt new technologies faster than less R&D intensive firms (Baldwin and Scott, 1987).

Third, a lot of interest has been attracted by international spillovers. International spillovers relate to the fact that the knowledge, ideas and innovations developed in a particular country can go beyond national boundaries and contribute to the productivity performance of other countries. In order to investigate the R&D externalities which arise in one country and benefit firms in other countries, researchers assume that R&D expenditures diffuse in proportion to the level of relationship between the firms of different countries (Cincera and Van Pottelsberghe, 2001). Hence, the construction of an international spillover capital is usually based on the weighted sum of R&D stocks of all firms located outside the country of the firm which receives the spillovers (Cincera 1998; Branstetter, 1996).

A representative example is the work of Coe and Helpman (1995). The researchers found that there are significant spillover effects between one country and another. The magnitude of these spillovers with respect to total factor productivity was between 0.01 and 0.12. In line with the work of Coe and Helpman (1995), a number of literature review papers (Mohnen, 1999; Cincera and Van Pottelsberghe, 2001) confirm that foreign R&D contributes substantially to the productivity performance of industrialized economies. They also emphasize that the spillover effects are particularly important for smaller countries, as well as for those countries with a high degree of openness concerning their imports. But it is not clear yet whether the external R&D is more important than the domestic one; although the elasticity of external R&D is often higher than that of domestic R&D, the opposite is usually found when the rates of return are computed. Unfortunately, as data on the spillover pools of other countries are not available to us, this chapter focuses on the spillover effects in the UK.

Another important issue relates to the negative effects of spillovers, which have not attracted much interest. As Mohnen (1996, p.51) points out 'R&D spillovers can increase or decrease the price that a producer can charge for his product, depending on whether the new product from outside R&D is substitutable or complementary to the firm's own product'. In other words, in cases in which the external R&D substitutes for the R&D that a firm has carried out, the impact of spillovers is liable to decrease, rather than increase, a firm's economic performance. Jaffe (1986) found evidence that the positive spillovers are confounded with negative effects. His results indicate that spillovers are often associated with lower profits, lower market value, increased competition as well as a higher depreciation rate of the old knowledge. Similarly, Bitzer and Geishecker (2006) found that negative intra-industry spillovers often dominate their positive impacts.

These findings, however, are not surprising as the R&D that a firm's rivals undertake improves not only the general pool of knowledge but also their own products, processes and competitiveness. R&D undertaken by a firm's competitors may reduce its profitability (De Bondt, 1996). Aitken and Harrison (1999) discussed the market-stealing effects of innovation. They argued that competition from technologically superior rivals may force a firm to reduce output. In turn, this may shift its cost curve higher, resulting in lower productivity performance.

Consistent with this view, McGahan and Silverman (2006) demonstrated that external innovations may negatively influence organizational performance either through 'direct market-stealing' or 'indirect appropriation through licensing'. Overall, as De Bondt (1996) emphasized, industrial research may impose negative externalities on competitors, even though positive knowledge transmission occurs. Unfortunately, positive and negative spillover effects vary across firms and theory does not indicate which effect is likely to dominate; that is, when the positive spillover effects outweigh the market-stealing (or negative) effects.

3. RESEARCH METHODS

3.1 Econometric Framework

As noted in the introduction, the rationale behind R&D spillovers is that 'the level of productivity achieved by one firm depends not only on its own research but also on the level of the pool of general knowledge accessible to it' (Griliches, 1992, p.34). This leads to a relatively simple production function which besides the ordinary capital (K), labour (L) and R&D capital (R) of a firm, also includes a measure of the aggregate R&D (S_{int}) undertaken by the firms of the industry to which the firm belongs (intra-industry spillovers):

$$Q = f(K, L, R, S_{int}) \qquad (10.1)$$

This model, however, becomes more complicated when it is recognized that 'we do not deal with a closed industry but with a whole array of firms and industries which borrow different amounts of knowledge from different sources according to their economic and technological distance from them' (Griliches, 1992, p.35). So an additional variable (S_{ext}) should be added in order to represent the R&D undertaken by the firms in all other industries (inter-industry spillovers):

$$Q = f(K, L, R, S_{int}, S_{ext})$$ (10.2)

The difficulty of estimating this model lies on the construction of the spillover variable (S_{ext}). The external R&D activities relevant to each firm will vary widely, depending on the 'closeness' between the i_{th} firm and all others firms in the same or different industries. It is important at this point to make a distinction between two types of R&D spillovers: rent spillovers and knowledge spillovers (Griliches, 1979; 1992; Scherer, 1982). Rent spillovers occur through trade and when the new products that a firm develops are used as inputs by other firms, and generally when a firm buys recently-developed products at a price which is lower than their true user value (Mohnen, 1999). For example, the products of the information technology (IT) industry have advanced the productivity of many other sectors (Brynjolfsson and Hitt, 2003). The effects of rent spillovers are also described by Los and Verspagen (2000, p.130):

> Due to competitive pressures, the producer of the innovation is often unable to capture the full price increase that results from efficiency gains for customers, due to the higher quality of the innovation relative to the old product. For example, a new personal computer that can perform certain calculations twice as fast as the existing ones, will often be sold at a price between once and twice the price of the existing machines. As an immediate consequence, the price per efficiency unit has fallen, and the productivity of the firms using the new computer will rise.

But these, however, cannot be considered as true spillovers. True spillovers are the knowledge spillovers, which according to Griliches (1992, p.36) 'are ideas borrowed by research teams of industry *i* from the research results of industry *j*'. In other words, knowledge spillovers are not incorporated in new products but occur when a firm exploits the knowledge and ideas that other firms of the same or other industries have developed. An important consequence is that a firm accesses the relevant knowledge without having to pay for it (Los and Verspagen, 2000). Nevertheless, it is difficult to make a distinction empirically between knowledge and rent spillovers (Van Pottelsberghe, 1997). We should also note that although the majority of studies focus on knowledge spillovers, the significance of rent spillovers should not be ignored because as Geroski (1991) found, the use of innovations in the UK had a more powerful impact than the production of innovations.

Returning to our previous discussion concerning the available approaches for measuring spillovers, the methods for constructing intra-industry S_{intra} and inter-industry S_{inter} spillover capitals to be found in the literature are two: a non-weighted (or asymmetric) method and a weighted (or symmetric) method. The first one is very simple. The R&D undertaken by firms of the industry that a firm belongs is aggregated to construct its intra-industry spillover capital. Similarly, the sum of the R&D undertaken by the firms of all other industries is used to construct the inter-industry spillover capital. The drawback of this method is that it uses similar weights to aggregate R&D undertaken by firms in different industries. For example, by using this method one assumes that for a computer manufacturer the usefulness of the R&D undertaken by firms in the electronics industry is similar to that undertaken by those, say, in the transportation industry.

The second method (weighted or symmetric) overcomes this drawback. The spillover capital is constructed separately for each firm, and is weighted according to the technological distance between the sender and recipient of knowledge spillovers (Cincera, 1998). A matrix W dimension n x n is usually constructed and used in order to calculate the spillover capital specific to a firm i:

$$S_i = \sum_{j=1}^{n} w_{ij} RE_j \qquad (10.3)$$

where n represents the number of firms (or industries); RE_j represents the R&D undertaken by j firm (or industry), whilst w_{ij} represents the technological distance between i and j. Nonetheless, it is very difficult to define the technological distance or closeness between firms of different industries. To what extent, for instance, are the research efforts of a metal manufacturing firm or a firm producing mechanical machinery useful to a firm in the electrical industry? It is essential to weight the R&D efforts in j_{th} industry borrowed by a firm in i_{th} industry. What weight though, can represent adequately the technological distance between disparate firms?

There is a wide variety of possible means of accomplishing this. According to Mohnen (1999), weights can be divided into two groups. Those of the first group are constructed according to the flow of capital goods, patents, innovations or citations between firms or industries. This is based on the argument that the more firm i buys the products of j, produces goods patented by j, uses innovations discovered by j and cites patents registered by j, the closer it is likely to be to j (Cincera, 1998; Mohnen, 1999). The weights of the second group are based on vectors that position firms (or industries) into different 'spaces'. These spaces may be categories of patents, R&D activities, lines of business or even the qualifications of their R&D scientists and engineers (Cincera, 1998).

Representative studies are those of Adams (1990), Goto and Suzuki (1989) and Jaffe (1986). Adams (1990) for example, having detailed data about the R&D personnel, constructed a map of technological proximity by grouping together firms which hired scientists with similar qualifications. By contrast, Goto and Suzuki (1989) used a weighting factor based on whether or not industries carried out the same kind of R&D. Jaffe (1986) constructed a technological-proximity matrix by using the distribution of each firm's patents over different categories of patents. As many researchers have emphasized, each of the above approaches has its drawbacks, as each of them puts emphasis on different aspects of an already unclear concept of technological distance. The best approach may be to construct vectors that take into account all the above factors. This is, however, subject to data availability.

Another way to investigate spillover effects more practically is firstly, to estimate the returns to R&D at both the firm-level and industry-level, and then to compare the difference. The extent to which the returns to R&D at the industry-level are higher than those at the firm-level indicates the degree of spillover effect. What is interesting however, is that the attempt of Mairesse and Mohnen (1990) to investigate spillovers using this method revealed that the coefficient of R&D at industry level was no higher than that at firm level. The authors argued that this result may be caused by the same depreciation rate which was set for both R&D and spillovers capital. As spillover capital embodies a large component of social returns, its depreciation rate should be much lower than that of R&D capital (Cincera, 1998). Nevertheless, Bernstein (1988), using a sample of seven Canadian industries, found that the social rates of return to R&D are higher than the private ones, thereby showing that R&D externalities do exist. Similarly, Bernstein and Nadiri (1989), using a sample of four US industries found that social returns exceed the private ones.

Given that the difficulty of formalizing R&D spillovers becomes greater when widening the notion of spillovers across industries, the crucial element of this exercise is to estimate the spillover flows. As discussed earlier, there two approaches to the construction of the spillover variables: a non-weighted approach and a weighted approach. In order to avoid the problem arising from aggregating external R&D using similar weights, the weight-based approach has been used to construct a different spillover capital for each firm within the research sample.

The framework employed here is similar to that described in Chapter 6 and used in Chapter 8. It is based on an extended Cobb-Douglas production function that includes a measure of each firm's own R&D capital (r_{it}), as well as a spillover component (S_{it}). The model expressed in logarithmic form is as follows:

$$q_{it} = a + ak_{it} + \beta l_{it} + \gamma r_{it} + \delta s_{it} + D_{industry} + D_{time} + \varepsilon_{it} \qquad (10.4)$$

In order to serve the objectives of the study, Equation 10.4 is re-written in terms of labour productivity:

$$(q_{it} - l_{it}) = a + a(k_{it} - l_{it}) + \gamma(r_{it} - l_{it}) + (\mu - 1)l_{it} + \delta(s_{it} - l_{it}) + D_{industry} + D_{time} + \varepsilon_{it} \ (10.5)$$

The sample used to estimate Equation 10.5 is that described in Chapter 7 (107 multinational corporations). The findings of this chapter can be considered as an extension of those of Chapter 8. The spillover component (S_{it}) of Equation 10.5 can represent different kinds of spillover effects. Two different specifications are considered here. The first includes two separate measures of spillover variables, one for intra-industry spillovers and another one for inter-industry spillovers. The second specification includes a measure of the total spillover capital (the sum of both intra-industry and inter-industry spillovers). The construction of the intra-industry and inter-industry spillover variables are described below.

3.2 Intra-industry Spillovers

The intra-industry spillover capital was constructed in order to investigate the extent to which R&D activities carried out in the industry to which the firm belongs, contribute to its productivity performance. Although this stock uses firm-specific information as do the existing micro level studies, it is not restricted to the aggregation of the R&D undertaken by the firms in our sample. Instead, it follows the work of Harhoff (2000) allowing all private R&D undertaken by UK firms to enter the spillover pool. Thus the constructed spillover capital not only captures the knowledge and ideas developed by the firms of our sample, but also includes the knowledge and ideas developed by the entire UK manufacturing sector.

Data for the total R&D undertaken by each two-digit or three-digit industry were acquired from the UK Office for National Statistics (ONS). In contrast to other studies that used the GDP price index to deflate R&D expenditures, we use the R&D price indices constructed in Chapter 5. Using these data, the method described in Chapter 6 was then used to construct an intra-industry stock of spillover capital for each firm separately. The depreciation rate of this stock was again set at 20 percent per year, and was corrected for double counting. Each firm's own R&D capital was deducted from the total intra-industry spillover capital. Thus each firm's final spillover capital ($S_{it,final}$) is the total spillover capital ($S_{it,total}$) of the industry to which it belongs minus its own R&D capital (R_{it}):

$$S_{it,final} = S_{it,total} - R_{it} \qquad (10.6)$$

3.3 Inter-industry Spillovers

As discussed earlier, firms not only borrow knowledge from their own industry, but also from firms of other industries (depending on the economic and technological distance from them; Griliches, 1992). The inter-industry spillover capital has been calculated as follows. Initially, a proximity matrix *W* with dimensions n x n was constructed to identify the technological distance between firms; that is, to identify the extent to which the knowledge and ideas developed in different industries were useful for each firm of our sample.

From all the weightings used in similar studies, the patent-based one is closer to the pure form of knowledge spillovers (Harhoff, 2000). Unfortunately, because data on patents were not available, it became necessary to use different weightings. Following the work of Terleckyj (1974), input-output data on the use of intermediate goods were utilized to construct a technological proximity matrix. The input-output table was obtained from the UK Office for National Statistics. It was a 122 x 122 dimensions table and included information on the intermediate goods used to produce 122 different categories of product.

Those products relevant to our study were grouped into the 15 two-digit or three-digit industries of our research sample. For example, products such as inorganic chemicals, organic chemicals and other chemical goods were incorporated into the chemical industry. Hence, a table of 15 x 15 dimensions was constructed. Each firm's capital of inter-industry spillovers is thus the weighted sum of 14 different R&D capital stocks:

$$S_i = \sum_{j=1}^{14} w_{ij} R_j \qquad (10.7)$$

R_j represents the R&D capital of industry j, whilst w_{ij} is the weighting factor of the technological distance between firm i and industry j taken from the input-output table. Once again, in order to deflate the R&D expenditures the R&D price indices constructed in Chapter 5 were used. The method used to construct the spillover stocks was that described in Chapter 6 with the depreciation rate again set at 20 percent per year.

4. FINDINGS

The following sections present the findings regarding the impact of spillovers on productivity performance. The first section presents the effects of total spillovers, whereas the next two sections present the impact of intra-industry and inter-industry spillovers respectively on productivity. Although both intra- and inter-industry variables are included in the model, in order to avoid any bias due to the inter-correlation of the two variables, the results are presented separately. We also investigate, in Section 4.4, the extent to which spillovers effects are influenced by the degree of a firm's internationalization.

4.1 Total Spillover Effects

Table 10.2 presents the main findings for the sample of 107 multinational corporations obtained by using the least squares method and the cross-sectional econometric specification (see Chapter 6). The first column reports the results found in Chapter 8. This means that only each firm's own R&D capital is included in the model. In order to determine the average contribution of external R&D to a firm's productivity, Model 2 estimates the total effect of spillovers. To do so, a spillover variable representing the total external knowledge available to each firm (that is, both intra- and inter-industry spillovers) is included in the regression.

As the fourth row indicates, the elasticity of total spillovers is positive at 0.06, confirming that when the whole sample is considered, the effects of spillovers are both economically and statistically insignificant. As the coefficient of spillovers is 0.06, it shows that when the within-industry knowledge stock increases by 1 percent, the labour productivity of a multinational corporation increases by an average of 0.06 percent. The findings also indicate that the multinational corporations of the sample can increase their productivity performance by building on the scientific knowledge and know-how transmitted by other firms, and by using the technologies developed by other companies within or outside their own industry. On the other hand, however, these results could be interpreted differently by an R&D director who might simply see the research activities of his own company improving rivals' performance.

The finding that the coefficient of spillovers is positive is not consistent with Wakelin's work (Wakelin, 2001). She found that the impact of spillovers on the productivity of 98 UK firms was statistically insignificant between 1988 and 1992. Our results also contradict those of Geroski (1991) at the industry-level, who found that the coefficient of spillovers was approximately zero. Nor are our findings in line with studies for other countries, such as those of Antonelli (1994) who provided evidence that spillovers had insignificant consequences for the productivity of 92 Italian firms. However, the results of Table 10.2 confirm data from many firm-level studies in the US and other industry-level findings for the UK, both of which suggest that the magnitude of the spillover effects is relatively high (Adams and Jaffe, 1996; Branstetter, 1996; Los and Verspagen, 2000; Anon Higon, 2004; Sterlacchini, 1989).

Table 10.2 The total effects of spillovers

	Model 1	Model 2	Model 3
Log (K/L)	0.20*** (0.02)	0.20*** (0.02)	0.19*** (0.02)
Log L	0.03*** (0.008)	0.07*** (0.02)	0.02^{ns} (0.02)
R&D elasticity	0.15*** (0.01)	0.16*** (0.01)	0.16*** (0.01)
Total spillover effects	-	0.06*** (0.02)	-
Total spillover effects (weighted by absorptive capacity)	-	-	0.00^{ns} (0.01)
Control for firm size	-	0.02^{ns} (0.02)	0.02^{ns} (0.02)
Control for technological opportunities	-	-0.05^{ns} (0.03)	-0.05^{ns} (0.03)
Control for time	yes	yes	yes
Control for industry	yes	yes	yes
R^2	0.37 (0.15)	0.35 (0.16)	0.35 (0.16)

Notes: ns = not significant, * 5% level of significance, ** 1% level of significance, *** 0.1% level of significance, the absence of a star indicates a level of significance of 10%.

The findings for the spillover variable of Model 3 go one step further. Many researchers have argued that some firms are very adept at drawing on external knowledge with considerable consequences for their productivity. According to the absorptive-capacity hypothesis of Cohen and Levinthal

(1989), the extent to which an organization can benefit from external knowledge depends on the level of its own research activities. Hence, the more R&D a firm undertakes, the more it is able to acquire and utilize other firms' knowledge. In order to test whether the data are consistent with the hypothesis of Cohen and Levinthal (1989), following the work of Harhoff (2000) an interaction variable was included. This variable is a measure of the intra-industry spillover capital weighted by each firm's own R&D; that is, $logS * logR$. Interestingly, the coefficient of spillover effects is now statistically insignificant, thereby providing no support to the hypothesis of absorptive capacity.

4.2 Intra-Industry Spillover Effects

Section 4.1 examined the effects of 'total' spillovers; that is, both intra- and inter-industry spillovers. This section analyzes separately the impacts of the R&D undertaken by intra-industry firms. Model 1 reports the results found in Chapter 8 (only each firm's own R&D capital is included in the model). Model 3 shows the findings concerning the intra-industry spillovers (without any weights). Although it had previously been found that the average (or total) effect of spillovers for the full sample was positive, the new findings revealed considerable differences. In contrast to the previous results, the findings of Model 3 clearly indicate that the contribution of within-industry knowledge to productivity performance at the firm-level is negative. It is worth noting, however, that even after the inclusion of the spillover variable the coefficient of own R&D remains stable at 0.15.

The spillover variable of Model 3, however, relies on the assumption that all R&D activities undertaken within the industry to which a firm belongs, are relevant and useful to the firm. Hence, it provides an unweighted measure of spillovers. However, the extent to which the within-industry knowledge is useful for a firm differs across industries. For instance, calculations based on the ONS input-output table showed that electrical and electronics firms buy approximately 40 percent of their intermediate inputs from their own industry. By contrast, only 9 percent of the intermediate inputs of minerals and instruments manufacturers are bought from their own industry.

Model 2 reports the findings when the intra-industry spillover capital is weighted according to the input-output flows. In other words, it is weighted according to the extent to which a firm buys intermediate goods from its own two- or three-digit industry. The coefficient of intra-industry spillovers is now statistically insignificant, thereby implying that the use of an un-weighted measure of spillovers may lead to a significant bias. As the new results suggest, intra-industry spillovers on average do not affect the productivity performance of multinational corporations.

Table 10.3 The intra-industry effects of spillovers

	Model 1	Model 2	Model 3	Model 4
Log (K/L)	0.20*** (0.02)	0.20*** (0.02)	0.20*** (0.02)	0.22*** (0.02)
Log L	0.03*** (0.008)	0.12*** (0.03)	-0.01^{ns} (0.05)	0.10** (0.04)
R&D elasticity	0.15*** (0.01)	0.17*** (0.01)	0.15*** (0.01)	0.28*** (0.04)
Intra-industry spillovers (IO weighted)	-	-0.02^{ns} (0.02)	-	-
Intra-industry spillovers (without weights)	-	-	-0.13*** (0.03)	-
Intra-industry spillovers (absorptive capacity)	-	-	-	-0.04*** (0.01)
Control for firm size	-	0.04* (0.02)	0.02^{ns} (0.02)	0.04* (0.02)
Control for tech. opportunities	-	0.20** (0.07)	0.10 (0.06)	0.12* (0.06)
Control for time	yes	yes	yes	yes
Control for industry	yes	yes	yes	yes
R^2	0.37 (0.15)	0.54 (0.12)	0.36 (0.15)	0.36 (0.15)

Notes: ns = not significant, * 5% level of significance, ** 1% level of significance, *** 0.1% level of significance, the absence of a star indicates a level of significance of 10%.

To confirm the findings of Model 2, we have re-calculated the results using a weight that takes into account each firm's absorptive capacity. Model 4 reports the findings. The new intra-industry spillover variable is statistically significant and negative at -0.04. Although the improved statistical significance of the spillover effects provides some support to the hypothesis of absorptive capacity, it is surprising that the coefficient is even lower. This may be a result of the fact that because each firm's own R&D capital is incorporated in the new variable, multi-collinearity problems ensue (the effects of which are severe since this changes the coefficient of R&D capital from 0.17 to 0.28).

Overall, the results from the three different models support that the intra-industry spillover effects measured in this study tend to be negative, suggesting that the R&D undertaken by their competitors has considerably negative consequences for their productivity. The findings are consistent with the arguments discussed in Section 2 that the R&D undertaken by a firm's competitors, by improving their products and processes, leads to increased competition, and in consequence it has negative effects on productivity. It also supports Mohnen (1996) who pointed that the effects of spillovers can be either positive or negative depending on whether the products from outside R&D are substitutes or complements for a firm's own products.

4.3 Inter-Industry Spillover Effects

Having investigated in the previous section the effects of *intra*-industry spillovers, the next step is to estimate the impact that *inter*-industry spillovers have on productivity performance. As Sterlacchini (1989) suggested, inter-industry spillovers are particularly important for industries that undertake little R&D, but buy goods embodying other industries' R&D. Table 10.4 presents the main findings for the sample of 107 multinational corporations. For comparison purposes, Model 1 reports the results when only each firm's own R&D capital is included in the model. Model 2 reports the findings for our main input-output weighted inter-industry spillover variable.

The use of appropriate weights is particularly important because, as our calculations have shown, there are industries such as motor vehicles, paper and printing, in which only 17 percent of their intermediate inputs are taken from the other 14 industries of the sample. On the other hand, in industries such as metals, up to 70 percent of their intermediate inputs are taken from other industries. As Table 10.4 indicates, the coefficient of the weighted measure of inter-industry spillovers is positive at 0.12 and statistically significant. Hence, on average the knowledge and ideas developed by firms in industries different from that to which a firm belongs have a very positive impact on its productivity performance. Nevertheless, we should note that when we employed an un-weighted measure of spillovers, the coeffient decreased significantly, confirming once again that the lack of such corrections may lead to biased estimates.

Generally, the findings of Table 10.4 confirm Geroski (1995) who has argued that as external new technologies can be used as a base for future discoveries, it is likely that spillovers will be complementary for a firm's own research activities, and will consequently have a positive effect on performance. On the other hand, as our findings indicate that the effects of inter-industry spillovers are positive and high, they stand in direct contrast with previous studies such as that of Bernstein (1988) for Canada that showed that intra-industry spillovers are more significant than inter-industry spillovers. Even though the usefulness of external R&D tends to be highest for a firm if it is undertaken by firms in the industry to which this firm belongs (Griliches, 1992), it seems that the negative effects of intense R&D competition outweigh the corresponding potential benefits.

Table 10.4 The inter-industry effects of spillovers

	Model 1	Model 2	Model 3
Log (K/L)	0.20*** (0.02)	0.20*** (0.03)	0.20*** (0.02)
Log L	0.03*** (0.008)	0.12*** (0.03)	0.06** (0.02)
R&D elasticity	0.15*** (0.01)	0.17*** (0.01)	0.16*** (0.01)
Inter-industry spillover effects (IO weighted)	-	0.12** (0.04)	-
Inter-industry spillover effects (without weights)	-	-	0.03** (0.01)
Control for firm size	-	0.04* (0.02)	0.02^{ns} (0.02)
Control for technological opportunities	-	0.20** (0.07)	-0.02^{ns} (0.02)
Control for time	yes	yes	yes
Control for industry	yes	yes	yes
R^2	0.37 (0.15)	0.54 (0.12)	0.34 (0.16)

Notes: ns = not significant, * 5% level of significance, ** 1% level of significance, *** 0.1% level of significance, the absence of a star indicates a level of significance of 10%.

To investigate whether the hypothesis of absorptive capacity is valid in the case of inter-industry spillovers, Model 1 of Table 10.5 describes what happens when the inter-industry spillover variable is weighted by each firm's own R&D capital. The effects of spillovers are now not significant, showing for one more time that the hypothesis of absorptive capacity is not confirmed with our data. The previous findings, however, should be interpreted cautiously. As discussed earlier, it is difficult to define empirically the concept of technological distance. So one cannot be sure of the extent to which our weighting matrix w_{ij} reflects the real technological relationship between firms. As many researchers have argued, it may be the case that firms benefit when they are very close or very distant from other companies.

Table 10.5 The inter-industry effects of spillovers (different weights)

	Model 1	Model 2	Model 3
Log (K/L)	0.21*** (0.03)	0.21*** (0.03)	0.21*** (0.03)
Log L	0.03^{ns} (0.02)	0.08** (0.03)	0.05* (0.0)
R&D elasticity	0.16*** (0.03)	0.16*** (0.01)	0.16*** (0.01)
Inter-industry spillover effects (absorptive capacity)	0.00^{ns} (0.01)	-	-
Inter-industry spillover effects (emphasis on distant industries)	-	0.05* (0.02)	-
Inter-industry spillover effects (emphasis on neighbour ind.)	-	-	0.02* (0.008)
Control for firm size	0.03^{ns} (0.02)	0.02^{ns} (0.02)	0.02^{ns} (0.02)
Control for technological opportunities	-0.05^{ns} (0.04)	-0.00^{ns} (0.04)	-0.00^{ns} (0.04)
Control for time	yes	yes	yes
Control for industry	yes	yes	yes
R^2	0.33 (0.16)	0.34 (0.16)	0.34 (0.16)

Notes: ns = not significant, * 5% level of significance, ** 1% level of significance, *** 0.1% level of significance, the absence of a star indicates a level of significance of 10%.

In order to investigate the sensitivity of our findings to changes in the definition of 'technological closeness', we followed the work of researchers such as Harhoff (2000) and used alternative weighting metrics that are nested within an exponential transformation. We transformed the weighting matrix w_{ij} as $w'_{ij}=w^{\alpha}_{ij}$ with $\alpha>0$. The rationale behind this transformation is that the distance between a firm's own R&D and external R&D might be a nonlinear function of the matrix w_{ij}. Hence, following previous studies, whilst the initial linearly-weighted spillover variable was based on $\alpha=1$, two new spillover variables were constructed for values of α equal to 0.33 and 2. When α takes values smaller than 1, it allows the R&D of 'distant' firms to be weighted more strongly in the constructed spillover variable. Conversely, when $\alpha>1$ then distant R&D activities are weighted less strongly (Harhoff, 2000).

The last two columns (Model 2 and Model 3) in Table 10.5 report the findings when the spillover variables with the alternative weighting metrics took the place of the initial inter-industry variable (see Model 2 in Table 10.4). The elasticity of spillovers for Model 2 (which gives emphasis to the R&D of distant firms) is significantly lower (at 0.05) than the elasticity found when the standard model was employed (at 0.12). Similarly, the elasticity of spillovers for Model 3 (based on the notion that R&D of neighbour firms is more important) decreased significantly at 0.02. At the same time, both variables became less (statistically) significant. These findings do not favour a broader definition of the spillover pool. In other words, it seems that multinational corporations are not capable of drawing knowledge successfully from very close or more distant industries. These results, however, contradict those of Harhoff (2000) who found that the impact of spillovers on productivity of German manufacturing firms remained relatively stable when alternative values of α were used.

4.4 Internationalization and Spillover Effects

Even though past studies recognized the importance of monitoring and using external knowledge and technologies, they often ignored the fact that depending on a number of factors, firms look at external inventions in different ways (Chesbrough, 2007). As discussed in Chapter 3 and empirically confirmed in Chapter 8, the degree of a firm's internationalization plays a crucial role. We have argued that multinational corporations have a number of firm-specific characteristics that allow them to develop new technologies successfully, and exploit the benefits of innovation better. Similarly, one may argue that there are a number of factors that may influence the assets, resources and market positions of highly internationalized companies and in turn, the impact that spillovers have on their productivity performance. In this section, we test whether a firm's ability to draw external knowledge successfully is influenced by its degree of internationalization (that is, the extent to which firms operate beyond their national borders; Kotabe et al., 2002). In order to do so, using the approach employed in Chapter 8, we split the sample into firms with a higher and lower degree of internationalization, and estimated the model for each subgroup separately. Table 10.6 reports the results for the total spillover effects.

Table 10.6 Degree of internationalization (DOI) and total spillovers

	Low DOI	High DOI
Log (K/L)	0.20*** (0.05)	0.20*** (0.03)
Log L	0.13* (0.05)	0.07** (0.03)
R&D elasticity	0.10*** (0.03)	0.18*** (0.01)
Total spillover effects	0.07^{ns} (0.05)	0.04 (0.02)
Control for firm size	-0.06^{ns} (0.04)	0.04* (0.02)
Control for technological opportunities	-0.18** (0.05)	0.02^{ns} (0.04)
Control for time	yes	yes
Control for industry	yes	yes
R^2	0.25 (0.18)	0.54 (0.13)

Notes: ns = not significant, * 5% level of significance, ** 1% level of significance, *** 0.1% level of significance, the absence of a star indicates a level of significance of 10%.

The findings indicate that the impact of total spillovers is for both sub-samples statistically insignificant, implying that they do not have important consequences for the productivity of multinational corporations. For this reason, we re-estimated the model using intra- and inter-industry variables. Table 10.7 reports the recalculated results. As the findings indicate, the R&D

undertaken by intra-industry firms does not have a significant impact on firm productivity performance. Nevertheless, the effects of inter-industry spillovers differ significantly across the two groups of firms. The relevant coefficient for those firms with a lower degree of internationalization is 0.28, whereas (in contrast to our expectations), the corresponding coefficient for those with greater degree of internationalization is markedly lower at 0.12.

Table 10.7 Degree of internationalization (DOI), intra- and inter-industry spillovers

	Low DOI	High DOI
Log (K/L)	0.22*** (0.05)	0.20*** (0.03)
Log L	0.28*** (0.08)	0.12*** (0.04)
R&D elasticity	0.10*** (0.03)	0.18*** (0.01)
Intra-industry spillover effects (IO weighted)	-0.03^{ns} (0.04)	-0.02^{ns} (0.02)
Inter-industry spillover effects (IO weighted)	0.28** (0.10)	0.12** (0.04)
Control for firm size	-0.06^{ns} (0.04)	0.04* (0.02)
Control for technological opportunities	0.19^{ns} (0.14)	0.20** (0.07)
Control for time	yes	yes
Control for industry	yes	yes
R^2	0.26 (0.18)	0.54 (0.13)

Notes: ns = not significant, * 5% level of significance, ** 1% level of significance, *** 0.1% level of significance, the absence of a star indicates a level of significance of 10%.

Even though the findings of Chapter 8 indicated that the economic returns to innovation are significantly higher for firms with a high degree of internationalization, it seems that the less internationalized firms can benefit even more from the technologies developed by inter-industry companies. This result might be explained by the fact that as this study examined the effects of R&D spillovers in the UK (rather than those of international spillovers), it may be the case that whereas less internationalized firms focus and build on the ideas, know-how and technologies developed in the UK, highly internationalized firms with dispersed R&D sites prefer to exploit the knowledge developed in other countries. Unfortunately, the lack of appropriate data does not allow us to confirm empirically this argument.

5. LIMITATIONS

Many of the limitations of this research are similar to those of previous studies. Besides the limitations related to the Cobb-Douglas framework (see Chapter 8), the source of most problems relates to the measurement of output and inputs. With regard to the measurement of output, sales may not capture immeasurable improvements such as improved quality and variety. Nor do official price indices fully account for its improvements. As a result, the estimated contribution of R&D spillovers to firms' productivity performance is likely to be lower than it should be. An additional downward bias may arise from the fact that due to the lack of data regarding the materials used in production, it was necessary to use sales, rather than value added. Similarly, the measurement of capital, labour and R&D capital is difficult to determine accurately. However, as the issues associated with these inputs have been discussed in detail in the previous chapters, we focus on the limitations associated with the measurement of the spillover flows.

One limitation is engendered by the fact that we identify the technological distance between firms by using input-output data. As has been emphasized by Griliches (1992), this weighting approach tends to underestimate the role of pure knowledge spillovers. This is because it is based on economic transactions between companies, rather than on technological association between firms (Van Meijl, 1995). So the spillover effects estimated here embody both knowledge and rent spillovers. Although the use of data about the extent to which one firm cites patents registered by other firms would be preferable, these were not available to us.

Nevertheless, we believe that spillover flows are so complicated that both patents and input-output data are crude ways to infer the degree to which one firm can embody external knowledge in developing its products and processes. Griliches (1992) emphasized that the knowledge pool that researchers construct is not in itself indicative of how much of this knowledge can be spilled over to other organizations, or who the potential recipients of the transmitted knowledge will be. This leads to a further limitation, associated with the fact that many firms in the sample are diversified. As a result, they may draw knowledge from a much wider pool than that constructed. Conversely, the smaller firms in the sample may draw knowledge from a much narrower product field. Quoting Griliches (1992, p.42): 'The small firm will have specialized in a much narrower niche than is described by the available SIC classification'. In such cases, no matter what weights were used, the knowledge pool hypothesized for each firm may include knowledge which is irrelevant and not useful to a particular firm.

Finally, as noted in the previous chapters, R&D is in itself aggregated in terms of composition as it includes activities such as basic, applied, product and process R&D. Hence, this study (like similar studies) cannot identify the types of R&D that are spilled more (or less) easily to other firms. For instance, it is likely that product R&D would 'leak' more easily to the external world. By contrast, possibly only a small part of process R&D is transmissible to other firms. The time needed for knowledge to diffuse also varies, depending on the type of R&D. Thus it seems worthwhile to estimate different spillover pools for each type of R&D, and re-estimate the model. This should make it feasible to identify those types of R&D with high social value; that is, R&D that can be spilled over easily and that makes a significant contribution to other firms' productivity. The results of this exercise could be then used by government agents to fund appropriate types of research that are more useful to society.

6. CONCLUSION AND FUTURE RESEARCH

Building on the argument that in order to unlock their potential, companies must actively search for and exploit external technologies and sources of knowledge (Chesbrough, 2003; 2007), this chapter assessed the impact of both intra-industry and inter-industry spillovers on the productivity performance of multinational corporations. The use of firm-level data allowed us to estimate the extent to which a firm (rather than an industry) benefits from the research efforts of other organizations. The analysis revealed a number of important findings that may improve the academic and managerial understanding of the spillovers-performance relationship.

First of all, the total effect of spillovers for the whole sample is positive and relatively high. Even though many previous studies have emphasized the importance of absorptive capacity, our data do not always support this hypothesis. The findings indicated that a linear measure of spillovers performs better than a broad or narrow spillover definition. When we estimated the intra- and inter-industry effects separately, we found both positive and negative spillovers. In other words, even though firms must create additional value by exploiting external sources of innovation (Chesbrough, 2007), our findings suggest that not all firms are able to do this.

To be specific, the productivity effects of the R&D undertaken by intra-industry competitors is either negative or statistically insignificant, suggesting that intense competition from rivals either outweighs or neutralizes the positive knowledge externalities. Conversely, the R&D undertaken by companies in more distantly related industries (whose products either complement a firm's own products or are not directly related to them) can have positive consequences for productivity performance, as shown by the fact that positive inter-industry spillovers were more significant than intra-industry ones.

We also find that spillover effects vary, depending on the degree of a firm's internationalization. Our analysis indicates that although intra-industry spillovers were insignificant for both sub-samples, there are greater benefits from inter-industry spillovers for firms with a lower degree of internationalization than for the more highly internationalized firms. An implication of this finding is that future theoretical predictions about knowledge externalities should be linked to a firm's international expansion. Equally, in order to examine the role of outside R&D more accurately, empirical research should take into account those factors.

The findings of this chapter when combined with the results of Chapter 8 provide a better understanding of the mechanisms underlying the relationship between the stock of scientific knowledge and productivity performance. As demonstrated in Chapter 8, R&D does have a significant direct impact on productivity performance. Firms that undertake R&D, however, may also benefit from the indirect R&D-effect of knowledge spillovers. These results suggest that in order to keep their technological leadership, multinational corporations should effectively incorporate external inventions in their R&D processes (Chesbrough, 2007). Many R&D directors have already started doing so by giving rewards to scientists who adopt ideas from elsewhere (De Bondt, 1996). It is also hoped that the research findings of this chapter may help the government to formulate policies that will enhance firms' innovative capacity and productivity performance. As Mohnen (1999) has emphasized, by understanding whether the spillovers transmitted by certain types of firms generate greater effects than those transmitted by other types of firms, the government might be able to assist the circulation of knowledge.

The work in this chapter can be extended in a number of ways. Even though emphasis was put on the role of knowledge produced by the industrial sector, much research is also undertaken by universities. Although academic research is only rarely directly translated into new products (Pavitt, 2001), in many industries there is a strong relationship between universities and industrial innovation (Klevorick et al., 1995). This has also been confirmed by the findings of Laursen and Salter (2004), that indicate that UK firms that undertake R&D draw knowledge from university research. Hence, it seems worthwhile to assess the extent to which academic research can advance firms' productivity.

Another way to extend this study is to investigate whether external R&D is a complementary to or a substitute for the firm's own research efforts. To do so, one could use models whose dependent variable is R&D spending (rather than output). Representative work in this field is that of Harhoff (2000) and Jaffe (1988). Similarly, the analysis of this chapter could be extended to include an international spillover capital, thereby assessing the effects of the R&D undertaken by firms in other countries. A final suggestion for future research relates to the measurement of spillover flows. One could perhaps reduce the probability of including irrelevant and not useful knowledge into a firm's spillover capital by interviewing R&D personnel in the firms, asking about their competitors and the sources of knowledge they use. A spillover capital that would be analogous to the knowledge sources that each firm indicated could then be constructed.

This would be a novel approach because (without including all the international spillover capital) it takes into account the knowledge and ideas developed by some non-UK firms. The rationale behind this suggestion is that a firm does not have the capacity to trace and assimilate all the knowledge developed by other firms. By contrast, it may be argued that it possibly focuses on the knowledge produced by a small number of firms. In that case, one would be able to measure much more accurately the relevant knowledge, and construct a spillover capital that is much more specific to each firm.

11. The Role of the Internet in Explaining Innovation Performance

The ability of a firm to develop new technologies defines to a great extent its competitiveness. Although there are many studies that present practical examples of how firms utilize the Internet to support their everyday research activities, there is not much theory to explain how and why the Internet improves innovation performance (or R&D efficiency). This chapter fills this void by exploring the association between the Internet and R&D efficiency. Initially, to provide a better unit of analysis, it adopts a feature-based approach to the Internet. Then it offers a conceptual framework which by using theoretical explanations, past empirical research and examples from practice explains how and why two features of the Internet ('search' and 'communication') improve three critical dimensions of R&D efficiency (cost, time and quality) and a firm's absorptive capacity. Finally, although it is difficult to provide econometric evidence (as the availability of data is limited), it offers some preliminary findings that can be used as a basis for future research. Note that many parts of this chapter have been reprinted from the study of Kafouros (2006; Journal of Technovation).

1. INTRODUCTION

During the last two decades, product life cycles have been shortened dramatically. For instance, during the 1980s the life cycle of semiconductor products shrank by 25 percent (Iansiti and West, 1997). The continually shorter product life cycles affected firms' profitability and forced them to improve the productivity of their Research and Development departments (R&D-efficiency), i.e. to accelerate the development cycle, reduce costs and improve quality. Firms responded by integrating into their development process new information and Internet technologies, the adoption of which resulted in more productive R&D departments. A vivid example of this is the automotive industry which during the 1990s decreased the average development cycle from 60 to only 18 months (Advanced Manufacturing, July 2001). The new technologies, and the informational changes that accompanied them, transformed the traditional way in which R&D individuals communicate and collect information. For instance, the previous 'mainframe' computing architecture was replaced by Internet-based systems enhancing the communication between R&D teams (OECD, 2001a). At the same time, the Internet became one of the largest sources of scientific and commercial information in the world.

Although the integration of Internet technologies has had a significant impact on the efficiency of R&D-process, the role of the Internet is disregarded by the R&D literatures. For instance, the R&D econometric literature has never quantified the impact of the Internet on R&D-efficiency. The literature relating to R&D spillovers investigates the role of external knowledge, but does not focus on the medium by which firms acquire and disseminate that knowledge. Similarly, although there are many technology and R&D management studies that present practical examples of how firms utilize the Internet to support their everyday research activities, there is little theory to explain how and why the Internet should improve R&D-efficiency. This chapter aims to fill that void. It contributes to research firstly by offering a theoretical framework that conceptualizes how and why the Internet improves the productivity of the R&D-process of manufacturing firms, and secondly by providing preliminary empirical evidence concerning the relationship between R&D-efficiency and the Internet.

2. LITERATURE REVIEW

There is little research that systematically investigates how the Internet affects R&D-efficiency. Two studies that are consistent with our objectives and which provide a basis for our analysis are those of Howe et al. (2000) and Kessler (2003). Howe et al. (2000) use the so-called stage-gate approach (an operational model for moving new products from ideas to launch) to demonstrate how the Internet and Intranet applications can support new product development. Kessler (2003) uses a different approach. He provides a knowledge-based framework for understanding the interaction between the Internet and R&D. Specifically, he investigates how the Internet through various knowledge flows affects the process speed, project efficiency and product quality. As it will be observed later, however, we use a different approach. We separate the Internet into two technological components (or features) and analyse the impact of those features on R&D-efficiency.

In addition to these two studies, there are many scattered observations, arguments and pieces of evidence indicating that R&D teams utilize the Internet to improve their productivity. Antonelli et al. (2000) point out that the Internet has changed the process of knowledge accumulation. Baujard et al. (1998) emphasize that the Internet makes information retrieval easier. Similarly, Mitchell (2000) argues that the Internet transforms the processes by which R&D teams acquire and create knowledge and Bakos (1991) argues that electronic marketplaces reduce the costs incurred to acquire information. Hellstrom et al. (2001) describe how a network database of cooperating projects was built by utilising the Internet. Sawhney and Prandelli (2000) explain how the Internet can be used to organize 'communities of creation' which provide a dynamic environment of knowledge creation and sharing.

Firms can also use virtual reality (as a simulation exercise) to imitate complex, time consuming and expensive processes (Gardiner and Ritchie, 1999). For instance, Dahan and Srivinasan (2000) describe an Internet-based method that helps firms to test different concepts and select the best one. Richir et al. (2001) demonstrate an analogous digital-design process that allows products to be kept virtual throughout the design process. The Internet can also facilitate better internal and external communication (Gupta, 1997). Hibbard and Carrillo (1998), for example, explain how online software can provide a network to communicate and share knowledge across departments and business units. Knowledge-sharing is significant for R&D-efficiency because, as Nonaka and Takeuchi (1995) emphasize, innovation is empowered when the knowledge accumulated from the 'outside' is shared within the firm. Similarly, Kodama (1999) argues that the use of information networks leads to innovation and value creation.

The Internet can change not only the final product but also the entire process of R&D. For example, Iansiti and McCormack (1997) demontrate that when product designers use the Internet, they adopt flexible processes which allow them to continue to improve the products even after implementation has begun. Thus the cost of and time for testing alternative options is reduced. Other researchers demonstrate that R&D teams use the Internet for online comparison of the available components as well as to communicate interactively with suppliers and customers (Ghosh, 1998; Plymale and Hartgrove, 1999). In summary, although there are many examples that show that firms utilize the Internet to support their product development, there is not much theory to explain how and why the Internet improves R&D-efficiency.

3. THEORETICAL FRAMEWORK

The studies we reviewed in the previous section emphasize that the Internet is important for both information acquisition and for internal and external communication. The examples in which R&D departments use Internet and Intranet networking tools, either to collect information or to communicate are plentiful and easy to identify. For instance, traditional mail has largely been replaced by electronic mail; virtual teams communicate and work from distance; Intranet networks are utilized to exchange documents, and individuals can access online journals, download documents and use the Web to monitor competitors' products and patents.

3.1 The Features of the Internet

In order to investigate how networking tools such as the above improve R&D-efficiency, they need to be categorized. Following authors who break down the structure of a technology according to its features (see DeSanctis and Poole, 1994; Griffith, 1999 among others), the impact of two major features of the Internet, 'search' and 'communication', will be investigated.

The 'search' feature gives access to more sources of information. It includes the networking tools and activities that are related to searching, finding, retrieving and collecting the required information; for example, access to online papers, search engines and knowledge databases.

The 'communication' feature affects the communication within R&D department, across departments and associated organizations. Vivid examples of the 'communication' feature are online communities, electronic mail, virtual discussion rooms and e-conferencing.

A feature-based approach provides the best method of analysis as any improvement of R&D is actually caused not by the whole Internet but by its features. Griffith (1999) confirms this view arguing that features are the building blocks or component parts of a technology. Similarly, Griffith and Northcraft (1994) argue that any technology is actually a combination of features. The concept of features is also used in other research fields. For example, marketing scholars study consumers using models in which products embody a bundle of characteristics or attributes (Griffith, 1999). Having identified the Internet features in this section, we illustrate below the dynamic connections between the features of the Internet and R&D-efficiency.

3.2 How does the Internet Influence Innovation Performance?

One way of understanding how the Internet improves R&D-efficiency is to focus on how its features affect the factors which determine R&D-efficiency. According to past literature, these factors are many (see Cooper and Kleinschmidt, 1995). However, in order to simplify our analysis we concentrate on the three classic measures of project success: (1) Cost, i.e. the financial requirements of the entire process, (2) Time, i.e. the time from the conceptualization stage of a product to its final introduction to the market, and (3) Quality, i.e. the degree to which the final product satisfies customers' preferences such as size, robustness, and ease of use. The following subsections explain how and why the Internet features affect these three critical dimensions of R&D-efficiency, and also describe how the Internet is associated with the concept of 'absorptive capacity'.

3.2.1 The connection between the 'search' feature and cost, time and quality

The 'search' feature of the Internet can dramatically reduce the cost of accessing, searching, retrieving and storing the required information by providing low cost sources of information such as e-books, forums, newsgroups and conferences. Individuals can at low cost request information from institutions, retrieve information from archives and keep themselves updated through automated newsletters. For instance, using the online community 'experts-exchange' (www.experts-exchange.com), R&D members can get answers to IT queries free of charge. Another example of how the Internet can reduce costs relates to library facilities. Until the late 1980s, R&D departments were forced to buy hardcopies of books, journals and catalogues of components. However, the cost of buying and storing hardcopies as well as the cost of maintaining and managing a within-firm library was very high. These costs were even higher for internationalized, and thus decentralized, firms that had to maintain libraries in each R&D centre. In recent years, however, the majority of the required books and journals are bought in electronic form. Therefore, the cost is dramatically lower because firstly, there is no need to buy several copies as they can be shared between individuals at any distance and secondly, e-copies do not need physical storage.

Access to suppliers' information is also less costly as their Web sites provide online knowledge databases and other valuable search tools. R&D teams can also use the Internet to identify potential suppliers for negligible costs. For instance Barua et al. (1997) searched for local area network suppliers to connect firm's offices. Using a Web search engine, they located 352 potential resellers whilst a search of the 'yellow pages' furnished only 14 firms. The cost of searching within-firm information is also lower. With the help of Intranets, databases and data-mining techniques, the knowledge created from past projects (or at least the explicit part of this knowledge) can be codified and stored in databases and thus easily accessed and shared at any time. Documentation allows individuals to digitalize what they know and thus enrich their firm's database (Nonaka and Takeuchi, 1995).

Furthermore, the 'search' feature of the Internet has a significant impact not only on cost but also on the time required for the completion of a project. For instance, in the electronic industry, the development of devices requires the use of the so-called 'data-books' (manuals of Integrated Circuits, IC). Until the late 1980s, a lot of time was spent by engineers to search these manuals. In recent years, however, data-books have become available online and engineers, by accessing the Web sites of IC manufacturers, can now find immediately what they need, access knowledge databases, download design tools and order the parts they need.

The time-consuming manual search has thus been replaced by sophisticated electronic search engines helping R&D teams to find the required information in less time. For example, British Telecom (BT) uses a system which summarizes documents down to 25 percent of the initial size. As a result, they can manage more efficiently the volume of information (Dennis et al., 1998). Furthermore, the retrieval of information is also easier and faster since the 'intangibility' of designs and documents allow them to be downloaded in almost no time at any distance from the source (Baujard et al., 1998). BT, for example, has used the Internet to reduce the turnaround time of information from weeks to days (Dennis et al., 1998). In summary, as Howe et al. (2000) argue, the easier access to data and documents has helped firms to reduce the development cycles and achieve lead time reductions.

Equally, the 'search' feature can improve product quality. The Internet is itself a large up-to-date library that increases the amount of information available to R&D teams. Firms are no longer restricted to internal resources. Instead, as Mitchell (2000) emphasizes, they can capture creativity and value from the global public. The within-firm sources of knowledge are also improved as by utilizing modern knowledge-management techniques and Intranet networks, firms can capture the knowledge of previous and current employees, thereby increasing the organizational memory (Kessler, 2003). The increased knowledge leads to improved quality as it allows teams to create, explore and test a much larger number of technological components, and choose the most appropriate ones according to the dimensions and characteristics that the final product requires (see Dahan and Srivinasan, 2000; Richir et al., 2001).

Network mechanisms can further improve quality. Iansiti and McCormack (1997) argue that these mechanisms enable the continuous flow of information about customer needs and preferences, and thus allow R&D teams to integrate changing customer requirements into the products. For example, Finch (1999) by analysing an archive of 1600 online discussions acquired valuable information that contributed to better understanding of how customers view a firm's product relative to competitors' products. R&D teams by accessing Web sites that provide demographic information and statistics about customer preferences (see for example www.researchinfo.com) can fine-tune products to satisfy customers' needs. Both Microsoft and AT&T use the services of Websitesurveys.com to collect data for consumer preferences (Howe et al., 2000) whilst BT publishes a customer-requirement document that informs R&D staff about the new preferences of customers (Dennis et al., 1998). In summary, by accessing larger sources of information R&D departments can increase the quality of products since they can collect more information, create more technological components and examine more possible versions of the final product.

Hence we may conclude that: The 'search' feature of the Internet can improve R&D-efficiency by decreasing the cost and the time devoted to access, search, retrieve and store the required information. It can also improve R&D-efficiency by increasing the quality of final products.

3.2.2 The connection between the 'communication' feature and cost, time and quality

The 'communication' feature of the Internet is also very significant as the success of development process is closely connected to efficient communication; that is, quantity and quality of communication (Damanpour, 1991; Gardiner and Ritchie, 1999). The 'communication' feature can dramatically reduce both the internal and external communication costs arising from coordination (particularly when R&D teams are in geographically dispersed locations). By allowing easy and direct links it can offer services inexpensively (Ghosh, 1998). For instance, electronic mail has replaced the traditional mail while the ordinary telephone is gradually been replaced by the Internet phone (voice over IP) that uses the Internet connection to deliver voice at any distance at very low cost.

The Internet and online software can also provide low cost communication across departments and business units (Hameri and Nihtila, 1997; Hibbard and Carrillo, 1998). Furthermore, a number of frequent face-to-face meetings across departments and organizations can now be carried out at distance as the Internet provides a virtual environment for video-conferencing and telecommuting (remote work). IBM by using video-conferencing technology has succeeded in decreasing dramatically travelling costs (Boutellier et al., 1998). In a similar way, the 'communication' feature can reduce the time required for the completion of a project by reducing the time R&D teams spend in communicating and coordinating with other teams, departments and associated organizations.

The time required for coordination is significant as in many cases the project team consists of hundreds of engineers from many different departments, firms and institutes (Hameri and Nihtila, 1997). Particularly when R&D teams, departments and suppliers are in geographically dispersed locations, the Internet by providing a virtual environment for e-conferencing, allows individuals to communicate at a distance decreasing the time that was spent on document exchange, face-to-face meetings and travelling. Unilever, for example, adopted a platform that informs members in real time about project progress using Lotus Notes (Ciborra and Patriotta, 1998). This can also reduce the need for simultaneous engineering that is costly.

The argument that electronic methods offer faster coverage as compared to traditional ones has also been demonstrated empirically. Hameri and Nihtila (1997), using data from a project database server found that the time lag between data entry and retrieval is almost zero. Many examples confirm that the Internet accelerates the development process by improving communication. Herman Miller, a multinational office furniture manufacturer, succeeded in reducing production time by creating a Web site that improved communication with suppliers (Howe et al., 2000). Furthermore, there is strong association between the 'communication' feature and quality. The Internet not only provides cheap and fast communication but also facilitates better communication. As Kessler (2003) argues, by providing channels that did not exist before, it circulates ideas and information. For instance, R&D individuals who use Internet telephones can send and receive text messages, depict pictures and graphs and communicate asynchronously with their colleagues in decentralized departments. In other cases, by using video-conference technology, online meetings can take place instead of simple phone calls.

There are many examples from industrial practice that confirm that the Internet by facilitating efficient communication at several organizational levels improves quality. Sweeney (1999) emphasizes that geographically dispersed teams in Ford Motor, do not just communicate but can examine rotating 3-D car models through the Internet. Similarly, Extranets serve as communicational channels to interact with customers and associate firms, receive feedback, identify changes in preferences and locate potential problems. Such information allows R&D teams to comprehend customers' perceptions, identify what dimensions of the product need to be changed, and customize it according to these preferences.

Based on these arguments, we propose that the 'communication' feature of the Internet can improve R&D-efficiency by decreasing the costs and the time R&D teams spend to communicate and coordinate with other teams, departments and associated organizations. In addition (like the 'search' feature), it improves R&D-efficiency by increasing the quality of final products.

3.2.3 The connection between the Internet and absorptive capacity

Another way of understanding how the Internet improves R&D-efficiency is to investigate how it is associated with the concept of absorptive capacity. According to Cohen and Levinthal (1990), absorptive capacity is a firm's ability to capture external information, assimilate it, and apply it to ongoing projects. They argue that there are three main factors that influence absorptive capacity: (1) a firm's existing-knowledge, (2) a firm's interface with external sources of knowledge, and (3) a firm's ability to transfer knowledge within and across departments. We argue that although the Internet cannot affect the first factor (which is mainly connected to a firm's previous investments in R&D), it can dramatically influence the other two.

The second factor refers to the acquisition of knowledge and to the elements which increase a firm's ability to access the external environment. This external knowledge embodies a number of different knowledge sources including the knowledge created by universities, government institutions and the R&D departments of other firms. However, the ability of a firm to access these sources is limited. The ease (or difficulty) of accessing them depends on the media that a firm uses to reach them. We term these media 'external channels' and we consider them as the firm's linkages to the external environment. We argue that the Internet improves the interaction of a firm with the external environment firstly by improving the already established external channels and secondly by providing channels which did not exist before. The improvement of the established external channels allows a firm to obtain more knowledge. For example, an already established interaction between a firm and its suppliers can be improved by electronic mail and other online tools. The Internet can also provide new external channels and offer linkages that were not available before (usually due to geographical constraints). So firms by using the Internet can study products made in other countries that could not otherwise be investigated easily. Firms can also use online communities and forums to interact with scientists from all over the world and therefore obtain a broader knowledge.

In addition, the Internet can affect the third main factor of absorptive capacity (a firm's ability to transfer knowledge within and across departments). This refers to the internal dissemination of the knowledge acquired from external sources and thus to a firm's ability to exploit this knowledge. The circulation of knowledge triggers the creation of new knowledge and fuels innovation (Nonaka and Takeuchi, 1995). The success of the R&D-process requires the efficient collaboration of not only R&D individuals and R&D teams, but also other departments such as the marketing and production (Mansfield, 1968a). The ease (or difficulty) of communication between different departments depends on what we term 'internal channels'; that is, the linkages between the different subunits of a firm.

We argue that the Internet can improve the established internal channels and additionally provide new ones. The improved internal channels enhance the efficiency of communication because (in addition to face-to-face contact) individuals can now use digital tools to exchange documents, data and designs. Representative examples of these channels are the electronic mail and the Intranets. Furthermore, the Internet provides new channels and gives the opportunity to individuals to reach members of the firm that could not be reached previously. A good example is that of virtual-teams, whereby despite their members being dispersed across a wide geographical region, they may still be able to work together and collaborate.

Based on these arguments, we propose that the internet increases the absorptive capacity of a firm by improving established external and internal channels, as well as by providing channels that did not previously exist. Thus it improves a firm's ability to access and acquire external knowledge as well as improving its ability to circulate knowledge within and across departments.

4. SEARCHING FOR EMPIRICAL EVIDENCE

The previous section explained how and why the two features of the Internet enhance the three critical dimensions of R&D-efficiency as well as the absorptive capacity of a firm. Having provided a theoretical explanation, the next step is to try to provide some evidence that the Internet does improve R&D-efficiency. Given that this association has not hitherto been explored econometrically, an econometric methodology as well as formal evidence is lacking. Accepting the validity of the arguments discussed previously, the contribution of R&D to productivity should have increased after the inception of commercial exploitation of the Internet in 1993 and as it was growing.

A proxy to represent the available online scientific knowledge such as patents and academic advances, as well as non-scientific knowledge like information for the commercial trends and demographics, may be the number of online Web sites available in a given year. A proxy to represent the links that the Internet provides (that is, how many individuals, firms, institutes and universities can communicate) could be the stock of communication equipment available to access the internet. This refers to the number of Internet hosts (that is, registered computers with IP address connected to the Internet). To observe in detail any potential time pattern in data, Table 11.1 presents the R&D elasticity per year starting from 1989 to 2002. These results are based on the method of ordinary least squares and the 'long' sample of 14 years (a description of this dataset can be found in Chapter 7).

The second column of Table 11.1 reveals a distinct pattern over time. Until 1995 the contribution of R&D to productivity performance was not more than 0.08. However, after 1995 it increased dramatically up to 0.29 (in 2001 and 2002). Although the commercial use of the Internet started in 1993, prior to 1995 the number of Web sites and hosts was small. After this date however, the number of Web sites and hosts began to increase and the Internet became a respectable source of knowledge as well as an important tool for communication. Although there are many possible causes for this discontinuity over time, it appears that the coefficient of R&D matches the growth of Web sites and hosts, and started to increase dramatically after 1995.

Table 11.1 R&D elasticity over time [a, b, c]

Year	R&D Elasticity
1989	0.03^{ns} (0.03)
1990	0.04^{ns} (0.03)
1991	0.07 (0.04)
1992	0.07 (0.04)
1993	0.06^{ns} (0.04)
1994	0.08 (0.04)
1995	0.11*** (0.04)
1996	0.11*** (0.04)
1997	0.15*** (0.04)
1998	0.17*** (0.04)
1999	0.23*** (0.05)
2000	0.24*** (0.06)
2001	0.29*** (0.05)
2002	0.29*** (0.05)

Notes:
[a] The dependent variable is labour productivity.
[b] ns = not significant, * 5% level of significance, ** 1% level of significance, *** 0.1% level of significance, the absence of a star indicates a level of significance of 10%.
[c] Control variables for time and industry have been included in the regression.

We also investigated a number of other factors that could have increased the coefficient of R&D over time. For example, this increase could have been fueled by an increase in R&D investments during the second time period (that is, after 1995). However, this argument was rejected because R&D-intensity in the first and second sub-periods was similar. Another possibility could be a lower cost of funding (through falling interest rates for example), which would decrease the total cost of R&D investments. However, in that case the coefficient of ordinary capital should also have increased during the second time-period; it was actually found to be stable. Similarly, the cost of R&D could be lower if the government had increased R&D expenditure. However, government expenditure on R&D in fact decreased during the 1990s (ONS, 2000). So this explanation must also be rejected. A third possibility is the improvement of productivity performance (or alternatively the effect of a business cycle). Examining the descriptive statistics of the sample, we found that neither the level nor the growth of labour productivity can explain the higher coefficient of R&D.

We also examined the possibility that this discontinuity over time is affected by a demand-side exogenous factor (Nagaoka, 2003). This could explain the change in coefficient as in 1993 the size of market increased considerably (being the year in which the agreement for the unification of Europe occurred). After unification, firms could reach more efficiently larger numbers of customers, increase their sales and thereby benefit from factors such as higher demand and economies of scale. We examined firms' average sales per year and although they started to increase after 1994, the increment was not large enough to explain the dramatic change of R&D elasticity.

We also considered the possibility that the elasticity of R&D was affected by the estimated R&D indices (the value of which declined after 1995; see Chapter 5). In order to investigate this, we re-estimated the model using the GDP price index. Once again, it was found that R&D elasticity increased after 1995, indicating that the estimated R&D indices were not the reason for this discontinuity. Another argument relates to the issue of appropriability. The higher R&D elasticity may be the result of the increased ability of firms to appropriate their research findings. But as the ability depends primarily on the concentration of the market (Mansfield, 1968a), it is difficult to argue that this radically changed within those few years. On the other hand, firms may be more able to appropriate their research findings simply because of a more efficient patent law. The primary legislation governing patent law in the UK is the 1977 Patents Act. Although this has been amended many times, there was no significant change to patent law around 1995 which could have significantly influenced the capability of firms to appropriate their research findings.

Although it is difficult to provide econometric evidence, a better method to analyse the association between the Internet and R&D-efficiency is to use moderated regression analysis and include an additional variable in the production function. By adding in the main Cobb-Douglas model a variable that will represent the Internet will not provide a solution because its coefficient will reflect the impact of the Internet on productivity performance, (rather than the impact of the Internet on R&D-efficiency). So a better method is to construct and include a variable that will embody the interaction of R&D and the Internet. This variable should incorporate a

Empirical Findings

firm's use of the Internet as a weighting factor for its R&D capital:

$$Q_{it} = f(K_{it}, L_{it}, IR_{it}) \qquad (11.1)$$

The variable (IR_{it}) should represent the R&D capital (R_{it}) of a firm i at time t weighted by a time-specific and firm-specific measure of the Internet (I_{it}). The main difficulty relates to the construction of such an Internet measure. As explained earlier, the Internet comprises two features. Hence two weighting factors must be incorporated in this variable; one to represent the search feature (S_{it}) and one to represent the communication feature (C_{it}). We weight the new R&D variable (IR_{it}) as follows:

$$IR_{it} = R_{it}(S_t + C_t) / 2 \qquad (11.2)$$

R_{it} stands for the R&D capital of each firm. As the only available data related to these variables are aggregate statistics concerning the use and growth of the Internet, S_t and C_t are represented by the number of web sites and internet hosts respectively. Table 11.2 presents the new results.

Table 11.2 Results for the Internet-weighted R&D [a, b, c]

	Model 1	Model 2
Log (K/L)	0.27*** (0.02)	0.27*** (0.02)
Log L	0.02ns (0.01)	0.02ns (0.01)
R&D Elasticity	0.12*** (0.01)	0.13*** (0.01)
Control for time	yes	yes
Control for industry	yes	yes
R^2	0.37 (0.17)	0.38 (0.17)

Notes:
[a] The dependent variable is labour productivity.
[b] ns = not significant, * 5% level of significance, ** 1% level of significance, *** 0.1% level of significance, the absence of a star indicates a level of significance of 10%.
[c] The coefficient of R&D of 0.12 is not identical to the coefficient of 0.14 that Chapter 9

reported. The reason for this is that in order to include the lagged variables, six years of the data were not included in the previous section, so consequently, the estimates in Chapter 9 are slightly higher.

Model 1 presents the coefficients when the usual R&D capital is used, while Model 2 reports the coefficients when the Internet-weighted measure of R&D capital (IR_{it}) is included in the model. The findings of Table 11.2 are not very encouraging as the coefficient of R&D increased only slightly from 0.12 to 0.13. However, it should be kept in mind that the proxies used (number of web sites and hosts) are a very crude measure of the size of the Internet. It is hoped that these differences will be higher when firm-level measures of the Internet are used. Due to lack of data, it is not possible at present to provide further evidence that the Internet has played an important role in enhancing R&D-efficiency.

What variables, however, might be used in the future to better investigate empirically the impact of the Internet on R&D-efficiency? An ideal method would be to find firm-level data regarding the use of the Internet within each firm of the sample. For example, one could collect statistics about the traffic (the volume of data transferred across the internet) and emails (the number of messages exchanged) from firms' servers. The Internet- and email-servers of each firm record very detailed statistics. One can retrieve, for instance, how many gigabytes of data have been downloaded from specific internet domains, e.g. the domains of the UK, European or World Patent Offices or from educational domains (ac.xx, edu.xx), thereby mapping to some extent these knowledge spillovers. However, because firms very rarely provide access to such confidential data, a number of alternative proxies which can be used as a basis for future research are discussed below.

The communication feature (C_{it}) that improves the communication within R&D department, across departments and associated organizations will vary depending not only on the firm but also on time. As discussed earlier, firms that possess a better infrastructure and understanding of technologies may use the Internet more effectively than other organizations that do not possess such technological understanding. In addition, as the Internet was gradually expanding across the world, the communication feature became more important. There are many variables that can be used as a proxy for the communication feature. However, from the numerous Internet indicators such as hosts, users, traffic, access and type of connections, reported in the literature (OECD, 1998), the number of Internet hosts seems to be the most representative of the total links that the Internet provides.

There are many issues, however, that should be taken into account. Many hosts will not be relevant to R&D departments, so a better measure may be to examine the hosts by second-level domains. For instance, given that it is likely that the most useful contacts of R&D departments are those established with universities, research centres and e-communities, the most relevant domains will be those of ac.xx, edu.xx, org, net and info. Additionally, the search feature (C_{it}) that represents the available online knowledge will also vary depending on the firm and time. Only a small percentage of the total Web sites available will be relevant to a firm's needs. The relevant Web sites will also vary over time and may possibly increase as the Internet becomes more popular. One variable which could represent the available online knowledge is the number of online Web sites. As in the previous case, since the majority of the information is acquired from the Web pages of universities, research institutes, online journals and conferences proceedings, as well as from innovation and patent databases, the most relevant Web sites will be those of ac.xx, edu.xx, org, net and info and these of search engines.

Although it is difficult to measure the number of academic and R&D related Web pages, the Journal of Cybermetrics using Network Information Centre (NIC) has approximated the number of different sub-domains including ac.xx and edu.xx. Unfortunately, time series data do not exist. Additionally, it would be useful to find statistics from academic journal hosts (like ebsco and science-direct) concerning the number of online papers per year and the number of online papers per academic field. Finally, it should be noted that the role of commercial Web sites is also important, and should not be ignored. As Leydesdorff (2001) emphasizes, innovations that can be retrieved in the patent and science citation databases, are frequently retrieved by firms using their commercial and trade names.

Because the association between the Internet and R&D-efficiency has not hitherto been examined econometrically, further investigation may significantly increase our understanding. Although the measurement of the Internet and the construction of the above proxies is a difficult task, there are a number of research sources that may help. The first attempt to construct Internet infrastructure indicators was made by OECD (1998). After 1998 a number of papers concerning the Internet use, e-commerce and business performance have been published by OECD (2000; 2001c). Moreover, the UK office for national statistics (ONS) carried out a survey about the Internet and e-commerce in UK firms in 2000 (ONS, 2002b) and many subsequent publications from ONS have followed. It should also be noted that the statistics required to construct the proxies discussed above do exist. The largest surveys about the Internet are carried out by Network Wizards on behalf of the Internet Systems Consortium (ISC). These surveys count, usually on an annual basis, the number of hosts. Using the raw data of these surveys, it is possible to identify the number of second-level academic domains within the UK. As the cost of this database is high and the task very large, further research will inevitably require research funding.

5. CONCLUSIONS

In this chapter, we investigate the relationship between the Internet and innovation performance. Initially, in order to provide a better unit of analysis, we adopt a feature-based approach to the Internet. Then we offer a conceptual framework which by using theoretical explanations, past empirical research and examples from practice explains how and why the two features of the Internet improve not only the three critical dimensions of R&D efficiency and but also a firm's absorptive capacity. Finally, we offer some preliminary empirical findings that can be used as a basis for future research. As the theoretical association between the Internet and R&D efficiency is largely unexplored, this chapter should be of particular interest to those social scientists that examined the impacts of technological change. It could also contribute to the knowledge-management and absorptive-capacity research fields as it explores how R&D departments by using the Internet, acquire information from external sources, disseminate it throughout the firm and empower the creation of knowledge through efficient communication and interaction. Besides the contribution to scholarly knowledge, there are also important implications for practice. As the current research suggests, the Internet may improve the R&D efficiency of multinational corporations. The integration of the Internet in R&D-process plays an important role.

However, more research (both case studies and econometric analysis) is needed to address a number of knowledge gaps. Case studies should answer questions such as 'For which stages of R&D-process is the integration of the Internet more important?' or 'On which dimension (cost, time, and quality) has the Internet the greatest impact?' On the other hand, econometric analysis should examine the extent to which the Internet improves R&D efficiency in different locations around the globe. In that case we will be able to answer questions like 'Is the Internet infrastructure of countries important for the improvement of R&D efficiency?'

12. Conclusion

What has this book investigated, and why is it important? What are the main findings emerging from the analysis? What are the limitations to these findings? Do multinational corporations' research efforts contribute to their own performance? Can firms benefit from the R&D undertaken by their intra-industry competitors and other inter-industry firms? What conclusions can be drawn from the findings? How may the results be used by managers and policy makers? In what ways can this research be extended? This chapter endeavours to answer these questions. The first section summarizes the findings of the research, whilst the second one communicates the limitations of the analysis. The contributions and implications of the investigation are discussed in the third section, and suggestions for decision- and policy-making are drawn from the results. The last section suggests possibilities for future research.

1. OVERVIEW OF THE FINDINGS: WHAT HAVE WE LEARNT?

Using a sample of UK multinational corporations, this book has examined the impacts of innovation and scientific knowledge on firm productivity performance. It has also examined the effects of knowledge externalities (or spillovers) and investigated the extent to which other firms' technological advances influence a firm's productivity performance. As discussed in the previous chapters, the evaluation of the impacts of R&D and spillovers using firm-level data was very important because it allowed us to estimate the extent to which a firm (rather than an industry or a country) benefits from its own R&D as well as from the research efforts of other firms.

Chapter 3 investigated the theoretical relationship between innovation and firm productivity performance. We noted that whilst some multinational corporations can turn innovation into a powerful competitive weapon, others find that the vast costs associated with innovation outweigh its potential advantages, indicating that for them, industrial research is merely a defense mechanism. Chapter 4 reviewed the past literature. In Chapter 5, we found that the costs of R&D inputs differed across industries. The inflation rate of

R&D in industries such as textiles and minerals was higher than that in industries such as aerospace, office equipment and pharmaceuticals. It was shown that there are clear differences between deflation by the GDP price index and deflation by the R&D price index. Although the GDP index followed an upward trend, this was not the case for the R&D price index which decreased after 1995 (whilst the GDP index continued to rise).

Moreover, their values were considerably different. The increase of the GDP price index was higher by comparison with the R&D price index. This finding is important as it contradicts the results of other studies that examined earlier time periods and found that the rise of the UK GDP price index was less than that of the corresponding R&D index. It was also shown that the use of R&D price indices has important implications for academic research and for the accurate measurement of the effects of R&D. Using the GDP price index biased the coefficient of R&D downwards, which confirms the need for R&D price indices and for better quality of data.

The third part of the book (empirical findings) provided answers to many of the research questions posed in the introduction. In Chapter 8, the evidence suggested that there was a strong relationship between labour productivity and R&D capital (or stock of scientific knowledge). The average elasticity of R&D for the whole sample was 0.15, indicating that the contribution of R&D to the labour productivity performance of the UK multinational corporations of the sample was positive and high. Generally, when this elasticity is compared with the findings reported for other countries, it appears to be slightly higher. The elasticity of R&D remained robust in almost every case under differing model and variables specifications, suggesting that these findings can be used with confidence. It is surprising and to some extent unfortunate, however, that although a lot of effort was put into the better measurement of the labour input, the estimates were not sensitive to those improvements.

Because this research was carried out at firm level, the findings show the private (rather than the social) returns to R&D. In other words, they indicate that when a MNC increases its R&D capital per employee by 1 percent, its labour productivity will increase by around 0.15 percent per year. As noted earlier, however, the R&D variable is itself aggregated. Hence, this elasticity indicates the average impact of the many different types of R&D. This emphasizes the need for more detailed data which may allow us in the future to estimate separately, the returns to basic research or those to process R&D.

Fourth, when each industry was examined separately, it was found that the effects of R&D varied widely, indicating once again the pitfalls of aggregation. As the findings indicated, R&D elasticity was quite high for the chemical and transportation industries. Yet R&D elasticity for the fifth sub-sample (the remaining industries) was found to be statistically insignificant.

However, in view of the heterogeneity of the firms within this group, we should not put a lot of confidence in this finding. The findings of Chapter 8 also provided a clear answer to the arguments regarding the role of firm size. The coefficient of R&D was significantly higher for larger MNCs, supporting the postulate that the effects of R&D are positively associated with firm size. The results also supported the hypothesis that the magnitude of the impact of R&D depends on the technological opportunities that a firm faces. The elasticity of R&D for technologically advanced firms was found to be much higher at 0.16, than that for low-tech firms, where it was 0.09. When we compared the monetary returns to R&D with the returns to other investments in fixed tangible assets, however, it was found that the monetary returns to R&D for low-tech firms were even higher than those for technologically advanced firms. The implication of this finding for academic research is important because, as discussed in Chapter 8, it shows that in cases where only the R&D elasticity is taken into account, the interpretations may be misleading. Moreover, the estimation of the monetary returns to R&D also implied that multinational corporations could have generated a higher output per employee if they had invested more in R&D. It was found that for every additional pound of ordinary capital per employee that a firm spent, its sales per employee would increase by 77 pence per year, whilst for every additional pound of R&D capital per employee, the sales per employee would grow by 94 pence per year.

We discussed the reasons why the returns to R&D for some industries and types of firms were considerably higher than those of other industries and firm types. The most likely explanations relate to economies of scale, to different dynamic capabilities and to the understanding of technologies, different technical know-how and managerial qualities across firms, as well as to different appropriability regimes across industries. Although it cannot be argued that only one is true or that one can assess for certain the veracity of each explanation, each does appear to have some merit.

This book has also investigated how competition influences the returns to innovation. The analysis confirmed that the economic benefits that a firm appropriates from its new technological developments depend on the competitive pressure that it faces. The findings indicated that when a market tends to have conditions of perfect-competition, the returns to a firm's own R&D are significantly lower than the economic returns enjoyed by companies in oligopolistic markets. Additionally, Chapter 8 investigated the role of internationalization in explaining innovation performance. The econometric results showed that in the case of less internationalized firms, the costs associated with the development of new technologies outweigh the potential benefits. In contrast, we found that the effects of innovation for highly internationalized firms were considerably higher, thereby confirming that internationalization is a firm-specific characteristic that affects the payoff from innovation.

Chapter 9 extended the research undertaken in Chapter 8. There were three sets of noteworthy results. First, the findings regarding the time lag of R&D suggested that the effects of R&D were maximized shortly after the investment in R&D had been made. Furthermore, the returns to R&D did not seem to decay as rapidly as might be expected. Even six years after an investment in R&D had been made, the elasticity of R&D remained relatively high. This suggested that firms may experience high returns to their R&D investments over a long period of time. When we examined whether a firm's degree of internationalization influences the lag structure of R&D, it was found that in contrast to our expectations, the returns to R&D decay very slowly for less international firms.

There were also a number of noteworthy findings regarding the impact of R&D spillovers on the productivity performance of multinational corporations. When the whole sample was analysed, it was found that the impact of total R&D spillovers on productivity performance at the firm level was positive and relatively high between 1995 and 2002. When we estimated the intra- and inter-industry effects separately, we found both positive and negative spillovers. The impacts of the R&D undertaken by intra-industry competitors were either negative or statistically insignificant.

As discussed in Chapter 10, this result confirms the argument that intense competition from rivals often outweighs the corresponding positive knowledge externalities. Nevertheless, we found that the R&D undertaken by companies in more distantly related industries had a positive impact on firms' productivity performance. When we re-estimated the results for different sub-samples, we found that spillovers varied, depending on the degree of a firm's internationalization. Even though intra-industry spillovers were insignificant for both sub-samples, we found the inter-industry spillovers to be greater for those firms with a lower degree of internationalization.

The book also examined the relationship between the Internet and R&D-efficiency. Our theoretical framework demonstrated how and why two features of the Internet (search and communication) improved the three critical dimensions of R&D-efficiency (cost, time, quality), as well as a firm's absorptive capacity. Some preliminary empirical evidence was also provided, which indicated that the Internet had indeed played a significant role in improving R&D-efficiency. Although the empirical findings could serve as a possible basis for future research, it should be recognized that the method used was a crude measure of Internet effects.

2. LIMITATIONS OF THE STUDY

The findings reported in the book are subject to a variety of limitations. As many of these limitations have been extensively discussed in the previous chapters, this section briefly summarizes the most important ones:

(1) The firm-level data that we employed here did not allow us to investigate the social returns to R&D. Nevertheless, the externalities which spill over to other firms were examined in Chapter 10.

(2) The measurement of output was not optimal, as sales (rather than value added) were used. The sales might not capture immeasurable improvements of output. Similarly, the imperfect output deflators did not fully account for improvements such as quality and variety in output. As a result, the estimated R&D elasticity was possibly biased downwards.

(3) The inputs of capital and labour were not corrected in order to take into account the effects of factors such as capacity utilization, the numbers of hours worked and the heterogeneity of employees in terms of education, age and experience.

(4) Besides the omitted input of intermediate materials, some other unobserved inputs (or control variables) such as managerial capabilities and the ability of R&D employees were also omitted.

(5) A sample selectivity bias might arise from the collection of the data.

(6) The smaller firms of the sample were still relatively large as all the firms were multinationals.

(7) Although firm-level data were used, a degree of aggregation still remained. The firms in the sample were multinationals, owning many smaller firms and operating in different countries, across which many parameters would inevitably vary.

(8) R&D expenditure could only represent the formal research effort. However, scientific knowledge is also determined by other sources of knowledge such as informal research and learning by doing.

(9) Many firms were diversified, producing a wide variety of products. One may therefore end up aggregating dissimilar firms and in consequence reduce the accuracy of the estimates.

(10) R&D expenditure is in itself aggregated as it is the sum of a variety of different R&D activities such as basic, applied, product, process and outsourced R&D. Hence, this study estimated the average impact of all the different types of R&D on the productivity performance of multinational corporations. As discussed in the previous chapters, more detailed data may allow us in the future to estimate, for example, the returns to basic and applied research or those to process and product R&D.

(11) Another limitation to the study relates to the quality of the data and the accounting treatment of R&D. As the reporting of R&D is to some extent voluntary (Stoneman and Toivanen, 2001), some potential selectivity bias may occur. Nevertheless, by taking into account the fact that the sample represented 80 percent of the total private R&D in the UK, it is not expected that this caused a significant bias.

(12) In order to examine R&D spillovers, the technological distance between firms was estimated by using input-output data. Although this weighting approach estimates adequately rent spillovers, it tends to underestimate the role of pure knowledge spillovers Griliches (1992).

(13) As Griliches (1992) emphasized, the constructed reservoir of knowledge available in an industry is not indicative of how much of this knowledge can be spilled over to other firms, or who the recipients of the transmitted knowledge are. For instance, the firms of the sample that were more diversified, they may draw knowledge from a pool which is much wider than the one constructed.

(14) Given that the firms in the sample were multinationals, there is a possibility that their R&D activities were undertaken overseas and not in the UK. In that case, the global nature of R&D may have biased the results because the R&D undertaken in, say, the state of Massachusetts might be more (or less) efficient that the R&D undertaken in the UK. Once again, more detailed data are needed to investigate this issue.

(15) The R&D included in the model is a simplified representation of R&D activity: research and development is undertaken by a singe agent who finances the project and is at the same time the creator, owner and user of the innovation. However, as Baussola (1999, p.87) emphasizes, R&D activity takes place either within firms, or through contractual agreement between firms.

3. IMPLICATIONS

The conclusions that have been produced chapter by chapter as well as a number of additional broader conclusions based on the findings of this research are provided here. As the empirical findings showed that industrial research activities contributed significantly to the productivity performance of multinational corporations, it would appear that despite the technological uncertainty and commercial risk involved in such investments (Geroski, 1995), it is worth investing in R&D. Even though some of the economic value and many of the potential benefits are forwarded to other firms and consumers, innovative firms can appropriate some of the advantages for themselves. These findings may encourage managers and policy makers to increase investments in R&D. For example, it was found that strategic investments in R&D could not only generate revenues for many years, but that these revenues were often much higher than those generated by other investments in fixed assets. In indicating that the contribution of R&D to firm performance is strong, the findings might help to stimulate private as well as public investments in R&D.

In contrast to other studies that found that R&D is of little consequence to the productivity of low-tech firms, we showed that low-tech firms can improve their performance and consequently competitiveness by investing in R&D. However, managers should bear in mind that a firm will not necessarily increase its productivity simply by investing in R&D. Those firms which experienced high returns to R&D may differ from other firms in ways that cannot be remedied fully in this way. The organizational culture and technological infrastructure could be complementary factors which allowed such high returns to R&D for some firms (Teece et al., 1997).

Furthermore, as the relationship between the Internet and R&D-productivity has not hitherto been explored econometrically or theoretically, the findings led to a number of potentially useful conclusions for R&D-management. It was shown that the integration of the Internet in the everyday processes is important in relation to the productivity of R&D departments. By integrating new Internet technologies in the process of R&D, managers can improve not only their firms' absorptive capacity but also the time and cost of R&D projects and the quality of the final products.

Concerning the overall impact of R&D, when the findings concerning the impact of a firm's own R&D are combined with the results of spillover effects, they provide a better understanding of the mechanisms underlying the relationship between innovative activity and firm productivity performance. However, this picture is complicated by the fact that both positive and negative spillover effects were found. Even so, many useful conclusions for managers may be drawn from these results. Firstly, the decision of managers of technologically advanced firms to invest heavily in R&D is once again justified; these firms benefited not only from their own research efforts but also from that undertaken by firms within, as well as outside, the industry to which they belong. Managers should note, however, that the impact of external R&D on productivity is less significant than the impact of their own research activities.

By contrast, the opposite is true in the case of smaller firms. Their managers should continue investing in R&D because although their firms' own research efforts were not particularly beneficial to productivity performance, these efforts enabled their firms to become more competitive using the knowledge transmitted by firms of the same and of other industries. This finding which indicated that spillover effects were even higher than the R&D undertaken by smaller firms, may also provide guidance relating to acquisition and merging policies. As smaller firms are very capable of exploiting other organizations' research efforts, managers of larger firms should be particularly careful when considering strategic options that involve merging smaller firms with the parent company because the effects may be different to those expected (the individual specific capabilities of smaller firms might be lost, for example).

In the case of both smaller and of technologically advanced firms, the positive externalities arising from R&D spillovers appear to outweigh the potential negative externalities from R&D competition (Cincera, 1998). This is of course desirable from a policy-making perspective because firms' productivity is further improved. Additionally, the managers of low-tech and larger firms should be warned that the R&D undertaken by other firms is liable to have negative consequences for the productivity performance of their firms. This result confirmed the arguments of Geroski (1995) who observed that external R&D could complement a firm's own R&D in some cases, but substitute for it in others. It might also be considered as an indication that the R&D departments of both low-tech and larger firms need to collaborate and formulate alliances rather than to compete.

As well as the implications for management, a number of important suggestions for policy making can be drawn from the findings. Perhaps the most interesting issue is whether it is possible that the government could close the UK productivity gap by increasing and focusing on R&D investments. As the research findings indicate, investment in R&D is indeed one way of accelerating productivity growth. The contribution of R&D to productivity appears to be very significant, so policy makers should be warned that a decline in R&D investments may turn out to be very costly to the UK economy. On the other hand, policy makers should also be aware that given the existence of international spillovers, UK investments in R&D are likely to benefit the productivity of other countries too (Cincera, 1998). Of course, it is impossible to force multinational corporations to internalize the results of their R&D.

It should be also emphasized that R&D policies must be formulated very carefully. In order to promote innovation and accelerate economic growth, they need to ensure that the contributions of own R&D as well as of R&D spillovers to productivity are both positive and high for all types of firms. Nevertheless, this is not the case for some of the firms of the sample. For example, the private returns to R&D, however estimated, were found to be low for smaller firms, indicating that they should be aided to improve their innovative capacity and their capability to appropriate the benefits of R&D.

As many researchers (Cincera, 1998; Rao et al., 2001) have emphasized, policy makers could support these firms either directly, by means of tax incentives and R&D subsidies that will decrease the cost of undertaking research; or indirectly by, for example, investing in public sector R&D, removing barriers to the commercialization of innovations, building better technological infrastructure, helping with the adoption and diffusion of new technologies, lowering patent costs and simplifying the patent filling procedure.

As recent evidence indicates, an efficient policy is to introduce carefully designed R&D tax incentives. Hall and Van Reenen (2000) surveyed the econometric evidence on the effects of tax incentives in OECD countries on the user cost of R&D, and concluded that a dollar in tax credit for R&D stimulates a dollar of additional R&D. Muellbauer and Cameron (1994) also surveyed the findings of past studies and concluded that R&D tax credits could be a cost-effective way of stimulating R&D investments. Similarly, Bloom et al. (2002) investigated the effects of tax changes on R&D spending in nine OECD countries (including the UK) over a 19 year period (1979–1997). They found that a 10 percent fall in the cost of R&D stimulates a 10 percent rise in level of R&D in the long-run.

Nevertheless, in order to accelerate productivity growth further, policy makers should eliminate negative spillover effects, especially for low-tech firms. One way of achieving this may be through the introduction of new incentives for collaborative R&D which will assist in the formulation of alliances and joint-venture R&D projects. As suggested by Mohnen (1999), an alternative way could be the formulation of policies that assist the circulation of knowledge and disseminate information concerning the advances of technology and science. Policy makers could also invest in knowledge infrastructure to facilitate and empower the flow of knowledge between universities and firms as suggested by Rao et al. (2001). As it is often suggested in order to accelerate economic performance, firms must work very closely with universities, thereby improving the mechanism that translates scientific knowledge into innovations and converting with ease newly developed knowledge into products (Cincera, 1998).

4. DIRECTIONS FOR FUTURE RESEARCH

The research undertaken in this book can be extended in a number of ways. To begin with, the production function used here could be enriched with better measures of output and additional measures of input. Data on the intermediate materials used in the production or alternatively data on value-added would allow us to estimate the impact of R&D on productivity performance better. In a similar vein, controlling for capacity utilization could allow the measurement R&D effects more accurately. It would also contribute to our understanding if more detailed data on the technological inputs used by the firms of our sample could be obtained.

Little research takes into account that many R&D projects are outsourced. So as well as a firm's internal R&D efforts, it would be of value to add into the empirical model the R&D activities that are outsourced either to other firms or to universities. This would allow the investigation as to whether the impact of in-house R&D on innovative capacity was greater than the corresponding impact of the outsourced R&D. As we have not taken this into account, it may bias the estimates. Moreover, as noted earlier, by using more detailed R&D data, it would be possible to break down R&D expenditure and estimate the effects of product, process, basic and applied R&D separately. It would also be useful to incorporate in the model a measure of computing capital (IT capital), which might enhance our understanding about the determinants of innovative activity, and the role of complementary assets.

Another way of extending this study would be to estimate the impact of R&D on profits and on production costs (rather than on productivity). As discussed in the previous chapters, the benefits of R&D are not fully reflected in productivity, but may also impact on firm profitability. On the other hand, cost-saving investments in R&D, such as process research, are likely to have a greater impact on production costs than on output. Hence, by employing these dependent variables, we would be able to assess the overall impact of R&D on a firm's economic performance and competitiveness.

The work on R&D spillovers can also be extended in many ways. One can assess the extent to which academic research can advance a firm's productivity. Another way to extend the current research is to investigate whether external R&D is a complement to, or a substitute for, a firm's own research efforts. Alternatively, one can investigate the effect of including an international spillover capital, thereby assessing the effects of the R&D undertaken by firms in other countries. Moreover, by recognising that diffusion of knowledge depends on the type of R&D investment (process, product, basic or applied), the impact of the spillovers generated by these different types of R&D could be evaluated. In this way, it would be possible to identify those types of R&D with high social value, which can therefore be spilled over easily and which provide a considerable contribution to the productivity performance of many firms. The results of this exercise could be then used by government agents to fund those types of research that are more beneficial for society.

Another opportunity for future research could be in the improvement of the measurement of spillover flows. The likelihood of including irrelevant knowledge into a firm's spillover capital could be reduced by interviewing the R&D employees, identifying firms' competitors and the sources of knowledge that they use. In this way, one could measure much more accurately the relevant knowledge that firms use and construct a spillover capital that would be much more specific to each firm. Additionally, statistics from firms' Internet servers might also be used as a complementary method of identifying the relevant sources of knowledge.

More research in terms of both case studies and econometric analysis could address a number of knowledge gaps regarding the role of the Internet. Case studies could answer questions such as 'For which stages of R&D-process is the integration of the Internet more important?' or 'On which dimension (cost, time, and quality) does the Internet have the greatest impact?'. Additionally, better econometric methods should be used to quantify the extent to which the Internet improves R&D-productivity. Other parameters, such as the Internet infrastructure of countries, should also be taken into account in this exercise.

The last suggestion for future research relates to the discussion of Chapter 3 that indicated that because a firm's research findings are often neutralized by its competitors' own research, innovation can be either a competitive weapon or a defense mechanism. Although online banking, for example, might not attract more customers to a bank (as all banks offer such services), there is likely to be a significant loss of customers if that bank terminated its online banking facilities. Hence, it would be of value to reformulate the main research question 'what is the impact of R&D on productivity?' as 'what happens to a firm's productivity if it ceases to undertake R&D?'. In other words, instead of taking into account only the level of a firm's research efforts, future studies should incorporate in their models the difference of this level from the average level of its competitors. This will permit future research to examine the circumstances under which the returns to R&D are maximized.

References

Acs, Z., D. Audretsch and M. Feldman (1993), 'Innovation and R&D spillovers', CEPR discussion paper no. 865.

Adams, J. (1990), 'Fundamental stocks of knowledge and productivity growth', *Journal of Political Economy*, **98** (4), 673-702.

Adams, J.D. and A.B Jaffe (1996), 'Bounding the effects of R&D: An investigation using matched establishment-firm data', *The RAND Journal of Economics*, **27** (4), 700-721.

Advanced Manufacturing (2001), 'Internet for industry', July 2001.

Aghion, P. and P. Howitt (1992), 'A model of growth theory through creative destruction', *Econometrica*, **60**, 323-351.

Aghion, P., C. Harris, P. Howitt and J. Vickers (2001), 'Competition, imitation and growth with step-by-step innovation', *Review of Economic Studies*, **68**, 467–92.

Aitken, B. and A. Harrison (1999), 'Do domestic firms benefit from foreign direct investment? Evidence from panel data', *American Economic Review*, **89**, 605-618.

Ando, A. (1971), 'On a problem of aggregation', *International Economic Review*, **12** (2), 306-311.

Anon Higon, D. (2004), 'The impact of research and development spillovers on UK manufacturing TFP', Aston Business School Research Papers RP0421, Birmingham, UK.

Antonelli, C. (1994), 'Technological districts localized spillovers and productivity growth. The Italian evidence on technological externalities in the core regions', *International Review of Applied Economics*, **8** (1), 18-30.

Antonelli, C., A. Geuna and W.E. Steinmueller (2000), 'Information and communication technologies and the production, distribution and use of knowledge', *International Journal of Technology Management*, **20**, 72–94.

Arrow, K. (1962), 'The economic implications of learning by doing', *Review of Economic Studies*, **29**, 155-173.

Audretsch, D. and M. Feldman (1994), 'Knowledge spillovers and the geography of innovation and production', CEPR discussion paper no. 953.

Bakos, J.Y. (1991), 'A strategic analysis of electronic marketplaces', *MIS Quarterly*, **15** (3), 295-310.

Baldwin, W. and J. Scott (1987), *Market Structure and Technological Change*, London, UK: Harwood Academic Publishers.

Barro, R. (1990), 'Government spending in a simple model of endogenous growth', *Journal of Political Economy*, **82** (6), 1095-1117.

Barua, A., S. Ravindran and A.B. Whinston (1997), 'Efficient selection of suppliers over the Internet', *Journal of Management Information Systems*, **13** (4), 117–137.

Basu, S. and J.G. Fernald (1997), 'Returns to scale in US production function: Estimates and implications', *Journal of Political Economy*, **105**, 249-283.

Baujard, O., V. Baujard, S. Aurel, C. Boyer and R.D. Appel (1998), 'Trends in medical information retrieval on Internet', *Computers in Biology and Medicine*,

28, 589-601.

Baussola, M. (1999), 'Technological change, diffusion and output growth', PhD Thesis, Warwick Business School, UK.

Bera, A.K. and C.M. Jarque (1981), 'An efficient large-sample test for normality of observations and regression residuals', working papers in econometrics no. 40, Australian National University, Canberra.

Berndt, E.R. (1991), *The Practice of Econometrics*, Reading, Massachusetts: Addison Wesley.

Bernstein, J. (1988), 'Costs of production, intra- and interindustry R&D spillovers: Canadian evidence', *Canadian Journal of Economics*, **21**, 324-347.

Bernstein, J. and M. Nadiri (1989), 'Research and development and intra-industry spillovers: An empirical application of dynamic duality', *Review of Economic Studies*, **56**, 249-269.

Bitzer, J. and I. Geishecker (2006), 'What drives trade-related R&D spillovers? Decomposing knowledge-diffusing trade flows', *Economics Letters*, **93** (1), 52-57.

Bloom, N., R. Griffith and J. Van Reenen (2002), 'Do R&D credits work? Evidence from a panel of countries 1979-97', *Journal of Public Economics*, **85** (1), 1-31.

Bonte, W. (2004), 'Spillovers from publicly financed business R&D: some empirical evidence from Germany', *Research Policy*, **33** (10), 1635-1655.

Bosworth, D. (1979), 'Recent trends in research and development in the United Kingdom', *Research Policy*, **8** (2), 164-185.

Boutellier, R., O. Gassmann, H. Macho and M. Roux (1998), 'Management of dispersed product development teams: The role of information technologies', *R&D Management*, **28** (1), 13-25.

Branstetter, L.G. (1996), 'Are knowledge spillovers international or intranational in scope? Microeconometric evidence from the Japan and the United States', National Bureau of Economic Research Working Paper 5800, USA.

Branstetter, L.G. and M. Sakakibara (2002), 'When do research consortia work well and why? Evidence from Japanese panel data', *The American Economic Review*, **92** (1), 143-159.

Bryan, W.R. (1967), 'Bank adjustments to monetary policy: Alternative estimates of the lag', *American Economic Review*, **57** (4), 855-864.

Brynjolfsson, E. and L. Hitt (1996), 'Paradox lost? Firm-level evidence on the returns to information systems spending', *Management Science*, **42** (4), 541-558.

Brynjolfsson, E. and L. Hitt (2000), 'Beyond computation: Information technology, organizational transformation and business performance', *Journal of Economic Perspectives*, **14** (4), 23-48.

Brynjolfsson, E. and L. Hitt (2003), 'Computing productivity: Firm-level evidence', *Review of Economics and Statistics*, **85** (4), 793-808.

Buckley, P.J. and M. Casson (1976), *The Future of the Multinational Enterprise*, London: Macmillan.

Cameron, G. (1996), 'On the measurement of real R&D - Divisia price indices for UK business enterprise R&D', *Research Evaluation*, **6** (3), 215-219.

Cameron, G. (2000), 'R&D and growth at the industry level', Nuffield College Economics Papers 2000-W4, University of Oxford, UK.

Caves, R.E. (1982), *Multinational Enterprise and Economic Analysis*, Cambridge: Cambridge University Press.

Chang, I. and G.C. Tiao (1983), 'Effect of exogenous interventions on the estimation of time series parameters', Proceedings of the Business and Economics Statistic Section, *American Statistical Association*, 532-537.

Chen, M.J. and D. Miller (1994), 'Competitive attack, retaliation and performance: An expectancy-valence framework', *Strategic Management Journal*, **15**, 85-102.

Cheng, J.L.C. and D.S. Bolon (1993), 'The management of multinational R&D: A neglected topic in international business research', *Journal of International Business Studies*, **24**, 1-18.

Chesbrough, H.W. (2003), *Open Innovation: The New Imperative for Creating and Profiting from Technology*, Boston: Harvard Business School Press.

Chesbrough, H.W. (2007), 'Why companies should have open business models', *MIT Sloan Management Review*, **48** (2), 22-28.

Christensen, L.R., D.W. Jorgenson and L.J. Lau (1973), 'Transcendental logarithmic production frontiers', *Review of Economics and Statistics*, **55**, 28-45.

Ciborra, C.U. and G. Patriotta (1998), 'Groupware and teamwork in R&D: Limits to learning and innovation', *R&D Management*, **28** (1), 43-52.

Cincera, M. (1998), 'Economic and Technological Performance of International Firms', PhD Thesis, Universite Libre of De Bruxelles.

Cincera, M. and B. Van Pottelsberghe (2001), 'International R&D spillovers: A survey', *Cahiers Economiques de Bruxelles*, **169** (1).

Clark, B. and Z. Griliches (1984), 'Productivity and R&D at the firm level in French manufacturing', in Zvi Griliches (ed.), *R&D, patents, and productivity*, Chicago: University of Chicago Press, pp. 393-416.

Cobb, C. and P. Douglas (1928), 'A Theory of production', *American Economic Review*, **18** (1), 139-65.

Cockburn, I. and Z. Griliches (1987), 'Industry effects and appropriability measures in the stock market's valuation of R&D and patents', National Bureau of Economic Research Working Paper 2465, USA.

Coe, D. and E. Helpman (1995), 'International R&D spillovers', *European Economic Review*, **39**, 859-887.

Cohen, W.M. and S. Klepper (1996), 'Firm size and the nature of innovation within industries: The case of product and process R&D', *The Review of Economics and Statistics*, **78** (2), 232-243.

Cohen, W.M. and D.A. Levinthal (1989), 'Innovation and learning: the two faces of R&D', *The Economic Journal*, **99**, 569–596.

Cohen, W.M. and D.A. Levinthal (1990), 'Absorptive Capacity: A new perspective on learning and innovation', *Administrative Science Quarterly*, **35** (1), 128–152.

Cooper, R.G. and E.J. Kleinschmidt (1995), 'Benchmarking the firm's critical success factors in new product development', *The Journal of Product Innovation Management*, **12**, 374-391.

Court, A.T. (1939), 'Hedonic price indices with automotive examples', in *The dynamics of automobile demand*, New York, General Motors Corporation, pp.99-117.

Crafts, N. and M. O'Mahony (2001), 'A perspective on UK productivity performance', *Fiscal Studies*, **22** (3), 271-306.

Cuneo, P. and J. Mairesse (1984), 'Productivity and R&D at the firm level in French manufacturing', in Zvi Griliches (ed.), *R&D, Patents, and Productivity*, Chicago: University of Chicago Press, pp. 375-392.

Dahan, E. and V. Srinivasan (2000), 'The predictive power of Internet-based product concept testing using visual depiction and animation', *The Journal of Product Innovation Management*, **17** (2), 99-109.

Damanpour, F. (1991), 'Organizational innovation: a meta-analysis of effects of determinants and moderators', *Academy of Management Journal*, **34**, 555–590.

De Bondt, R. (1996), 'Spillovers and innovative activities', *International Journal of Industrial Organisation*, **15**, 1-28.

Dennis, R.M., P. Flavin and G.J. Davies (1998), 'Online R&D management: The way forward', *R&D Management*, **28** (1), 27-35.

DeSanctis, G. and M.S. Poole (1994), 'Capturing the complexity in advanced technology use: Adaptive structuration theory', *Organization Science*, **5**, 121-147.

Dilling-Hansen, M., T. Eriksson and E.S. Madsen (2000), 'The Impact of R&D on productivity: Evidence from Danish firm-level data', *International Advances in Economic Research*, **6** (2).

Dye, R. (1986), 'Proprietary and non proprietary disclosures', *Journal of Business*, **59** (2), 331-366.

Eisenhardt, K. and J. Martin (2000), 'Dynamic capabilities: What are they?', *Strategic Management Journal*, **21**, 1105-1121.

Federico, P.J. (1958), 'Renewal fees and other patent fees in foreign countries', Subcommittee of Patents, Trademarks, and Copyrights of the committee of Judiciary, United States Senate, study no. 17, Washington D.C.: Government Printing Office.

Finch, B.J. (1999), 'Internet discussions as a source for consumer product, customer involvement and quality information: An exploratory study', *Journal of Operations Management*, **17** (5), 535–536.

Fisch, J.H. (2003), 'Optimal dispersion of R&D activities in multinational corporations with a genetic algorithm', *Research Policy*, **32** (8), 1381-1396.

Freeman, C. (1982), *The Economics of Industrial Innovation*, London: Pinter.

Frohman, A.L. (1982), 'Technology as a competitive weapon', *Harvard Business Review*, **60** (1), 97-104.

Fuchs, V. (1963), 'Capital-labour substitution: A note', *Review of Economics and Statistics*, **45**, 436-8.

Gardiner, P.D. and J.M. Ritchie (1999), 'Project planning in a virtual world: information management metamorphosis or technology going too far?', *International Journal of Information Management*, **19** (6), 485.

Geroski, P.A. (1991), 'Innovation and the sectoral sources of UK productivity growth', *The Economic Journal*, **101**, 1438-1451.

Geroski, P.A. (1995), 'Markets for technology: Knowledge, innovation, and appropriability', in Paul Stoneman (ed.), *Handbook of the Economics of Innovation and Technological Change*, Oxford: Blackwell, pp. 90-131.

Ghosh, S. (1998), 'Making business sense of the Internet', *Harvard Business Review*, **76** (2), 126–135.

Goto, A. and K. Suzuki (1989), 'R&D capital, rate of return on R&D investment and spillover of R&D on Japanese manufacturing industries', *The Review of Economics and Statistics*, **71** (4), 555-564.

Granstrand, O., L. Hikanson and S. Sjolander (1993), 'Internationalization of R&D - A survey of some recent research', *Research Policy*, **22** (5), 413-430.

Grant, R.M. (1987), 'Multinationality and performance among British manufacturing companies', *Journal of International Business Studies*, **22**, 249-263.

Gray, R.H. (1985), 'Accounting for R&D: A review of experiences with SSAP 13', London, Research Board of the ICAEW.

Greenhalgh, C. and M. Rogers (2006), 'The value of innovation: The interaction of competition, R&D and IP', *Research Policy*, **35** (4), 562-580.

Griffith, T.L. (1999), 'Technology features as triggers for sensemaking', *Academy of Management Review*, **21** (3), 472-488.

Griffith, T.L. and G.B. Northcraft (1994), 'Distinguishing between the forest and the trees: Media, features and methodology in electronic communication research', *Organization Science*, **5**, 272-285.

Griffith, R., S. Redding and J.Van Reenen (2004), 'Mapping the two faces of R&D: productivity growth in a panel of OECD industries', *The review of Economics and Statistics*, **86** (4), 883-895.

Griliches, Z. (1961), 'Hedonic price indexes for automobiles: An econometric analysis of quality change', in Price Statistics Review Committee NBER, *The Price Statistics of the Federal Government: Review, Appraisal, and Recommendations*, General Series no. 73, New York, pp.173-96.

Griliches, Z. (1964), 'Research expenditure, education and the aggregated agricultural production function', *American Economic Review*, **54** (6), 961-974.

Griliches, Z. (1973), 'Research expenditures and growth accounting', in Z. Williams (ed.), *Science and Technology in Economic Growth*, London: Macmillan, pp.59-95.

Griliches, Z. (1979), 'Issues in assessing the contribution of research and development to productivity growth', *Bell Journal of Economics*, **10**, 92-116.

Griliches, Z. (1980), 'Returns to research and development expenditures in the private sector', in J. Kendrick and B. Vaccara (eds), *New Developments in Productivity Measurement and Analysis*, Chicago: University of Chicago Press, pp.339-374.

Griliches, Z. (1984), 'Data problems in econometrics', National Bureau of Economic Research Technical Working Paper 39, USA.

Griliches, Z. (1986), 'Productivity, R&D, and basic research at the firm level in the 1970s', *American Economic Review*, **76** (1), 141-154.

Griliches, Z. (1992), 'The search for R&D spillovers', *Scandinavian Journal of Economics*, **94**, 29-47.

Griliches, Z. (1995), 'R&D and productivity: Econometric results and econometric and measurement issues', in Paul Stoneman (ed.), *Handbook of the Economics of Innovation and Technological Change*, Oxford: Blackwell, pp.52-89.

Griliches, Z. and F. Lichtenberg (1984), 'R&D and productivity at the industry level: Is there still a relationship?', in Zvi Griliches (ed.), *R&D, Patents, and Productivity*, Chicago: University of Chicago Press, pp.465-496.

Griliches, Z. and J. Mairesse (1983), 'Comparing productivity growth: An exploration of French and US industrial and firm data', *European Economic Review*, **21**, 89-119.

Griliches, Z. and J. Mairesse (1984), 'Productivity and R&D at the firm level', in Zvi Griliches (ed.), *R&D, Patents, and Productivity*, Chicago: University of Chicago Press, pp.339-374.

Griliches, Z. and J. Mairesse (1990), 'R&D and productivity growth: comparing Japanese and US manufacturing firms', in C. Hulten (ed.), *Productivity growth in Japan and the United States*, Chicago: University of Chicago Press, pp.317-348.

Griliches, Z. and V. Ringstad (1971), *Economies of Scale and the Form of the Production Function*, Amsterdam: North Holland.

Griliches, Z., A. Pakes and B. Hall (1987), 'The value of patents as indicators of inventive activity', in P. Dasgupta and P. Stoneman (eds.), *Economic Policy and Technological Performance*, Cambridge: Cambridge Press, pp.97-124.

Gujarati, D.N. (1995), *Basic Econometrics*, New York: McGraw-Hill.

Gupta, U.G. (1997), 'The new revolution: Intranets, not Internets', *Product and Inventory Management Journal*, **38** (2), 16–20.

Hall, B. (1990), 'The manufacturing sector master file: 1959-1987 documentation',

National Bureau of Economic Research Working Paper 3366, USA.

Hall, B. (1993), 'Industrial R&D during the 1980s: Did the rate of return fall?', *Brookings Papers on Economic Activity (Microeconomics)*, **2**, 289-343.

Hall, B., Z. Griliches and J.A. Hausman (1986), 'Patents and R&D: Is there a lag?', *International Economic Review*, **27** (2), 265-284.

Hall, B. and J. Mairesse (1995), 'Exploring the relationship between R&D and productivity in French manufacturing firms', *Journal of Econometrics*, **65**, 263-293.

Hall, B. and J. Van Reenen (2000), 'How effective are fiscal incentives for R&D? A review of the evidence', *Research Policy*, **29** (4), 449-469.

Hambrick, D.C. and I.C. Macmillan (1985), 'Efficiency of product R&D in business units: The role of strategic context', *Academy of Management Journal*, **28** (3), 527-547.

Hameri, A.P. and J. Nihtila (1997), 'Distributed new product development project based on Internet and World-Wide Web: A case study', *Journal of Product Innovation Management*, **14** (2), 77–87.

Harhoff, D. (1998), 'R&D and productivity in German manufacturing firms', *Economics of Innovation and New Technology*, **6**, 28–49.

Harhoff, D. (2000), 'R&D spillovers, technological proximity, and productivity growth: Evidence from German panel data', *Schmalenbach Business Review*, **52** (3), 238-260.

Harhoff, D., J. Henkel and E. Von Hippel (2003), 'Profiting from voluntary information spillovers: How users benefit by freely revealing their innovations', *Research Policy*, **32** (10), 1753–1769.

Hebden, J. (1983), *Application of Econometrics*, Oxford: Philip Allan.

Hellstrom, T., J. Eckerstein and A. Helm (2001), 'R&D management through network mapping: Using the Internet to identify strategic network actors in cooperative research networks', *R&D Management*, **31**(3), 257-263.

Hibbard, J. and K.M. Carrillo (1998), 'Knowledge revolution', Information Week 663, January 5, 49-54.

Hill, P. (1988), 'Recent developments in index number theory and practice', Organization for Economic Co-Operation and Development Economic Studies no. 10.

Hitt, M.A., R.E. Hoskisson and R.D. Ireland (1994), 'A mid-range theory of the interactive effects of international and product diversification on innovation and performance', *Journal of Management*, **20**, 297-326.

HM Treasury (2003), 'Productivity in the UK: The Evidence and the Government's Approach'

Howe, V., R.G. Mathieu and J. Parker (2000), 'Supporting new product development with the Internet'. *Industrial Management and Data Systems*, **100** (6), 277-284.

Iansiti, M. and A. McCormack (1997), 'Developing product on Internet time', *Harvard Business Review*, **75** (5), 108-117.

Iansiti, M. and J. West (1997), 'Technology Integration: Turning great research into great products', *Harvard Business Review*, **75** (3), 69-79.

Jaffe, A. (1986), 'Technological opportunity and spillovers of R&D', *American Economic Review*, **76** (5), 984-1001.

Jaffe, A. (1989), 'Real effect of academic research', *American Economic Review*, **79**, 957-70.

Jankowski, J. (1993), 'Do we need a price index for industrial R&D?', *Research Policy*, **22** (3), 195-205.

Jorgenson, D.W. (1963), 'Capital theory and investment behavior', *The American Economic Review*, Papers and Proceedings of the Seventy Fifth Annual Meeting of the American Economic Association, **53** (2), 247-259.

Jorgenson, D.W. and Z. Griliches (1967), 'The explanation of productivity change', *The Review of Economic Studies*, **34** (3), 249-83.

Kafouros, M.I. (2005), 'R&D and productivity growth: Evidence from the UK, Economics of Innovation and New Technology, **14** (6), 479-497.

Kafouros, M.I. (2006), 'The Impact of the Internet on R&D-Efficiency: Theory and Evidence', *Technovation*, **26** (7), 827-835.

Kamien, M., and N. Schwartz (1982), *Market Structure and Innovation*, Cambridge: Cambridge University Press.

Karshenas, M. and P. Stoneman (1995), 'Technological diffusion', in Paul Stoneman (ed.), *Handbook of the Economics of Innovation and Technological Change*, Oxford: Blackwell, pp.265-297.

Kessler, E.H. (2003), 'Leveraging e-R&D processes: A knowledge-based view', *Technovation*, **23**, 905-915.

Kleinknecht, A. (1987), 'Measuring R&D in small firms: How much are we missing?', *The Journal of Industrial Economics*, **86**, 253-256.

Klevorick, A.K., R.C. Levin, R.R. Nelson and S.G. Winter (1995), 'On the sources and significance of interindustry differences in technological opportunities', *Research Policy*, **24** (2), 185-205.

Kodama, M. (1999), 'Customer value creation through community-based information networks', *International Journal of Information Management*, **19**, 495-508.

Koenker, R. (1981), 'A note on studentizing a test for heteroskedasticity', *Journal of Econometrics*, **17**, 107-12.

Kotabe, M., S. Srinivasan and P.S. Aulakh (2002), 'Multinationality and firm performance: The moderating role of R&D and marketing capabilities', *Journal of International Business Studies*, **33** (1), 79-97.

Kuemmerle, W. (1997), 'Building effective R&D capabilities abroad', *Harvard Business Review*, **75** (2), 61-70.

Laursen, K. and A. Salter (2004), 'Searching low and high: What types of firms use universities as a source of innovation?', *Research Policy*, **33** (8), 1201-1215.

Laursen, K. and A. Salter (2006), 'Open for innovation: The role of openness in explaining innovation performance among UK manufacturing firms', *Strategic Management Journal*, **27** (2), 131-150.

Lev, B. and T. Sougiannis (1996), 'The capitalization, amortization and value-relevance of R&D', *Journal of Accounting and Economics*, **21**, 107-138.

Levin, R.C., A.K. Klevorick, R.R. Nelson and S.G. Winter (1987), 'Appropriating the returns from industrial research and development', *Brookings Papers on Economic Activity*, **3**, 783-820.

Levin, R.C. (1988), 'Appropriability, R&D spending, and technological performance', *American Economic Review*, **78**, 424-428.

Levy, D.M. and N.E. Terleckyj (1983), 'Effects of government R&D on private R&D investment and productivity: A macroeconomic analysis', *Bell Journal of Economics*, **14**, 551-61.

Leydesdorff, L. (2001), 'Indicators of Innovation in a Knowledge based Economy', *Cybermetrics*, **5** (1).

Lichtenberg, F. (1984), 'The relationship between federal contract R&D and company R&D', *The American Economic Review*, **74** (2), 73-78.

Lichtenberg, F. and Z. Griliches (1989), 'Errors of measurement in output deflators',

Journal of Business and Economics Statistics, **7** (1).

Lichtenberg, F. and D. Siegel (1991), 'The impact of R&D investment on Productivity: New evidence using linked R&D-LRD data', *Economic Inquiry*, **29** (2), 203.

Link, A. (1981), *Research and Development Activity in US Manufacturing*, New York: Praeger.

Link, A. (1982), 'Productivity growth, environmental regulations and the composition of R&D', *The Bell Journal of Economics*, **13** (2), 548-554.

Link, A. (1983), 'Inter-firm technology flows and productivity growth', *Economics Letter*, **11**, 179-184.

Los, B. and B. Verspagen (2000), 'R&D spillovers and productivity: Evidence from U.S. manufacturing microdata', *Empirical Economics*, **25**, 127-148.

Lu J.W. and P.W. Beamish (2004), 'International diversification and firm performance: The s-curve hypothesis', *Academy of Management Journal*, **47** (4), 598-609.

Lucas, R. (1988), 'On the mechanics of economic development', *Journal of Monetary Economics*, **22**, 3-42.

Mairesse, J. and B. Hall (1996), 'Estimating the productivity of research and development in French and US manufacturing firms: An exploration of simultaneity issues with GMM methods', in K. Wagner and B. Van Ark (eds), *International Productivity Differences and their Explanations*, Elsevier Science, pp.285-315.

Mairesse, J. and P. Mohnen (1990), '*Recherche-Développement et Productivité - Un Survol de la Littérature Econométrique*', *Economie et Statistique*, 99-108.

Mairesse, J. and M. Sassenou (1991), 'R&D and productivity: A survey of econometric studies at the firm level', *The Science Technology and Industry Review*, **8**, 317-348.

Mansfield, E. (1965), 'Rates of return from industrial research and development', *American Economic Review*, **55**, 110-122.

Mansfield, E. (1968a), *The Economics of Technological Change*, New York: Norton.

Mansfield, E. (1968b), *Industrial Research and Technological Innovation: An Econometric Analysis*, New York: Norton.

Mansfield, E. (1980), 'Basic research and productivity increase in manufacturing', *The American Economic Review*, **70** (5), 863-873.

Mansfield, E. (1981), 'Composition of R&D expenditures: Relationship to size of firm, concentration, and innovative output', *The Review of Economics and Statistics*, **63** (4), 610-615.

Mansfield, E. (1984), 'R&D and innovation: Some empirical findings', in Zvi Griliches (ed), *R&D, Patents, and Productivity*, Chicago: University of Chicago Press, pp.127-148.

Mansfield, E. (1987), 'Price indexes for R&D inputs, 1969-83', *Management Science*, **33** (1), 124-129.

Mansfield, E. (1988), 'Industrial R&D in Japan and the United States: A comparative study', *The American Economic Review*, papers and proceedings of the one hundredth annual meeting of the American Economic Association, **78** (2), 223-228.

Mansfield, E. (1991), 'Academic research and industrial innovation', *Research Policy*, **20** (1), 1-12.

McGahan, A.M. and B.S. Silverman (2006), 'Profiting from technological innovation by others: The effect of competitor patenting on firm value', *Research Policy*, **35**

(8), 1222-1242.

McVicar, D. (2002), 'Spillovers and foreign direct investment in UK manufacturing', *Applied Economics Letters*, **9**, 297-300.

Minasian, J. (1962), 'The economics of research and development', in Richard Nelson (ed.), *The Rate and Direction of Inventive Activity: Economic and Social Factors*, Princeton University Press, pp.93-142.

Minasian, J. (1969), 'Research and development, production functions and rates of return', *American Economic Review*, **55**, 80-85.

Mitchell, G.R. (2000), 'Industrial R&D strategy for the 21st century', *Research Technology Management*, **43** (1), 31-35.

Mohnen, P. (1996), 'R&D Externalities and Productivity Growth', STI Review, 18, 39-66.

Mohnen, P. (1999), 'International R&D spillovers and economic growth', Université du Québec à Montréal and CIRANO.

Muellbauer, J. and G. Cameron (1994), 'Innovation and productivity in UK manufacturing', Memorandum for the House of Commons Select Committee on Science and Technology, Oxford, UK.

Nadiri, M.I. (1993), 'Innovations and technological spillovers', National Bureau of Economic Research working paper 4423, USA.

Nagaoka S. (2003), 'Determinants of R&D and its productivity: Identifying demand and supply channels', Hitotsubashi University working paper.

Nelson, R.R. (1959), 'The Simple economics of basic scientific research', *Journal of Political Economy*, **67**, 297-306.

Nelson, R.R. (1982), 'The Role of Knowledge in R&D Efficiency', *The Quarterly Journal of Economics*, **97** (3), 453-470.

Nevens, T.M., G.L. Summe, B. Uttal (1990), 'Commercializing technology: What the best companies do', *Harvard Business Review*, **68** (4), 154-163.

Nixon, B. (1997), 'The accounting treatment of research and development expenditure: Views of UK company accountants', *European Accounting Review*, **6** (2), 265-277.

Nonaka, I. and H. Takeuchi (1995), *The Knowledge-Creating Company*, Oxford University Press.

Odagiri, H. (1983), 'R&D expenditures, royalty payments and sales growth in Japanese manufacturing corporations', *The Journal of Industrial Economics*, **32** (1), 61-71.

Odagiri, H. and H. Iwata (1986), 'The impact of R&D on productivity increase in Japanese manufacturing companies', *Research Policy*, **15** (1), 13-19.

OECD (1998), 'Internet infrastructure indicators', Organization for Economic Co-Operation and Development, Paris.

OECD (2000), 'Local access pricing and e-commerce', Organization for Economic Co-Operation and Development, Paris.

OECD (2001a), 'Science, technology and industry scoreboard: Towards a knowledge-based economy', Organization for Economic Co-Operation and Development, Paris.

OECD (2001b), 'Measuring productivity: OECD manual', Organization for Economic Co-Operation and Development, Paris.

OECD (2001c), 'The Internet and Business Performance', Organization for Economic Co-Operation and Development, Paris.

OECD (2002), 'Frascati Manual', Organization for Economic Co-Operation and Development, Paris.

ONS (2000), 'Research and Experimental Development Statistics', UK Office for National Statistics, UK.

ONS (2002a), 'Research and Development in UK businesses: Business Monitor MA14', UK Office for National Statistics, UK.

ONS (2002b), 'E-Commerce Inquiry to Business 2000', UK Office for National Statistics, UK.

Pakes, A. and M. Schankerman (1984), 'The rate of obsolescence of patents, research gestation lags, and the private rate of return to research resources', in Zvi Griliches (ed.), *R&D, Patents and Productivity*, Chicago: University of Chicago Press, pp.98-112.

Pavitt, K. (1990), 'What we know about the strategic management of technology', *California Management Review*, Spring, 17-26.

Pavitt, K. (2001), 'Public policies to support basic research: What can the rest of the world learn from US theory and practice? (and what they should not learn)', *Industrial and Corporate Change*, 10, 761-779.

Pavitt, K., M. Robson and J. Townsend (1987), 'The size distribution of innovating firms in the UK: 1945-1983', *The Journal of Industrial Economics*, 55, 291-316.

Piergiovanni, R., E. Santarelli and M. Vivarelli (1997), 'From which source do small firms derive their innovative inputs? Some evidence from Italian industry', *Review of Industrial Organization*, 12, 243-258.

Plymale, J. and R. Hartgrove (1999), 'The web, our shared global engineering infrastructure', *Printed Circuit Design*, 16 (11), 24-27.

Porter, E.M. (1980), *Competitive Strategy: Techniques for Analyzing Industries and Competitors*, New York: The Free Press.

Price R.M. (1996), 'Technology and strategic advantage', *California Management Review*, 38 (3), 38-56.

R&D Scoreboard (2003), 'The Top 700 UK and 700 international companies by R&D investment', Department of Trade and Industry, UK.

R&D Scoreboard (2006), 'The top 800 UK and 1250 global companies by R&D investment', Department of Trade and Industry, UK.

Rao, S., A. Ahmad, W. Horsman and P. Kaptein-Russell (2001), 'The Importance of innovation for productivity', Micro-Economic Policy Analysis Branch Industry, Canada.

Raut, L. (1995), 'R&D spillovers and productivity growth: Evidence from Indian private firms', *Journal of Development Economics*, 48 (1), 1-23.

Ravenscraft D., F.M. Scherer (1982), 'The lag structure of economic returns to research and development', *Applied Economics*, 14, 603-620.

Richir, S., B. Taraval and H. Samier (2001), 'Information networks and technological innovation for industrial products', *International Journal of Technology Management*, 21 (3/4), 420-427.

Roberts, H. (2000), 'Laspeyres and his index', The European Conference on Economic History, Rotterdam, The Netherlands, 201-213.

Romer, P. (1986), 'Increasing returns and long term growth', *Journal of Political Economy*, 94 (5), 1002-1037.

Rosenberg, N. (1990), 'Why do firms do basic research (with their own money)?', *Research Policy*, 19 (2), 165-174.

Rugman, A.M. (1981), *Inside the Multinationals: The Economics of International Markets*, London: Croom Helm.

Sakurai, N., E. Ioannidis and G. Papacostantinou (1996), 'The impact of R&D and technology diffusion on productivity growth: Evidence for 10 OECD countries in the 1970s and 1980s', Organization for Economic Co-Operation and Development, Paris.

Santos, J., Y. Doz and P. Williamson (2004), 'Is your innovation process global?', *Sloan Management Review*, **45** (4), 31-37.

Sargent, T.C. and E.R. Rodriguez (2000), 'Labour or total factor productivity: Do we need to choose?', *International Productivity Monitor*, **1**, 41-44.

Sassenou, M. (1988), 'Recherche-developpment et productivity dans les enterprizes Japonaises: Une etude econometrique sur donnees de panel', PhD Thesis, Ecole des Hautes Etudes en Sciences Sociales, Paris.

Sawhney, M. and E. Prandelli (2000), 'Communities of creation: Managing distributed innovation in turbulent markets', *California Management Review*, **42** (4), 24–54.

Schankerman, M. (1981), 'The Effect of Double Counting and Expensing on the Measured Returns to R&D', *Review of Economics and Statistics*, **63** (3), 454-458.

Scherer, F.M. (1965), 'Firm size, market structure, opportunity and the output of patented inventions', *American Economic Review*, **55**, 1097-1125.

Scherer, F.M (1982), 'Inter-industry technology flows and productivity growth', *The Review of Economics and Statistics*, **64** (4), 627-634.

Schott, K. (1976), 'Investment in private industrial research and development in Britain', *Journal of Industrial Economics*, **25** (2), 81-99.

Schumpeter, J.A. (1950), *Capitalism, Socialism and Democracy*, New York: Harper and Row.

Scott, J.T. (1984), 'Firm versus industry variability in R&D intensity', in Zvi Griliches (ed.), *R&D, Patents, and Productivity*, Chicago: University of Chicago Press, pp.233-248.

Singh, N. and H. Trieu (1996), 'The role of R&D in explaining total factor productivity growth in Japan, South Korea, and Taiwan', University of California Santa Cruz, Economics Department working paper.

Solow, R. (1957), 'Technical change and the aggregate production function', *Review of Economics and Statistics*, **39**, 312-20.

Sorenson O. and L. Fleming (2004), 'Science and the diffusion of knowledge', *Research Policy*, **33** (10), 1615-1634.

SSAP-13 (1989), 'Accounting for research and development', Statement of Standard Accounting Practice no.13, The Institute of Chartered Accountants, England.

Sterlacchini, A. (1989), 'R&D, innovations, and total factor productivity growth in british manufacturing', *Applied Economics*, **21**, 1549-1562.

Stigler, G. (1947), *Trends in Output and Employment*, New York: National Bureau of Economic Research.

Stoneman, P. (1991), 'The use of a Levy/Grant system as an alternative to tax based incentives to R&D', *Research Policy*, **20** (3), 195-201.

Stoneman Paul (ed.) (1995), *Handbook of the Economics of Innovation and Technological Change*, Oxford: Blackwell.

Stoneman, P. and N. Francis (1994), 'Double deflation and the measurement of output and productivity in UK manufacturing 1979-89', *International Journal of the Economics of Business*, **1** (3), 423-437.

Stoneman, P. and O. Toivanen (2001), 'The impact of revised recommended accounting practices on R&D reporting by UK firms', *The International Journal of the Economics of Business*, **8** (1), 123-136.

Sweeney, T. (1999), 'R&D-Net helps Ford, Bechtel to innovate', Internetweek, 78 (6), 69.

Tang, J. (2006), 'Competition and Innovation Behaviour', *Research Policy*, **35** (1), 68-82.

Teece, D.J. (1986), 'Profiting from technological innovation: Implications for integration, collaboration, licensing and public policy', *Research Policy*, **15** (6), 285-305.

Teece, D.J., G. Pisano and A. Shuen (1997), 'Dynamic capabilities and strategic management', *Strategic Management Journal*, **18** (7), 509-533.

Terleckyj, N.E. (1974), 'Effects of R&D on the productivity growth of industries: An explanatory study', Washington, D.C., National Planning Association.

Theil, H. (1954), *Linear Aggregation of Economic Relation*, Amsterdam: North-Holland.

Thomas, R.L. (1993), *Introductory Econometrics: Theory and Applications*, London: Longman.

US Bureau of Labour Statistics (1993), 'Trends in multifactor productivity, 1948-81', BLS Bulletin 2178, USA.

Van Meijl, H. (1995), 'Endogenous technological change: The case of information technologies', PhD Thesis, University of Limburg, Maastricht.

Van Pottelsberghe de la Potterie, B. (1997), 'Issues in assessing the effect of interindustry R&D spillovers', *Economic Systems Research*, **9** (4), 331-356.

Van Reenen, J. (1997), 'Why has Britain had slower R&D growth?', *Research Policy*, **26** (4), 493-507.

Vase, P. (2001), 'ICT deflation and growth: A sensitivity analysis', Economic Methodology Branch, Office for National Statistics, UK.

Verspagen, B. (1995), 'R&D and productivity: A broad cross-section cross-country look', *Journal of Productivity Analysis*, **6**, 117-135.

von Zedtwitz, M. and O. Gassmann (2002), 'Market versus technology drive in R&D internationalization: Four different patterns of managing research and development', *Research Policy*, **31** (4), 569-588.

Wagner, L.U. (1968), 'Problems in estimating research and development investments and stock', Proceedings of the Business and Economic Statistics Section, Washington, D.C., ASA, 189-197.

Wakelin, K. (2001), 'Productivity growth and R&D expenditure in UK manufacturing firms', *Research Policy*, **30** (7), 1079-1090.

Wang, J. and K. Tsai (2003), 'Productivity growth and R&D expenditure in Taiwan's manufacturing firms', National Bureau of Economic Research Working Paper 9724, USA.

Waugh, F.V. (1928), 'Quality factors influencing vegetable prices', *Journal of Farm Economics*, **10**, 185-196.

Williams, B.R. (1973), *Science and Technology in Economic Growth*, London: MacMillan.

Williams, J.R. (1992), 'How sustainable is your competitive advantage?', *California Management Review*, **34** (2), 29-51.

Zellner, A. and C. Montmarquette (1971), 'A study of some aspects of temporal aggregation problem in econometric analyses', *The Review of Economics and Statistics*, **53** (4), 335-342.

Index